The Camondo Legacy

The Passions of a Paris Collector

Extract from Moïse de Camondo's Will

'Wishing to perpetuate the memory of my father Count Nissim de Camondo and that of my unfortunate son, Lieutenant Pilot Nissim de Camondo, killed in aerial combat on 5 September 1917, I bequeath my house such as it is at the time of my death to the Musée des Arts Décoratifs. My house is to be given the name Nissim de Camondo, the name of my son for whom this house and its collections were intended. With this bequest to the State of my house and the collections it contains, it is my wish to keep together as a whole the work to which I have devoted myself: the recreation of an 18th-century artistic residence. To my mind this reconstruction should serve to keep in France, in a setting created specially for this purpose, the most beautiful objects that I have been able to gather of this decorative art which has been one of France's glories, during the period I have loved above all others.'

The Camondo Legacy
The Passions of a Paris Collector

Edited by
Marie-Noël de Gary

Photographs by
Jean-Marie del Moral

Thames & Hudson

We would like to express our deepest thanks to all those who, in recent years,
have lent their support, offered their advice and shared their expert knowledge:

Françoise Arquié, Thierry Algrin, Pierre Arizzoli-Clémentel, Françoise-Anne Bachelier, François and Aline Bachelier, Laurence Baruch, Vincent Bastien, François Baudequin, Christian Baulez, Catherine Beau, Lorraine de Boisanger, Dominique Borgeaud, Roland Bossard, Valérie Bouisson, Sylvie Bourrat, Jean-Marc Boyer, Rémi Brazet, Monica Burckhardt, Yves Carlier, Xavier Chiron, Caroline Civetta, Isabelle de Conihout, Ghislaine Corbi, Pierre Costerg, Stéphanie Cubain, Pierre-François Dayot, Suzanne Delaunay, Vincent Droguet, Emmanuel Ducamp, Stéphane Ducoux, Jean-Louis Dumas, Rena Dumas, Jean-Paul Fabre, Bernard Frizza, Régis Fromaget, Olivier Gabet, Charlotte Gere, Hubert Goldschmidt, Hélène Guéné-Loyer, Françoise Heilbrun, Sophie Heudron, Benoit Jenn, Daniëlle Kilsuk-Grosheide, the Kraemer family, Alastair Laing, David Langeois, Ulrich Leben, Sylvie Legrand-Rossi, Marie-Christine Lesguillier-Colinet, Véronique Lévesque, Marie-Flore Levoir, Gérard Mabille, Nathalie Manuel, Alexis Marcovics, Laure de Margerie, Francine Mariani-Ducray, Sarah Medlam, Anne-Marie Milliot, Olivier Morel, Sophie Motsch, Pascale Ogée, Bénédicte Ottinger, Philippe Palasi, Renaud Paul-Dauphin, Hélène Pasquet Le Guen, Sylvie Pasquier, Carole Pécoux, Joséphine Pellas, Stéphane Petrov, Anne-Emmanuelle Piton, Denis Plouvier, Gilles Plum, the Duke de Polignac, Diane Porthault, Anne L. Poulet, Tamara Préaud, Béatrice Quette, Nicole de Reyniès, Marie-Laure de Rochebrune, Hélène de Saint-Pierre, Xavier Salmon, Carolyn Sargentson, Anne Sefrioui, Suzanne Slesin, Régine Soulier, Laure Soustiel, Claire Scemla-Claveranne, Jean Stucker, Guilhem Scherf, Selma Schwartz, Alexandre Tharaud, Sophie Tranié, David Wharry, Baron Guy de Wouters,

and all the staff at Les Arts Décoratifs.

Published with the support of Friends of the Musées des Arts Décoratifs, Inc.

Les Arts Décoratifs
Hélène David-Weill, *President*
Sophie Durrleman, *Chief Executive Officer*
Béatrice Salmon, *Director of the Museums*
Renata Cortinovis, *Director of Development*

Editor: Chloé Demey
Design: Pascale Ogée
Translation: David Wharry

First published in the United Kingdom in 2008 by Thames & Hudson Ltd, 181A High Holborn, London WC1V 7QX

www.thamesandhudson.com

British Library Cataloguing-in-Publication Data
A catalogue record for this book is available from the British Library

ISBN: 978-0-500-51410-8

Printed and bound in France

Contents

Abbreviation: AMNC for Archives of the Musée Nissim de Camondo

*We would like to express our gratitude to all those whose support has contributed
to the Musée Nissim de Camondo and the conservation of its collections.*

M. Didier Aaron

M. and Mme Antoine Bernheim

M. Pierre Champenois

The Marquis and Marquise de Clermont-
    Tonnerre

M. and Mme Michel David-Weill

Baron and Baronne William Desazars
    de Montgailhard

M. Jean Gismondi

Mr. and Mrs. John Gutfreund

Mrs. Howard Keck

Mr. and Mrs. Stephen Kellen

Mr. and Mrs. Henry Kravis

M. Étienne Lévy

M. Michel Meyer

M. Yves Mikaeloff

M. Jacques Perrin

M. and Mme Frank Richardson

Baron Élie de Rothschild

Baron Edmond de Rothschild

M. Henri Samuel

M. Maurice Segoura

M. and Mme Bernard Steinitz

Mrs. Charles Wrightsman

Firmenich et Cie

Friends of French Art

The J. Paul Getty Trust

The Florence Gould Foundation

Kraemer Antiquaires

Honda France

Honda Motors Ltd

Jean-Marie Rossi-Aveline

Syndicat National des Antiquaires

The Roy and Niuta Titus Foundation

The house that Moïse de Camondo built, in the heart of the Plaine Monceau district, shows how completely his family had assimilated the French way of life and thinking since their arrival in Paris in 1870. Choosing the most beautiful furniture and the finest objects of the 18th century from antique dealers, he proved his exceptional powers of understanding and sensitivity with regard to a culture that was foreign to his own.

By leaving his house and collections to the French state, Moïse de Camondo bequeathed his life's work. He wanted the public, whether French or foreign, to have the opportunity to get to know and admire the outstanding taste, knowledge and creativity of French craftsmen of the 18th century, as he had done himself.

In one way, this is no different to the gesture made by a long line of donors whose gifts have enabled the the Musée des Arts Décoratifs collections to exist: communicating their choice with taste and passion, donating something that has been enjoyed for a long time in the intimacy of a single place. The Musée Nissim de Camondo is exceptional. Its collections are not cold and lifeless, they live and breathe. They represent in equal parts a sum of knowledge, a heartfelt passion, a feeling for beauty, a sense of proportion, elation and refinement; they express an infinite yearning.

Walking around the Count de Camondo's residence, the visitor is not only dazzled by the wealth and beauty that surrounds him, and by the acute vision of the art of the 18th century possessed by a man who lived at the turn of the 19th and 20th centuries, but also by his desire that his house should benefit from the latest in modern fittings. The Musée Nissim de Camondo is an undeniable gem, a testament to an era when art and life's pleasures were combined in both the past and the present.

Hélène DAVID-WEILL

Photographs of Lieutenant Nissim de Camondo in the Large Study.

This book explores all the aspects of the Musée Nissim de Camondo that make it so exceptional; it is a tribute to its founder, Moïse de Camondo, and to all those who have supported it since it opened.

The house's architecture, with its original combination of tradition and modern comfort throughout, including in its servants' quarters, is examined here in detail. Numerous previously unpublished documents from the museum's archives allow us to piece together the personal history of Moïse de Camondo and his family, his tastes as a collector, and daily life in this grand mansion in the early 20th century. Reverence for the past and for the modern-mindedness of the house's inhabitants are harmoniously combined in every room, both public and private.

Looking around the house today, one may feel more like a guest than a visitor. This is thanks to the energy and talent of Marie-Noël de Gary, who has cared for this house for eleven years, observing to the letter Moïse de Camondo's express wish to show everybody the art of the 18th century, the period he 'loved above all others'.

Over a period of three years, Jean-Marie del Moral has photographed the way that the light, in different seasons and at different times of day, moves around each room and reveals its contents, giving each object a distinctive quality. In his choice of details, he does justice to the beauty and textures of materials and the subtle forms of 18th-century French art, whilst inviting us to share one man's passion for the objects he collected.

Béatrice SALMON

Moïse de Camondo

Moïse de Camondo's residence in rue de Monceau marked the culmination of an exceptional and tragic destiny. Who could have imagined that the creator of this showcase, of this quintessence of one of the high points of French art, was born on the shores of the Bosporus? Born into a Jewish family renowned for its philanthropy, he distinguished himself by his passion for his adoptive country and for one of its most refined expressions, its 18th-century art.

In the many-faceted collectors' world Moïse de Camondo cut a singular figure. He recreated the decor of a bygone age in the hope that it could become the setting of his own family history and regarded his recreation of France's aristocratic past as a total work of art.

From Istanbul to Paris *Sophie Le Tarnec and Nora Şeni*

◄ Abraham Salomon de Camondo. Visiting-card format photograph by Abdullah brothers, Pera, Constantinople, *c.* 1868. Although Abraham Salomon's exact date of birth is unknown, he was probably born around 1781. We do know, however, that he officially took over the running of Isaac Camondo & Co., bequeathed to him by his brother, in 1832. It took a fearless temperament to assert his authority, savoir-faire and fortune at this moment in history. The Ottoman state was shaken by institutional reforms, its Jewish communities were impoverished and the capital was still divided into Turkish, Greek and Armenian districts. Since Abraham Salomon's only son Raphael had died in 1866, this capable, cultivated and cosmopolitan man transferred his paternal affection and ambitions to his young grandsons Abraham Behor and Nissim, whom he groomed to become his extremely efficient business associates.

p. 20:

Moïse de Camondo.

Abraham Salomon and
Nissim de Camondo shortly
before their departure for Paris.
Visiting-card format photograph
by Abdullah Brothers, Pera,
Constantinople, c. 1868.
Venerated by his grandsons

Nissim and Abraham Behor,
'Grand Papa' Abraham Salomon
presided lovingly over his family.
He initiated his grandsons in the
world of finance but also guided
them in their roles as prominent
members of the Ottoman Jewish

community. But Abraham Behor
and Nissim's charitable
undertakings took a different
form from the traditional model.
Heirs of the Enlightenment,
they believed in Progress. They
focused their attention on
education, attempting to draw
their fellow Jews out of cultural
isolation to become citizens of the
country in which they lived.

The Camondo family
mausoleum at Haskoy.
Abraham Salomon died in Paris
in 1873. In accordance with his
wishes, his remains were taken
to Constantinople, where
the government gave him
a grand official funeral befitting

a statesman. He was buried
in this mausoleum, now in ruins,
which he had built on the heights
of the Golden Horn. He also
created a seminary, the *Yeshiva
Maghen Abraham*, where prayers
for the repose of his soul were
to be said after his death.

'The Rothschilds of the East'

Moïse de Camondo was born in Istanbul in 1860 into a family known as 'the Rothschilds of the East'. The comparison with that other major 19th-century banking dynasty was certainly perfectly appropriate. Like the Rothschilds, the Camondos were rich and talented financiers. Moïse's grandfather, uncle and father amassed one of the greatest fortunes of the Ottoman Empire, based as much on banking as the family's immense real estate interests.[1] Again like the Rothschilds they were also philanthropists. Practitioners of that very particular form of charity that was the hallmark of the 19th-century European elite, they created schools, hospitals and clinics, with the aim of preventing suffering rather than alleviating it. Banking and philanthropy were both strong influences on the world in which Moïse spent his early years. The family bank, Isaac Camondo & Co., was officially founded in 1832 by his great grandfather Abraham Salomon. Moïse lived near the bank in a fine stone-built residence in Galata, the cosmopolitan financial quarter next to the port of Istanbul.

Moïse grew up in times of great financial excitement. His father Nissim and uncle Abraham Behor had both joined their grandfather's business when they were very young, and had successfully managed to reconcile their bank's interests with their open-minded spirit and the reformist climate

that prevailed in the Ottoman government from 1839. They had close ties to the government ministers behind this new initiative and shared their determination to bypass that overriding Ottoman trait: resistance to innovation.[2] The Ottoman government elite were as attracted by modernity as Abraham Salomon was, and finance was one of the first fields that had to be brought up to date.[3] The Sublime Porte (the old diplomatic name for the sultan's court) began drawing up the necessary conditions for the creation of a modern banking system. The result was an unprecedented period of growth of the sector in which Abraham Salomon Camondo and Greek and Levantine financiers, all Istanbul *sarrafs* (moneylenders and changers),

would be the leading figures. These new conditions, strengthened by a second series of measures after the Crimean War (1853–55), attracted bankers from Paris and London. The Pereire brothers and James de Rothschild were among the first to send representatives to the shores of the Bosporus, and Moïse's great-grandfather, father and uncle fuelled this boom with unstoppable energy. Some ten banks were created in Istanbul in the 1860s, including the Société Générale de l'Empire Ottoman, of which the Camondos became shareholders alongside Greek Orthodox financiers, Crédit Lyonnais and the Imperial Ottoman Bank, which was granted the status of a central bank.

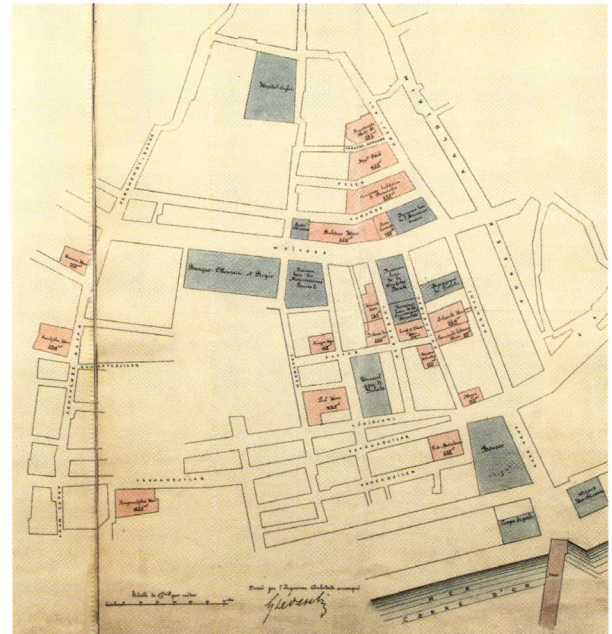

The Camondos were also the driving force behind the urban improvements that transformed Istanbul from the mid-19th century onwards. The Crimean War had enabled the Ottoman capital to see itself through the eyes of the Europeans who had begun to arrive there in great numbers. High-ranking officers of the forces of the Entente Cordiale, journalists, and princes present in the role of observers, all had to put up with a lack of hotels, uneven paving in badly-lit streets and stray dogs. Galata's cosmopolitan Levantine population was mortified by this. Hardly had the smoke of the cannons at Sebastopol cleared when the district's dignitaries put pressure on the Sublime Porte to bring the state of their city up to contemporary European standards. The result was the very official 'Commission for Order in the City',[4] created in 1855 with Abraham Salomon Camondo as one of its ten founder members. This commission was given the task of improving the poor conditions that had been so dramatically brought to light during the war. Work began on an experimental basis in Galata and the neighbouring Levantine district of Pera. From 1855 to 1865, streets were levelled, pavement laid, street lighting installed, and property confiscated and demolished to build new office buildings or *han*. Within a decade, the quarter had been transformed into a modern, luxurious financial district.

The impact of the growth of the banking sector on urban development can be traced to the

◄ The Camondo Steps, Istanbul. These steps, among the enduring legacies left by the Camondos in the Galata district, linked their residence to the banking street below. During a ceremony in 2004 attended by representatives of the Jewish community, the city of Istanbul unveiled a plaque officially naming these steps the Camondo Steps. This gesture may be seen as the first sign of a willingness to revive their memory in Turkey and celebrate their presence in Galata.

19th century and the great financial centres.[5] Streets, banks, mansions, flights of steps, *hans*, *hammams*: the Camondos left their mark all over the Galata district. Attracted by their achievements, envious banking houses flocked to acquire offices in or near the Camondo buildings, thereby definitively establishing the district as a financial hub. All the new banks that opened in Constantinople from 1865 did so within the perimeter south of Galata formed by Felek and Kürekçiler streets, within which nine of the ten Camondo *hans* were located. Four of the six new banks moved into these *hans*.

The family had flights of steps built that led from their mansion down to the streets that were lined with new, austere Viennese-style buildings. The 'Camondo Steps', whose amply curved handrails were later immortalized in a photograph by Cartier-Bresson, still link upper and lower Galata. At the top of these steps stands the *konak*, the mansion where Moïse was born, at 6 Camondo Street, 'with an adjoining pavilion in which there is an oratory and baths, opposite the winter garden'.[6] This large stone house was to have a strange future: first it was to be the childhood home of a future Parisian patron of the arts, whose heart belonged to the 18th century; and then, from the 1880s, it was to become one of the most important schools to be founded by the Universal Israelite Alliance in Istanbul.

The mark the Camondos made on Galata went far beyond these real-estate investments. Abraham

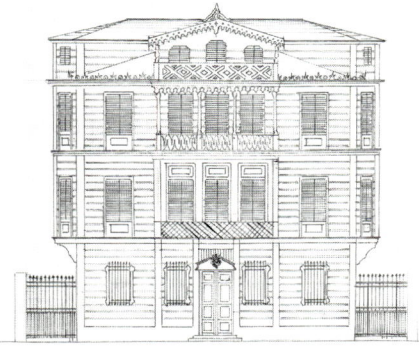

Nissim de Camondo's *yali* at Yenikoy.
Left: drawing of the façade by Hippocrates Papavossilion, tracing paper mounted on canvas, ink and gouache, *c.* 1908.
Below: a photograph of the house taken in about 1860.
In Istanbul, Moïse's days were spent according to the season: during the winter he would stay in the austere banking district in Galata, and he would spend the summer in the sun and fresh sea air at their *yali* on the Bosporus. His great-grandfather Abraham Salomon took up residence on the heights of Camlica, on the Asian side, while his father and uncle lived at Yenikoy on the European shore, in two neighbouring villas. There Moïse would play with his cousin Isaac in the large gardens overlooking the sea. These sumptuously furnished seaside residences, entirely built in wood, were let to Ottoman financiers during the summer months after the family moved to Paris.

Buyuk Dere in the 19th century.
Abraham Salomon built a synagogue in this town near Yenikoy on the Bosporus, where his grandsons had *yalis* near the summer residences of the French and British embassies. He supported the community on the island of Rhodes by building a school and synagogue, the *Kadosh Camondo*, at Lindos.

Salomon and his grandsons took the bold and innovative decision to invest in urban transport. In 1851, Abraham Salomon took part in the creation of the famous *Sirket-I Hayriye* steamer company, a semi-public company whose ferries accelerated the rhythm of life in Constantinople considerably. Two decades later, Abraham Behor, Moïse's uncle, built the city's first tramway and founded the Constantinople Tramway Company with some of his Greek associates in the Société Générale.[7] Horse-drawn trams now linked the banking quarter to other districts, and throughout the rest of the city, the crucible of their prosperity, the Camondos' elegance and efficiency soon made itself felt.

From charity to philanthropy

The Rothschilds and the Camondos both believed that the role of the ruling class was to spread benefits to all. Throughout the 19th century James de Rothschild in Paris and Moïse's father and uncle in Constantinople set up philanthropic institutions, rather than simply performing acts of charity, in France and the Middle East. As a pious man, grandfather Abraham Salomon obeyed the traditional Jewish rules governing *tzedakah* (charity). He established synagogues, shelters and funds for the destitute. His religious faith underpinned all his charitable acts, such as his financing of the reprinting of *Mea'm Lo'ez*, the Torah anthology aimed at a

'A strange city, Constantinople. Splendour and misery, tears and joys; the arbitrary more than elsewhere, and also more freedom – people of four different origins live together there without hating one another too much: Turks, Armenians, Greeks and Jews, children of the same land and tolerating each other much better than people from diverse provinces and political parties do in our country.'

Gérard de Nerval, *Voyage en Orient*.

secular public. But his grandsons, Abraham Behor and Nissim, had an entirely different idea of the responsibility of the elite within society. Inspired by the emancipation of the Jews in France and England, they were determined to lead the Jews of the Ottoman Empire towards full citizenship. The project was ambitious and ahead of its time since all Muslims and non-Muslims in the Empire were still subjects of their own 'nations'. The school became the prime instrument of this quasi-Utopia. James de Rothschild's emissary, Albert Cohn, had devoted himself to a vast project of 'regeneration' through education and work; he stopped off in Istanbul on his way to Jerusalem in 1854. With the Camondos, he co-founded a modern primary school there in the

Hasköy quarter, on the banks of the Golden Horn. Abraham Behor, twenty-seven years old and a man of the Enlightenment, took sole charge of this school two years later, providing it with a vast building for up to 450 pupils, including facilities for 50 boarders. The care of this institution, which he would fondly refer to as 'my school', became an almost sacred mission for him.[8] Very clear principles guided him: the Jews' use of Spanish, which they had continued to speak after fleeing the kingdom of Isabella of Castile in 1492, had led them to experience a profound sense of insularity.[9] From now on they were to be taught Turkish and French, which would help to bring them out of their isolation and integrate into the Ottoman environment and the European world.

◀ Countess Abraham Behor de Camondo, née Regina Baruh. Photograph by Abdullah Brothers, Pera, Constantinople, *c*. 1860. Abraham Behor married Regina Baruh on 3 September 1847 in Constantinople. They had two children, Clarisse, born in 1848, and Isaac, born in 1851.

▶ Countess Nissim de Camondo, née Elise Fernandez. Photograph by A. Liébert, Paris, *c*. 1870. Nissim married Elise Fernandez, born in Salonica, on 20 February 1885 in Constantinople. They had a son, Moïse, born in 1860.

▶ Moïse and Isaac de Camondo. Photograph by Abdullah Brothers, Pera, Constantinople, *c*. 1865. The Camondo family did not produce offspring in great numbers, which made for a fragile dynastic line. Isaac and Moïse, both only sons, were always close despite their very different characters and lifestyles. Moïse's admiration, care and affection for his elder cousin grew as the years went by.

At that time, Jewish philanthropic institutions were being set up in Paris: the Universal Israelite Alliance was founded in 1860.[10] Like his brother Abraham Behor, who had been appointed president of the Alliance's regional committee in Constantinople, Nissim threw himself energetically into the educational cause.[11] Until their deaths in 1889, both men consistently promoted education amongst their fellow Jews and collaborated with the Universal Israelite Alliance, whose ideas they shared. During the same period, their Greek Orthodox counterparts in Istanbul pursued similar goals, founding schools and employing modern teaching methods. But the comparison ends there, since the Camondo brothers were not guided by a sense of identity.[12]

Destination Paris

Although they were profoundly involved in Ottoman business and local philanthropy, the Camondos left Istanbul for Paris in 1869. Even the new, rebuilt Galata was too limited to satisfy their longing for the wider, European world. Prompted by the modernization of the banking sector, the Ottoman state was now turning to French and English banks rather than financiers in Constantinople. So Abraham Behor decided to become a European financier himself and set up a banking house in France. His younger brother, Moïse's father, was right behind him. The prospect of establishing themselves successfully in the City of Light had a

▲ Abraham Behor (left) and Nissim (right) de Camondo. Colodion prints reworked with gouache, c. 1870. As business associates and neighbours, constantly exchanging information, asking one another's opinion and encouraging one another, Nissim and Abraham Behor built their lives side by side.

They drew strength from their extraordinary mutual affection. It was unthinkable that business developments or life events could separate them. 'I accept for myself what you want to do for yourself,' Nissim wrote to his brother. 'Our interests and those of our children are the same. I do not want to separate them.' The strength of their bond struck their

contemporaries: 'Although they resembled one another little physically, the two brothers were very close friends. Count Abraham was stout and stocky while his brother was tall' (*L'Écho de Paris*, 16 December 1889). The two brothers died in 1889, only months apart.

▲ The Camondo coat of arms. Since their temporary exile in Trieste in the late 18th century, the Camondos had kept their status as 'protégés' of Austria-Hungary. They became Italian citizens in 1865, since Abraham Salomon had supported Italian reunification. In 1867 Victor Emmanuel II granted him the hereditary title of count, a coat of arms and a motto, *Fides et caritas*. Another decree in 1870 created Nissim count, again a hereditary title, and a motto, *Caritas et fides*. While he was preparing his family's move to Paris, Abraham Behor wrote to his brother: 'The carriages are ready, I am having the coat of arms put on the landaus, with just the crest on my coupé, and on Isaac's only the crown.'

magical appeal. Their enthusiasm was contagious: their venerable 'Grand Papa', now over eighty, also packed his bags and hired a private railway carriage to Vienna, accompanied by Dr Castro, a friend of the family, who was assigned the role of travelling companion.

The departure of the elderly banker was a major event in Istanbul. Nissim wrote to his brother how much he 'regretted that grand papa's departure was so public'.[13] The two brothers corresponded almost daily in French, giving accounts of their activities. Thanks to this correspondence, the various stages of their move to Paris can be followed in some detail. Abraham Behor initially rented a mansion close to the Arc de Triomphe, at 7 rue de Presbourg.

He looked after the stabling of his and Nissim's horses so that he could rent a residence opposite his, at number 6, and furniture, oriental carpets, exquisite objects, prayer shawls, *sefarim* (holy books) and other religious objects, and silverware hallmarked in Istanbul were shipped from Galata to Paris. The two brothers flaunted their ascendancy. They hired butlers who had served in the noblest houses, sent specialists to London to buy horses, and ordered carriages.[14] The coat of arms they had engraved on them was the visible sign of Victor Emmanuel's gratitude for Abraham Salomon's fervent support for Italian unity:[15] in 1867, he had granted him the hereditary title of count, a coat of arms and a motto, *Fides et Caritas* (Faith and Charity).

The Camondos' arrival did not go unnoticed. 'Coming straight from the land of legend, they started by depositing 40 million francs at the Banque de France.'[16] The bank moved into offices in rue Lafayette, and very soon the two brothers, as part of their shared plan for Parisian integration, set their heart on the new Plaine Monceau district. The park had been redesigned in 1861 and part of the garden had been acquired by the banker Émile Pereire, who immediately sold it off in plots to the financial and industrial haute bourgeoisie. For the Camondos it was therefore *the* place to live.

In June 1870, Abraham Behor bought a 4,000-square-metre plot of land at 61 rue de Monceau and Nissim acquired the adjoining plot and mansion at number 63. They consulted Denis-Louis Destors, an architect with a wealthy private clientele; the monumental residence he designed for Abraham Behor was finished in 1875. The banker, his wife Régina, his mother, his daughter Clarisse, her husband Léon Alfassa and their children moved into the main part of the house, set between the front courtyard and the garden at the back, and Isaac moved into the wing they called the 'Petit Hôtel' (small mansion). The interior decoration was designed with their social life in mind. On the ground floor, there was a series of linked reception rooms with painted ceilings and abundant mouldings, gilding and arabesques. Nissim also enlisted Destors' services for the refurbishment of

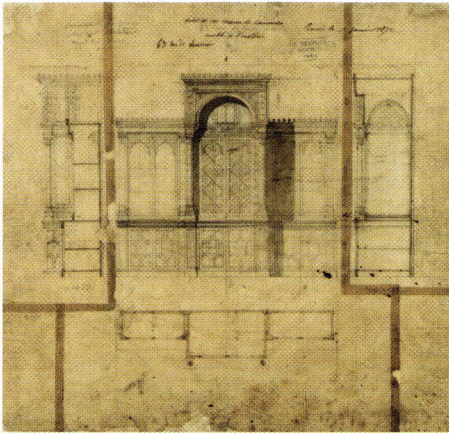

▼ Alphonse Hirsch, *Family Portrait*, oil on canvas, 1875.
The painter Alphonse Hirsch, a Japoniste and friend of the Camondos, probably painted Rachel, Albert and Georges Alfassa with their governess in the conservatory of their uncle Nissim's mansion at 63 rue de Monceau. This picture, shown in Paris at the 1876 Salon, is a priceless record of the interior decoration of the residence in which Moïse grew up and which he had demolished after his mother died.

Nestling among all the plants are two marble sculptures from his father's collection: Calvi's *Sleeping Child* and a bust of a woman by Cordier. The pair of bronze torchères in the form of storks mounted on tortoises and the black wood furniture show his Japoniste taste. All these objects were sold at auction on 21, 22 and 23 November 1910.

▲ Denis-Louis Destors, *Design for the Oratory*, pen and black ink on tracing paper, c. 1875.
Nissim de Camondo commissioned Denis-Louis Destors to design the family oratory at 63 rue de Monceau. The two brothers dutifully observed the Sephardic liturgical traditions handed down by their ancestors. Priceless objects that they had brought from Turkey were used during worship. After their parents died, Isaac and Moïse, who no longer practised their faith, decided to part with them. They donated some to the Musée de Cluny (which loaned them to the Musée d'art et d'histoire du Judaïsme) and others to the Portuguese synagogue in rue Buffault. The Near East and Judaism, the two major elements of their identity, had now been given up altogether.

his mansion at number 63, originally built in 1864 by the former owner, Adolphe Violet. An oratory was designed, where Grand Papa, the two brothers and their family gathered for worship. The house, in which Moïse spent his youth, was to be demolished in 1910. The only surviving account of it is the somewhat acid description Zola gives in his novel *La Curée*, in which 'this still-new and pale building', the residence of Saccard, has 'the pallid features and rich, silly importance of an upstart.'[17] Both houses rapidly became receptacles for a profusion of furniture in all styles and an incongruous assortment of *objets d'art*. The fashion of the moment was for mixing genres: a Renaissance hall with Louis XIV furnishings in the drawing room, 'Turkish style'

in the smoking room and 'Japanese style' in the conservatory. In Abraham Behor's house, a Chinese boudoir with red lacquer walls was filled with Far Eastern ceramics, furniture and objects.[18] The two brothers had embarked on the next phase of integration: they had become collectors and passionate connoisseurs of Japonisme and, eager to be recognized as such, were often seen at the gallery of the art dealer Paul Durand-Ruel and at prestigious auctions.[19] Accompanied by the young Isaac, they were noticed by the Goncourt brothers at the gallery of Auguste and Philippe Sichel, dealers specializing in 'Japonaiseries'.[20]

Their imposing residences and expensive collections were ideal stage sets for lavish hospitality.

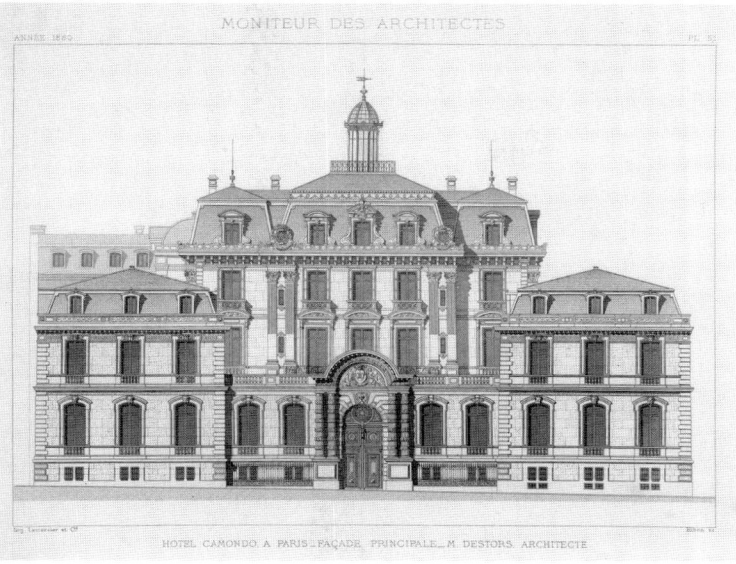

HOTEL CAMONDO A PARIS. FAÇADE PRINCIPALE. M. DESTORS ARCHITECTE

◄ The street façade of Hôtel Camondo, 61 rue de Monceau, *Moniteur des architectes*, 1880. Abraham Behor de Camondo commissioned Denis-Louis Destors to build him a house on the plot at 61 rue de Monceau. The architect submitted plans in 1871. Destors belonged to a generation of self-proclaimed eclectic architects who would freely employ many styles in the same building. In 1875, the Société Centrale des Architectes awarded him the silver medal for 'private architecture' for the Camondo house, and to the great satisfaction of its owner, the plans for the mansion drew an admiring crowd at the Universal Exhibition.

▲ The garden façade of Hôtel Camondo, 61 rue de Monceau, during construction, *c.* 1876. Abraham Behor and his family moved into their new residence in October 1875. The mansion is an imposing three-storey edifice in dressed stone, with a mansard roof surmounted by a lantern with a weather vane. All its façades are richly decorated. On the garden side, the first-floor windows are flanked by caryatids depicting the seasons. On the right, the iron and glass conservatory can be seen, an extremely fashionable feature of many of the new mansions built on the Plaine Monceau. The mansion's façades and roof were listed in 1979 but unfortunately the conservatory, the lantern and all the interior decoration were removed several years earlier.

p. 34-35 :
The garden façade
as it is today.

33

▲ The main drawing room, 61 rue de Monceau, *c.* 1876. This vast reception room opening directly onto the garden was the hub of the family's brilliant social life. The parquets were laid with two Persian carpets, probably from the Camondo residences in Galata. The Louis XIV-style furniture, ordered from Fourdinois, was upholstered in cut velvet with a garnet-coloured design on a gold ground, bought from Tassinari et Châtel. The same fabric was used for the curtains. Above the doors, decorated with gilded arabesques by E. Collignon, were paintings by H. Lévy (*The Libation, The Poet, The Centaur*) and on the ceiling three works by J.P. Blanc, winner of the Grand Prix de Rome in 1867 (*The Triumph of Civilization, Science* and *Industry*). The chandeliers were copper and imitation rock crystal, and on the mantelpiece of the imposing fireplace was a colossal clock with bronze figures symbolizing Prosperity.

▲ Giambattista Tiepolo, *The Wrathful Warrior*, oil on canvas, first half of the 18th century, auctioned on 1 February 1893, no. 27. One hundred and eight pictures were sold at the auction of Abraham Behor's collection of paintings. They included the 17th-century French, Italian, Flemish and Dutch schools, with works by the Barbizon School, the Orientalists and the Pompiers illustrating his taste for contemporary painting and preference for officially recognized painters such as Diaz de la Peña, Dupré, Corot, Chintreuil, Fromentin and Ziem. There was also a Jongkind, bought by Isaac.

▼ Interior of 61 rue de Monceau, *c.*1876.
A pair of pink marble columns at the foot of the monumental staircase was inspired by the Palais Garnier, with atlantes symbolizing Strength and Abundance supporting the vault. The staircase is lit by vase-shaped gas torchères mounted on gilt bronze consoles supported by caryatids. In the preceding antechamber there are Chinese vases on console tables (Abraham Behor was a passionate collector of Far Eastern art). When the mansion and its furniture were sold in 1893, Moïse bought some of these vases, notably the ones visible on the console table on the right.

▼ Vases with dragon-shaped handles, porcelain with enamelled overglaze decoration, China, Qianlong Period (1736–95). Moïse de Camondo acquired this vase at the auction on 1, 2 and 3 February 1893, no. 118.

The aristocratic and financial Tout-Paris, who soon came flocking to dinners and balls, went into raptures over their munificence: 'At Countess Camondo's ball last year, guests were given jewellery as well.'[21]

With apparently limitless means and boundless energy, everything seemed to contribute to their absolute success. With great application, the two brothers made Paris their own, fastidiously adopting the manner and lifestyle of the aristocracy and the customs of the world of high finance. They went hunting, took the waters and spent the winter on the French Riviera. Honours and decorations were heaped on them and they were revered and courted.[22] Nissim's tall, dashing profile was to be seen at the Opéra, concerts, the theatre and at the races. His magnificent carriages were a triumph. Society chroniclers had a field day: 'The great days of the Bois de Boulogne are back again. The rendezvous along the tree-lined avenues around Étoile was extremely lively. Among the most elegant carriages was Count de Camondo's, with two large, rather solemn but very beautiful bays!'[23] But anti-Semitic writers, then ferocious in their attacks, were quick to rail against 'this Levantine Turkeret', and denigrated Carolus-Duran's 'cunning and pallid'[24] portrait of him.[25]

Abraham Behor tirelessly combined his life in Paris and his business and philanthropic activities in Istanbul. Professionally and politically,

▼ Isaac de Camondo, photograph by A. Bert, Paris, c. 1890.
'One metre sixty-four, grey eyes, coloured complexion, round chin and oval face.' This description and the photograph of the forty-two-year-old Isaac on his hunting permit give the impression of an elegant, even stylish man whose gaze conveys a sharp mind and cheerful disposition. He never married, ignoring his father's supplications and thus putting at risk the continuation of a family line that was not to survive the tragedies of the 20th century.

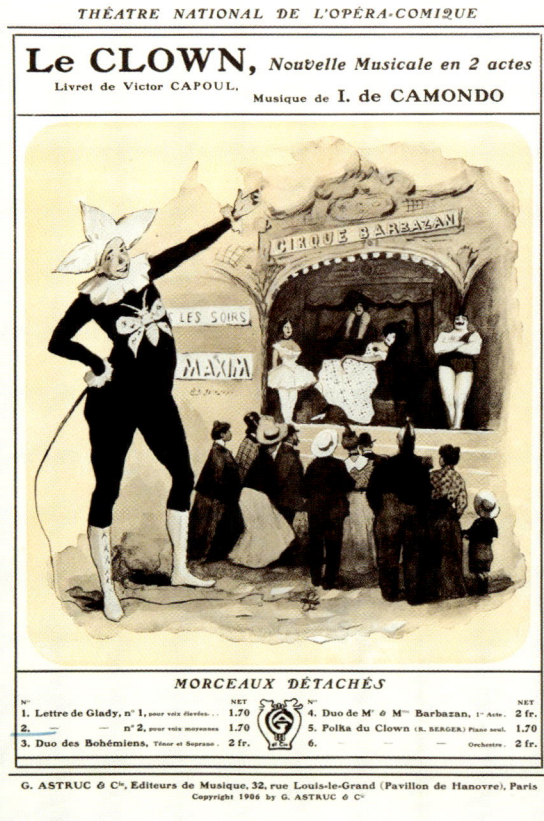

THÉÂTRE NATIONAL DE L'OPÉRA-COMIQUE

Le CLOWN, Nouvelle Musicale en 2 actes
Livret de Victor CAPOUL.
Musique de I. de CAMONDO

MORCEAUX DÉTACHÉS

G. ASTRUC & Cⁱᵉ, Editeurs de Musique, 32, rue Louis-le-Grand (Pavillon de Hanovre), Paris
Copyright 1906 by G. ASTRUC & Cⁱᵉ

▲ Le Clown, programme cover, 1908.
With some twenty orchestral, vocal and instrumental works already to his credit, Isaac de Camondo composed an opera, Le Clown, with a libretto by Victor Capoul. It was premiered in 1906 at the Nouveau Théâtre, directed by Albert Carré, director of the Opéra-Comique, and performed again in 1908 and 1909.
The opera then toured in the provinces and abroad the following years. It has never been performed since.

he remained extremely active. In their quest for assimilation, the Camondo brothers had by no means given up their composite Oriental, Judaic and philanthropic identity. But the foundations for total success were suddenly shaken by a bankruptcy caused by the cavalier attitude of Abraham Behor's son-in-law, Léon Alfassa.[26] Their reputation was badly bruised and their enthusiasm dampened, and this affected the serenity of their last years. They both died in 1889. To their sons Isaac and Moïse, for whom Turkey was no more than a dim and exotic memory, they bequeathed their wealth, titles, and love of art and the French Republic, but their philanthropy was soon to be superseded by patronage of the arts.

Isaac de Camondo, aesthete and music lover

Isaac, a young Parisian banker trained by his father and uncle and who shared the family's dazzling lifestyle, was only thirty-nine when he took charge of the family business. The future of the bank, links with Turkey and the family's charitable activities were of little concern compared to his passion for art. Since his youth, Isaac had been a collector.[27] He was an enlightened, prolific and characteristically eclectic buyer. At first a keen Japoniste, he bought sculpture, lacquerwork and ceramics and an impressive collection of prints. He went on to develop a passion for 18th-century furniture.

The main drawing room of Isaac de Camondo's home, 82 avenue des Champs-Élysées, c.1910.
Unlike his cousin Moïse, Isaac de Camondo lived in rented apartments after the sale of his father's mansion. In 1907, he was obliged to leave his home in rue Gluck, and the efficient and devoted Léonce Tédeschi, who took care of the family's business, soon found him the apartment at 82 avenue des Champs-Élysées: 'I visited this apartment which is absolutely admirable and, in my view, it is exactly what you require.' Photographs show the practically and comfortably furnished surroundings in which Isaac spent the rest of his days. His collections were arranged in 'museological' order. The furniture and objets d'art in the large drawing room were mostly acquired at the auction of the Baron Double collection.

In 1881, he was the most prominent buyer at the auction of the Baron Double collection. He acquired a large number of tables, chests of drawers and chairs and – most notably – the star item, the famous *Three Graces* clock. Then came his fascination with Impressionism, which he discovered in 1892 and 1893 at the galleries of Durand-Ruel, Ambroise Vollard and the Bernheim brothers. His favourite painters were initially Jongkind and Boudin, then his enthusiasm turned to Degas, Manet and Monet.

But the walls of the 'Petit Hôtel', the wing of the mansion in rue de Monceau which Abraham Behor had allotted to him, were probably never hung with famous Impressionist paintings.[28] The house was sold in 1893 due to family disagreements over his father's will, and Isaac moved to rue Gluck, close to the artist's entrance of the Paris Opéra. He entertained lavishly. Artists, museum curators and politicians flocked to admire his residence, where the master of the house regaled his guests with refined oriental dishes. Everyone was dazzled: 'Isaac de Camondo...lived in three adjoining apartments in rue Gluck, designed and fitted out for his collections like the museum in Amsterdam is for the Rembrandts... The dining room was, like his drawing rooms, a picture gallery.'[29] The proximity of the Opéra was no coincidence: music was Isaac's other passion. He was described as the 'prototype of the season-ticket holder' and a 'born patron of dance and music'.[30] Isaac, who had composed since his

youth, emulated Strauss and Offenbach until his combined discoveries of Wagner and Impressionism spurred him to create 'the musical equivalent of a picture'. The success of his melodies encouraged him to write an opera, *Le Clown*. It played to packed houses and the critics sang his praises: 'Monsieur de Camondo is an Impressionist who conveys what he feels with a truly powerful freshness of sound. He does not create a melodic sketch and then weigh it down with vibrant colours. One senses that his polychromatic vigour is spontaneous. He has light in his imagination.'[31] He and his publisher, Gabriel Astruc, both descendants of founders of the Universal Israelite Alliance, had known each other since childhood and shared the same love of music.

Isaac enabled his friend to complete his projects, and the Théâtre des Champs-Elysées was the fruit of their long collaboration.[32]

Although his passion for collecting never waned, he no longer hid his intentions: the Louvre would inherit everything. 'All this is yours', he said to his curator friends. In 1896, he cofounded the Société des Amis du Louvre and was one of its vice-presidents. The following year, he donated part of his collection to the museum while retaining the right of usufruct, and repeated this gesture in 1903 and 1906. However, to the great dismay of his father, he never married.

He kept his word: after his death in 1911, his entire art collection was bequeathed to the Louvre.

◄ Invitation to the inauguration of the Isaac de Camondo rooms at the Louvre, with an illustration of the *Three Graces* clock. The bequest was accepted by decree on 23 November 1911. The installation of the collection in the museum was not completed until two months before the outbreak of war and the official inauguration took place on 16 January 1920. Most of these works are now on display in the Louvre's Objets d'Art Department, in the Musée Guimet, the Musée d'Orsay and at the Château de Versailles.

► Statutes of Isaac Camondo & Co., 1899.
In 1869, the Camondos registered the bank's head office at 31 rue Lafayette, Paris. The statutes describe it as a 'Commercial Company in collective name', for the purpose of banking and all industrial operations of finance and commerce. The share capital was divided between its associates, Abraham Behor and his brother Nissim. These statutes were renewed several times; in 1899, Moïse and his cousin Isaac were the two associates, but they lacked their parents' dynamism and the Camondos' power in the world of finance gradually waned.

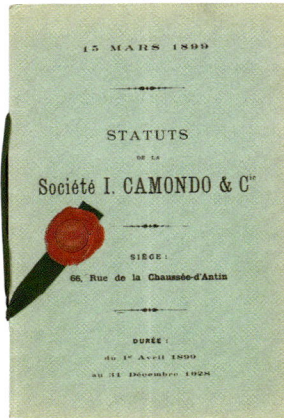

But he attached two conditions: its acceptance in its entirety and display in a space to be named after him for a period of fifty years. This was a novel obligation which finally led to his generosity being forgotten, but it enabled the venerable establishment to side-step the rule against showing contemporary works. Eighteenth-century furniture, medieval and Renaissance sculpture, Far Eastern objects and Japanese prints and ceramics were displayed in seven rooms on the second floor of the Louvre, along with more controversial works: around a hundred Impressionist paintings drawings and etchings. Apollinaire, probably one of the few to be delighted by this, wrote: 'The true modern museum in Paris is now the Louvre'.[33] Unshakeable confidence in the

▲ Léonce Tédeschi, photograph by F. Ponzetti, Genoa, 1892. The Camondos' trusted Constantinople-born administrator Léonce Tédeschi entered the family's service in Paris in the 1880s. He was a senior executive of the bank by 1889. Ever-present both in arranging financial affairs and the most private details of Isaac's daily life (he described him as a 'second self'), Tédeschi performed the same duties for Moïse, serving as their precise and painstaking factotum with unwavering dedication, even devotion.

'But the Jews' adaptation to the milieu – to the country – in which they lived was not solely a measure of exterior protection but an inner need. Their longing to be a part of a nation and need to feel secure in a place where they were no longer considered foreigners prompted them to attach themselves passionately to the culture of their surrounding environment.'

Stefan Zweig, *The World of Yesterday*, 1948.

talent of his painter friends meant more to Isaac than his own claim to fame and posterity.

The philanthropy of the preceding generations towards their community now expressed itself in patronage of the arts. By offering this artistic heritage, Isaac made it available to all. But in doing so, he strayed from the Rothschild family model, which demanded that evidence of its generosity should last forever. Concerned solely with his own fulfilment, he chose a personal destiny and ultimately compromised the survival of his family.

Moïse de Camondo, the sad fate of a gentleman

Tall, with a stern and distinguished appearance, naturally elegant in his speech and manners, Moïse was a courteous man. Although he had a certain deadpan humour, he was firm, sometimes even abrupt in his demands. He greatly admired his creative and capricious cousin, who was nine years older than him, but they were very different. Isaac was an inventive extrovert who followed his instincts and dared to satisfy his whim for innovation; Moïse was reserved, discreet, and conventional in his tastes. The responsibility for passing on the family name weighed heavily on him and tempered his behaviour.

His marriage to Irène Cahen d'Anvers on 14 October 1891, at the town hall of the 16th arrondissement, then the next day at the Israelite temple in rue de la Victoire, was rightly understood as a necessary and carefully considered act full of hope for the future. *Le Gaulois*[34] reported all the details of the splendid reception given at the Cahen d'Anvers' mansion in rue de Bassano, in the drawing rooms whose ornate panelling once adorned the Hôtel de Mayenne. It was here in rue de Bassano that Irène's mother, née Louise de Morpurgo, habitually entertained writers, politicians and artists. Charles Ephrussi introduced them to Renoir, whom the Cahen d'Anvers commissioned to paint their daughters' portraits.[35] Irène was painted in two sittings when she was eight.[36]

The young couple led a luxurious and nomadic life, spending their first winter at Cannes, then temporarily renting a mansion in rue de Constantine before moving to avenue d'Iéna. On 23 July 1892, Irène gave birth to a son, named Nissim after his paternal grandfather. They led a carefree, fashionable existence, spending their summers at Deauville or cruising in the Mediterranean on *Géraldine*, the elegant three-masted schooner Moïse had bought with his father-in-law, Louis Cahen d'Anvers. Two years later, their daughter Béatrice was born, and the same year, Moïse was appointed consul general of Serbia by Milan Obrenovich IV, an extravagant royal client of Isaac Camondo & Co. A capricious and rather

▼ Villa Béatrice, *c.*1910.
This brick and stone house with
its steeply pitched roofs was built
in the 19th century on the ruins
of a seigneurial château in the
village of Aumont, in the heart of

Halatte Forest near Senlis.
Moïse, who was extremely fond
of the area, bought it in 1904 and
named it Villa Béatrice. He came
regularly with children and
friends to this comfortable

house, where they lived
pleasantly and simply, relaxing
here every weekend or for
holidays. Hunting, riding and
tennis were their main pastimes.
Moïse and his children indulged

their passion for bloodsports
to the full, with regular shoots
on the estate, and riding to
hounds twice a week in Halatte
Forest with the 'Par Monts et
Vallons' hunt.

▼ Béatrice de Camondo
with her English governess and
the laundry maid, Eugénie
Kautzmann, in the villa's laundry
room.

unscrupulous figure, Count de Takovo – the title he used during his exile in Paris – was often invited to the Camondos' home, where Isaac introduced him to modern art. In 1894, he regained power and returned to Belgrade, where he ruled until his death in 1901. It was during this period that Moïse accepted the post of consul, then in 1900 that of general commissioner for Serbia at the Universal Exhibition.

Throughout this period, though, Moïse did not neglect his banking activities. Keeping up his father's habits, he continued to issue his stock exchange orders at the Café Anglais and to manage current business. Yet the dynamism and fiery spirit that had characterized the previous generation were

now mere memories. Moïse was also plagued by marital problems. In 1897, he and his wife were officially separated and they divorced in 1902. Isaac, his health failing, also gave up the world of business. When his cousin died in 1911, Moïse found himself alone as head of the bank and took over at Crédit Franco-Canadien, the Compagnie du Gaz, the Compagnie de Ciment Portland et Boulonnais and in the firms in which Isaac Camondo & Co. had a major stake. But the impetus had now gone forever and his taste for finance and risk-taking gave way to the simple and overcautious management of the family fortune. When Nissim died, Moïse had no qualms about shutting down Isaac Camondo & Co.[37]

guests were invited each weekend and returned home delighted, some even proclaiming it the finest hunting in France![40]

When not in the country with his children, Moïse got away from Paris. Over the years, he travelled less and less on business and increasingly for pleasure: St Moritz in December, Monte Carlo in January, then from June until late August, he would take his children with him to Biarritz, Dinard, La Bourboule and Pourville, sometimes in the company of friends. He took the waters at Evian, Aix-les-Bains and Contrexéville. A keen sailor since his youth, he sailed the length and breadth of the Channel, the North Sea and the Mediterranean on his steam yacht *Le Rover* and later on *Le Géraldine*, or

as a guest of his friend Pérignon on *La Fauvette*. Although he still went sailing, he increasingly opted for cultural cruises on board comfortable steamships.

His passion for the 18th century therefore in no way affected his lifestyle. A man of his time, he was a resolute modernist, who took great delight in technical progress and machines. He was a passionate motorist, was flattered to be recognized as such, and chose his cars for their powerful engines and elegant coachwork. He wrote to André Citroën: 'I am keen to inform you that I authorize you to include my name in the list of references in the brochure you are preparing.'[41] In 1901, he took part in the Paris–Berlin race and regretted not being able to

▼ Jean-Baptiste Oudry, *Uncoupling the Old Pack at the Petite Patte d'Oie Crossroads in Compiègne Forest*, oil on canvas, 1739 (detail).

▼ Foxhunting, Saint-Hubert, 1910.

Codified as early as the 14th century and a sign of royal power, hunting continued after the fall of the monarchy, becoming the preserve of a social and sporting elite. It has been an inexhaustible source of inspiration for artists, as illustrated by Jean-Baptiste Oudry's oil sketches of *The Royal Hunts of Louis XV,* executed after drawings from life, and among the jewels of Moïse de Camondo's collection; hunting customs and dress codes were handed down with full respect for tradition.

► Béatrice Reinach, 1933. From 1897, Béatrice, an accomplished horsewoman, was a member of the Lyons-Halatte hunt, whose motto was 'Par Monts et Vallons' ('Over Hill and Dale'). In their blue livery, they hunted mainly in Halatte Forest and with Prince Murat's and Gaston Menier's hunts at Chantilly, and later with Baron James de Rothschild's hounds at Compiègne. From 1885 to 1930, the master of the hunt was Count Bertrand de Valon. It was subsequently run by a committee, whose president was the Marquise de Chasseloup-Laubat.

participate in the Paris–Vienna race the following year as the racing chassis of his car was not delivered in time. When he moved into rue de Monceau, there were five cars in the garage designed for them: a Renault landaulet and limousine, a coupé, a double phaeton and a Panhard limousine. The two full-time chauffeur-mechanics who lodged in the outbuildings took care of their maintenance and sometimes drove them. Camille Clermont and Jules Guzzi carried out these well-paid duties competently for many years. From the 1920s onwards they usually looked after three cars, which Moïse regularly changed after lengthy deliberation for the latest models: a Torpedo Voisin, Talbot and Citroën coupés, then a Bugatti cabriolet, etc.[42]

After 1910 the design and construction of his new mansion in rue de Monceau took up all the energy and attention of Moïse and his entourage. During the summer of 1913, he and his children moved into the new residence, which promised to be a superb and lively home. By the following spring everything was finished, but hardly had the string of receptions for their curious and dazzled guests begun than war broke out, plunging the world into limbo.

Flight Lieutenant Nissim de Camondo

In 1914, Nissim, now twenty-two, had just completed his military service and begun training as a banker in

◄ Nissim and Béatrice de Camondo, René Seligmann and Oscar Roditi at St Moritz, 1913. Stefan Zweig's *World of Yesterday* describes a secure and carefree world: 'Never had Europe been more powerful, richer, more beautiful, never had it believed more firmly in an even better future.'

▼ Nissim de Camondo in the trenches, Bois-en-Hache, Aix-Noulette, November 1915.
'I hope that our turn in the trenches is over for a few days, as it really is a dirty mess, especially at night, with one's feet in water and the fog that seeps right into you.'
Letter from Nissim to Moïse de Camondo, 7 November 1915.

▼ Nissim de Camondo, observer-photographer of MF 33 Squadron, Le Plessis-Belleville, April 1916.
'I am pleased because my photos are good and are proving invaluable. … I am starting to become rather popular.'
Letter from Nissim to Moïse de Camondo, 16 April 1916.

▼ Nissim de Camondo, pilot, 1917.
'Monsieur, this morning, your son left on a photographic reconnaissance mission. He took with him Lieutenant Desessard, with whom he habitually flew and who was also an excellent gunner. We saw the machine gain altitude then head towards the enemy lines. Two hours later, they had not returned.'
Letter from Lieutenant Rotival to Moïse de Camondo, 5 September 1917.

the stocks department of the Banque de Paris et des Pays-Bas. Athletic, energetic, 'a fine huntsman, an elegant and bold horseman, charming both in his bearing and manners',[43] he enlisted immediately, driven by a joyful and sincere sense of patriotism. Whenever he had a moment's respite, he wrote to Moïse and Béatrice, whom he knew were fraught with anxiety. This correspondence, religiously preserved, describes the daily events he had to confront.[44] His accounts are alert and lively, with precise and colourful descriptions, the tone simple and direct. They are full of affection and tenderness for his family and reveal his intensely close relationship with his father, whom he addresses as 'tu' and showers with affectionate nicknames – a far cry from the distant and pompous respect that was de rigueur in most French aristocratic families. Offensives, retreats, battles, the cold, the violence of combat – nothing seemed to sap Nissim's enthusiasm and courage during the first year of war. He was promoted to second-lieutenant and assigned to the 21st Dragoon. But the mud of the trenches, fatigue and the deaths of his comrades finally tempered his optimism. In this icy, damp hell where 'danger was permanent and without glory', he decided to 'apply to join the air force as an observer'.[45] As the war wore on and intensified, it also became more modern. The air force, initially neglected, began to play an important role in the conflict; Nissim was sent on reconnaissance, bombing and combat missions. He

◄ Nissim and Béatrice
de Camondo in the park
at Château de Champs-
sur-Marne, the home
of their grandparents,
the Cahen d'Anvers,
spring 1916.
'My darling Bella, I think
of you all the time; I always
have your photo with me
and I kiss you with all
my heart.'
Letter from Nissim
to Béatrice,
16 November 1914.

did everything he could to overcome the resistance of his commanding officer and his father's reservations. His application was approved on 11 January 1916, and he was attached as an observer to squadron MF 33, whose insignia, an axe, took its cue from a play on words on the name of its squadron leader, Captain A. Bordage (in French 'à l'abordage!' means 'up lads and at 'em!'). A new and infinitely more exhilarating life began: 'I am sure,' he wrote to his father, 'that if you got into a plane, you would love it. It is a marvellous sensation and what is curious is the great impression of security one feels.'[46] And yet, 'one has to imagine the two-seaters in which we, as observers, went to war then. …Two holes. The pilot in front, his passenger behind. Between them two or three metres of smooth fuselage swept by the airstream behind the propeller. No question of a parachute. The observer would therefore run a double risk of death – his own and the pilot's. When the pilot was killed, the observer could do nothing but crash into the ground with the blind, mad plane'.[47]

Nineteen-sixteen was the year of Verdun. Nissim was praised for the quality of his photographs which were 'proving invaluable'.[48] He was promoted to lieutenant and was awarded his pilot's licence. In September 1917, Moïse was informed that his son was missing in action: 'This horrific war is for all of us, alas, a source of affliction, anxiety and anguish. I have myself been

Béatrice and Léon Reinach, 1933. In 1919, Béatrice married Léon Reinach, one of the sons of Théodore Reinach, a famous Hellenic scholar and member of the Institut de France. The couple lived with Moïse at 63 rue de Monceau. In 1923, after the birth of their second child, they moved to Neuilly-sur-Seine.

in utter agony, ever since my son, an army pilot, disappeared on the 5th behind enemy lines after an air battle. I have had no news since and the hopes we had, great though they were, are never enough, the period of waiting in which one entertains every possible conjecture being the most depressing'.[49] He would not be certain that his son had died until the beginning of October. 'From the beginning of the war,' he wrote 'a sombre foreboding, almost a sense of certainty had taken root in my mind, but with time, as the years went by, a sort of hope set in. Unfortunately it was dashed. His reckless courage was mentioned not once but five times in dispatches, and each time, instead of filling me with joy and pride it only deepened my fears. As you can see, this catastrophe has broken me and changed all my plans.'[50] The death of his only son, to whom he was to have given everything, robbed him of his flesh and blood and emptied his life of meaning.

The war dragged on and the menace of German long-range heavy artillery hung over Paris. Moïse de Camondo had to protect his mansion and safeguard his collections.[51] The efforts he put into this rescue operation momentarily distracted him from his 'unspeakable bitterness'.[52] Another event consoled him: Béatrice became engaged to Léon Reinach shortly after the Armistice. For Moïse this marriage was 'a great satisfaction and one less worry'.[53] Léon's illustrious family had served the worlds of art and politics with talent and intelligence. His father,

▼ Moïse de Camondo with his grandchildren and son-in-law, Léon Reinach, at Aumont, 1932. Moïse was an affectionate and

attentive grandfather and his grandchildren Fanny and Bertrand Reinach frequently stayed at Aumont. Just as he was in Paris,

Moïse was a meticulous host, taking great care over the upkeep of this property and the surrounding grounds.

Théodore Reinach, who held a doctorate and was a member of the Institut de France, built Villa Kérylos, a synthesis of Hellenistic art and his imagination, at Beaulieu on the Rivieria;[54] his uncle Joseph had been Gambetta's principal private secretary and, importantly, a Dreyfusard from the beginning. But as with the Camondos, political posturing and public appointments no longer motivated Reinachs' descendants. Béatrice was a reserved young woman, and Léon a man of discretion. 'He is a musician and a complete stranger to trade and business,' Moïse wrote.[55] The young couple lived at 63 rue de Monceau until 1924, where their two children, Fanny and Bertrand, added a touch of freshness and gaiety.[56]

Moïse, ever the attentive and affectionate grandfather, enjoyed their stays at Aumont. He himself no longer hunted but Béatrice had taken up the baton. An outstanding horsewoman, from September until late spring she rode with the 'Par Monts et Vallons' hunt, some of whose members were her closest friends. Young Fanny followed just as passionately in her wake.

Worn down by mourning and suffering, Moïse retired from society life. His friends were now mainly art lovers and gourmets. He recovered his taste for travel and wrote long descriptions of the pains he took to enrich the confidential guide of the Club des Cents, of which he was a member.

Like Isaac, he had become a personality in artistic officialdom and was often busy in his duties

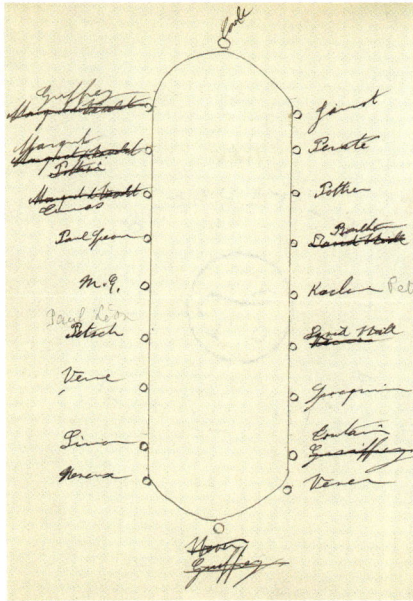

► ▼ Table plan and menu, 1933. Every year, usually in June, Moïse invited curators from the Musée du Louvre and members of the Conseil des Musées Nationaux to lunch; great care was taken over the seating plan and menu.

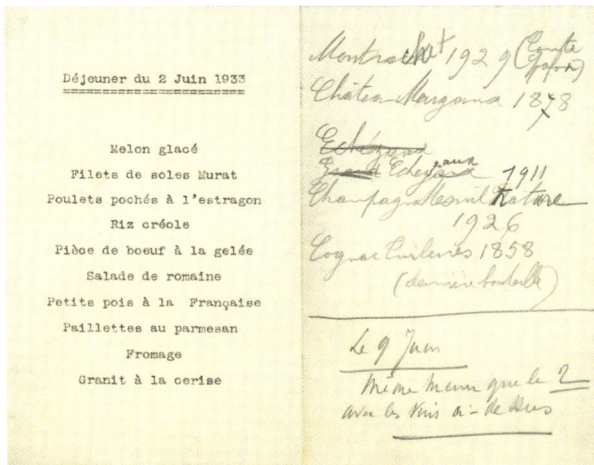

Déjeuner du 2 Juin 1933

Melon glacé
Filets de soles Murat
Poulets pochés à l'estragon
Riz créole
Pièce de boeuf à la gelée
Salade de romaine
Petits pois à la Française
Paillettes au parmesan
Fromage
Granit à la cerise

▼ The Blue Drawing Room.
After Béatrice and Léon Reinach moved to Neuilly, Moïse de Camondo made a comfortable and refined room for himself in his daughter's former bedroom and boudoir. He wrote his letters at this writing table, watched over by Nissim's photograph.

as a member of the board of the Société des Amis du Louvre, the Union Centrale des Arts Décoratifs and the Conseil des Musées Nationaux. He continued to acquire works at a steady rate despite Nissim's death. His son's memory obsessed him, yet as time went by, few people recognized the smiling young officer in the photographs he hung everywhere. The idea of dedicating the house and his collection to the memory of his son, of transforming it into a haven that would be immune from time and death, began to take shape in his mind.

The more this quest absorbed him during his last years the more sumptuous his residence became, devoted as it was to the 18th century. Exciting effects, the unexpected and the spontaneous found no place here – they would have been incongruous. Besides, the Reinachs had moved to Neuilly-sur-Seine and Moïse himself seldom lived at the house. However, each spring he invited curators and collectors, rarely more than twenty at a time, to his 'Louvre' and 'Marsan' lunches. The invitations were sent out three weeks before, the seating plan was the result of lengthy deliberation, and once the menu had been decided on, Moïse the connoisseur chose the wine. He also entertained his gourmet friends in the Club des Cents. The chef had to outdo himself to regale their refined palates. Apart from these formal and rigorously orchestrated events, only a few scholars of 18th-century art and close friends ever entered this timeless temple.

◄ Bertrand Reinach, 1938.
◄ Fanny Reinach at the races during the German Occupation. On 20 November 1943, Fanny, twenty-three, and Bertrand, twenty, were held prisoner at Drancy for almost a year, before being sent to Auschwitz with their father on convoy 62. Their mother Béatrice left on convoy 69 on 7 March 1944.

► Fanny Reinach on Pamplemousse, 1 August 1942. Fanny, like her mother, was a passionate horsewoman. She was an extremely accomplished rider, hunted to hounds and took part in riding competitions from a young age. Her riding exploits, recorded on film and kept in photograph albums, continued seemingly unhindered by the war and the Occupation.

On 21 December 1936, in the presence of numerous prominent figures from the art world, the education minister Jean Zay inaugurated the Musée Nissim de Camondo, whose management had been entrusted by its donor to the Union Centrale des Arts Décoratifs. Moïse had passed away the year before and Béatrice had supervised the execution of his will. She was proud that her father's mansion and collections had been donated to the nation. The new museum was a rare and enchanting place, a synthesis of modernism and the 'sweetness of living' praised by Talleyrand, and also the final triumph of the Camondo family, whose history was now at an end.

Nissim's death had been its pretext and possibly a premonition of the tragic end awaiting the family's last descendants. 'I was born in a museum,' Moïse's granddaughter Fanny confided to a friend at Drancy, the French 'waiting room' for the German death camps, where she, then 22 years old, her brother and her parents were imprisoned in 1942.[57] They left for Auschwitz on convoys 62 and 69, never to return. Their deaths were the ultimate justification for the Musée Nissim de Camondo.

► Nissim de Camondo's bedroom.
When the museum opened in 1936, in Nissim's former apartment only the office was opened to the public. It was devoted to family history and souvenirs. On the commode are photographs of Lieutenant Nissim de Camondo and his grandfather Count Nissim de Camondo. The bronze equestrian statue by Georges Malissard depicts his sister Béatrice Reinach in 1923. It was donated in 1967 by her cousin Irène Anspach.

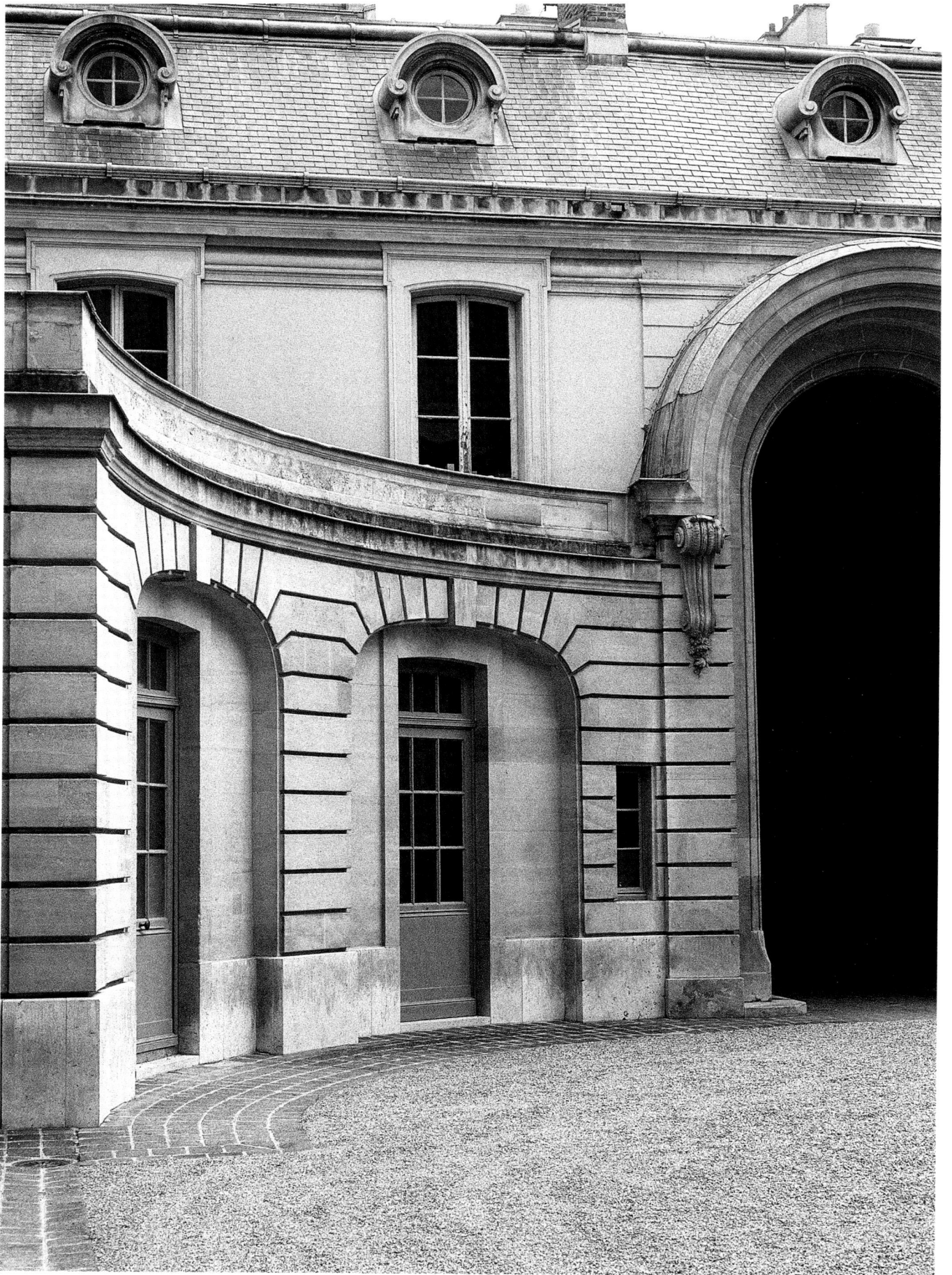

A Mansion in the 18th-Century Style *François Loyer*

On the edge of the park

When Moïse de Camondo inherited the family mansion after his mother's death on 18 June 1910, he immediately decided to rebuild it to create a more suitable setting for the works of art he had amassed during his career as a collector. Such a bold decision may seem surprising, for two reasons. Firstly, one might have imagined that a son would be more faithful both to his mother's memory and to his childhood home; and secondly, this rather unexpected return to the edge of the Parc Monceau ran counter to the trend at the time, which had seen the slow shift of Paris's residential areas to the west. Rather than the fashionable avenue du Bois, from whose grand mansions one could watch an endless procession of elegance, or the terraces of the avenue d'Iéna overlooking the Champ-de-Mars (the latest fashionable place to be seen), Moïse preferred the old-world prestige of boulevard Malesherbes, in the heart of the Rive Droite.[1] This decision was all the more striking given that his uncle Abraham Behor's prestigious mansion, on the adjoining plot, had been sold in 1893.[2] Moïse therefore had no great reason to come back and set up home in the shadow of the ambitious property next door, that had now passed into other hands. If he did so, it was for reasons other than underlining the social prestige and financial power of the dynasty of bankers to which he belonged.[3]

But did he really build it for himself? The answer to this question gives a better understanding of how original his decision was. From the start, the house he wanted to build was conceived as the setting for the prestigious collection he meant to bequeath to subsequent generations. Although officially intended for his son Nissim, this elegant residence was close to the other artistic foundations in the district: its immediate neighbour, the Musée Cernuschi,[4] and the prestigious Hôtel Jacquemart-André.[5] The choice of location speaks volumes about its owner's intentions: although the Palais de Chaillot site did not become the 'hill of the arts' that the Duchess de Galliera had envisaged twenty years earlier, the greenery of the Parc Monceau was now poised to take its place.[6]

The area had undoubtedly enjoyed a good reputation for some years. Since the beginning of the 19th century, its central location (about half a mile from place de la Madeleine) had made it a significant property development, especially as the still unfinished boulevard Malesherbes led to it almost in a straight line. From then on, the great temptation was to extend it to provide access to the Plaine Monceau area on the edge of Paris, and in the process create prestigious properties around the park.[7] The park itself, which dated back to the 18th century, had remained the property of the Orléans family until 1852, when it was decided to expropriate it, a decision which became effective in 1859. Redesigned in 1861 by the engineer Adolphe Alphand and reduced to half of its original size, it became the most luxurious park in Paris, with ornate iron gates designed by the architect Gabriel Davioud. Inspired by English gardens, the plan was to surround it with mansions that would enjoy private access during public opening hours. Yet the sale of plots around its southern side, masterfully carried out by the Pereire brothers, Émile and Isaac, took some time.[8] The first of these prestigious mansions were not built until the beginning of the Third Republic: the residences of Abraham Behor de Camondo, Émile-Justin Menier, Henri Cernuschi, Auguste Dreyfus, Émile Pereire and Joseph Reinach.[9] Despite the building of these mansions around the Parc Monceau, the jewel of Haussmann's Paris and so easy to imagine as belonging to the Second Empire, the project in fact dates from the moment of its fall.[10]

p. 56:
The rear of the outbuildings,
seen from the courtyard.

TERRAINS
DU PARC MONCEAU

The mansion at 63 rue de Monceau, at least in its original state, before its reconstruction by Sergent in 1911, was one of the earliest of the Parc Monceau residences. The plot was bought from Émile Pereire in 1863 by the entrepreneur Adolphe Violet, who built the house which Nissim de Camondo bought in 1870.[11] Although the name of the architect is unknown, his classical rationalist style is more than reminiscent of Jean-Louis Pascal and Gabriel Crétin, and also Charles Questel.[12] Its owner was a public works contractor who specialized in the supply of marble;[13] it was probably his acquisition of the Tinseau quarry at Damparis near Dôle in the Jura (a source of hard, frost-resistant limestone particularly sought after for laying the foundations of large buildings) which prompted him to sell the house only six years after it was built.[14]

The Hôtel Violet's architecture clashed with the setting, particularly with respect to its relative simplicity compared to its ambitious neighbours. The extremely long and narrow plot (approximately 80 by 25 metres) was ill-suited for a large mansion set in a garden, especially as it curved along the edge of the park. Three years after it was built, the owner exchanged land with Émile Pereire in order to widen and straighten the rear part of the property overlooking the park.[15] The main entrance was in rue de Monceau, but a secondary service entrance was also provided in the mews at 105 boulevard

► The 63 rue de Monceau entrance. The original outbuildings were retained.

◄ The division of plots on the south side of the Parc Monceau, c. 1868.
Émile Pereire acquired half of the former Orléans estate, which had been converted into a public park by Adolphe Alphand in 1861. In 1868, many of the plots (in pink on the plan) still had not been sold. Number 63 rue de Valois-du-Roule (now rue de Monceau) then belonged to Adolphe Violet. Numbers 61 and 63 were bought by the Camondo brothers in 1870.
Colour lithograph (scale 1:1000)
Bibliothèque historique de la Ville de Paris.

► The outbuildings, seen from the house.
The outbuildings, built by Adophe Violet in 1863, have kept their original appearance, with the tall entrance and semicircular ground floor set against the surrounding rectangular construction. René Sergent merely redesigned the false arcades with low arches and supporting structure to harmonize with the façade of the new house.

Malesherbes. The architect had a choice – either to construct a pavilion or to build a mansion in the space between two neighbouring residences. He opted for a building that adjoined one residence on the west side and was detached on the other, opposite the service entrance. This suggests that twin buildings may have been planned at numbers 61 and 63, a rather modest solution for such a location.

The outbuildings, with their monumental Louis XV-style gateway, were built facing the street (where they can still be seen today).[16] The style is sober, extremely restrained and undecorated.[17] The very deep gateway insulates the building from the street (in the manner of the Ancien Régime, and not employed since the Restoration, when the pavilion was preferred). The rather abrupt gateway is one of the building's original features.[18] The enclosure of the front of the courtyard is much more pronounced than in Eugène Pereire's neighbouring mansion, which simply has railings between two outlying pavilions framing the perspective.[19]

The gateway opens onto a square courtyard enclosed at the front by the semicircular rear of the outbuildings and at the back of which there originally stood an imposing, two-storey square pavilion with a shallow porch and a broad flight of steps with a glass canopy. The interior layout was clear-cut: an entrance hall entirely for ease of circulation, contrasting with the deep volumes of

◄ Plan of the plot
(1:500), 1900.
The juxtaposition of the
two mansions on their
respective plots prior to
Sergent's changes.

▼ Plan of the mansions at
61 and 63 rue de Monceau,
undated, black ink and
watercolour with pencil marks.
Probably drawn up by the
architect Denis-Louis Destors
when the two plots were
acquired, this plan shows the
position of Abraham Behor de
Camondo's future mansion and
the precise dimensions of its
neighbour, the former Hôtel
Violet, acquired by his brother
Nissim.

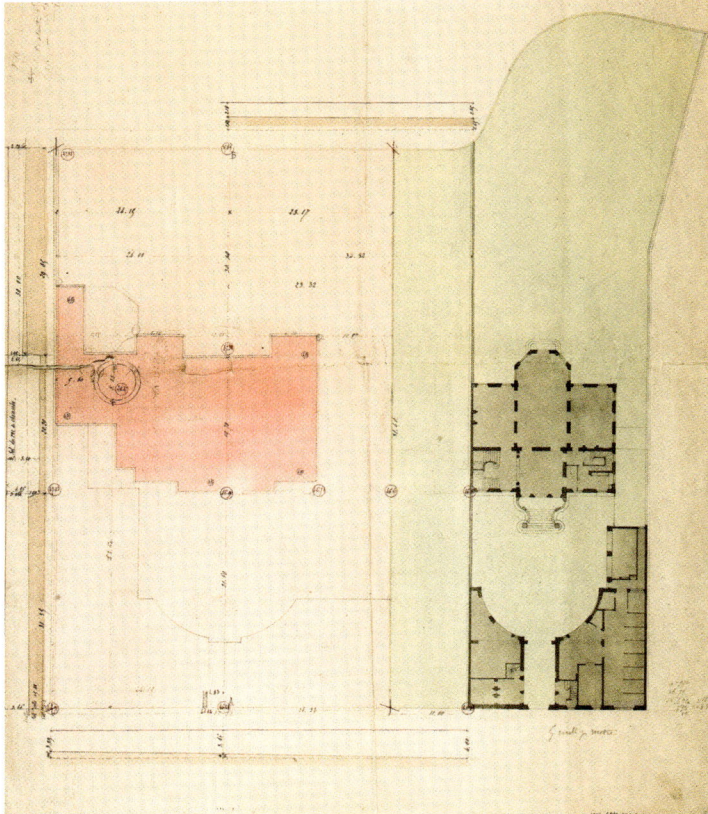

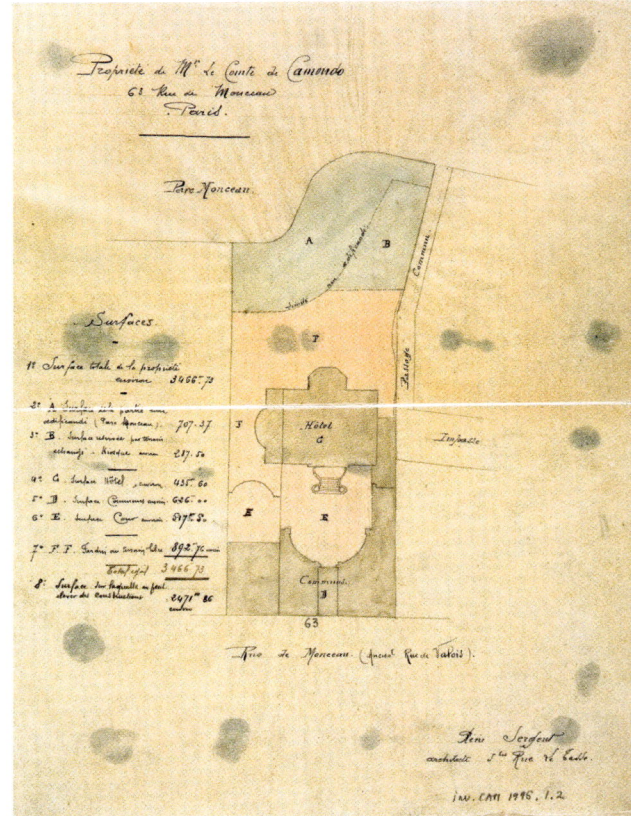

the rooms overlooking the park. On one side of
the hall was a fine staircase set against the wall,
and on the other the service staircase and servants'
quarters off the side corridor. On the garden side
of the house, the large drawing room was aligned
on an axis with the small drawing room and
the dining room on either side of it. The private
apartments on the first floor must have been
especially comfortable, with several bathrooms
benefiting from running water.[20]

This rather compact building (if judged
only by the simplicity of its ground plan) was
gradually expanded.[21] In 1872, Nissim de Camondo
also exchanged land, this time with his brother
Abraham Behor, who had just acquired the plot at
number 61 to build his own mansion.[22] The idea
was to separate the two buildings with a strip of
land, on which twin stables could be built on rue de
Monceau. The architect, Denis-Louis Destors,
skilfully extended the existing façade to match the
level of the neighbouring mansion, which he had
also designed. The brothers' two houses together,
one large and one small, give the impression of
a particularly fine double mansion. But Nissim
de Camondo did not stop there. The following
year he built a conservatory on the right of the
courtyard, on the mews side. Finally, in 1874, he
built a fourth façade, disguising the original gable
end on the west side. Taking advantage of the
annexed land, the architect was able to create a

► Plan of the upper ground floor, blueprint after the original, dated 22 September 1910. On this plan of the reconstruction, René Sergent marked the position of the existing building in red ink (the foundations were reused at the client's request). Here one can see that he kept the original plan as unchanged as possible, merely adding a wing at right angles on the park side, extending as far as the Hôtel Cernuschi next door, and widening it with service rooms on the right. He skilfully succeeded in placing the rotunda at the junction of the two façades overlooking the park, on the very spot where the central bay of the original building had stood.

◄ Plan of the plot before the demolition of the Violet mansion, showing the areas with planning permission and the limit of the non-aedificandi area. Undated [1910], tracing paper, pencil and watercolour.

protruding semi-rotunda with a dome to fill it out. The principle of twinned, adjoining mansions was developed into the idea of two vast separate buildings whose subtle interplay makes one forget the various projects and changes of mind that followed the initial construction.

The house of a rich collector

This was the building that Moïse de Camondo decided to demolish and rebuild thirty years later, but without altering the overall ground plan. The outbuildings on the street were kept as they were; only the architecture of the mansion itself changed. The new construction, built on the same foundations, was enlarged with the addition of service rooms on the east side, and extended at the back by a wing built at right angles with views of the park. The idea was to build a 'house of a rich collector'.[23] For over twenty years, Moïse de Camondo had been collecting the art of the second half of the 18th century, in a manner that

APRÉS LA COURSE_Beaucoup d'atteles mais peu d'élus

the Goncourt brothers would have approved of.[24] Interested almost exclusively in furniture and the decorative arts, he maintained close relations with the greatest antique dealers of his time, such as the Seligmanns and the Duveens.[25] He was certainly not the only one to have fallen in love with 18th-century art. The couturier Jacques Doucet preceded him, before selling off his collection in 1912. He had his rivals, too: his cousin Isaac de Camondo,[26] the Cognacq-Jays[27] and Edward and Julia Tuck.[28] But here his parents-in-law, the Cahen d'Anvers, must also be mentioned who devoted their lives to the restoration of the Château de Champs-sur-Marne, a masterpiece of early 18th-century French art.

The tradition of collectors and patrons (in the way that the Rothschilds had established in the mid-19th century) found surprisingly fertile ground in business circles, where most of today's great public collections originated. Appropriating what had been a princely privilege under the Ancien Régime, the financiers of the time thought nothing of investing colossal sums in prestigious purchases from which they drew no profit whatsoever, since most of the collections they acquired were eventually donated to public collections. The ambition that drove them to acquire exceptional works reflects as much their lifestyle (of which horseracing, yachting, hunting and balls were an integral part) as their refined

vision of culture, directly associated in their view with their patronage of the arts. Circumstances justified this, especially as their religious origin laid them open to extremely violent attacks, particularly after the Dreyfus Affair (1897) had unleashed an upsurge of passionate anti-Semitism of which they became choice victims.[29] One way of responding to this was to amass collections which celebrated France's grandeur and the greatest moments of its history, especially that period of refinement par excellence, the 18th century.[30]

The world these collectors frequented was in some ways a surprising one. The Tout-Paris to which they belonged was aristocratic only in name. The title bestowed on the Camondos by the Italian court thirty years earlier may have given their fortune more lustre, but nobody believed in this honorific nobility. The great lineages had already begun boosting their family fortunes by entering into advantageous alliances with industrial and financial dynasties, particularly American ones. The order of the day was already a far cry from the court of Versailles under the Ancien Régime and much closer to the 'two hundred families' later denounced by the Front Populaire.[31] The intermixing of the upper classes certainly did not affect either the elite's prejudices or its lifestyle but it did change its culture, which became much more open to the world of art; hence its members sometimes forged close ties with artists and art dealers. They belonged to the same world, a truer world than the conventions and social etiquette with which they had to comply on a daily basis. In this two-tier universe, art was a refuge, and often a consolation for personal tragedy, as Moïse de Camondo would later discover. It is hardly surprising, therefore, that he addressed an antique dealer by his first name in his private correspondence, or that he had absolute confidence in his intermediaries during his transactions, allowing him to acquire exceptional works, on the advice of a wide range of specialists including numerous museum curators keen to see such masterpieces brought together in a single collection, thereby ensuring their preservation and enhancement. From the outset, the reconstruction of the house in rue de Monceau was part of a long-term project, the creation piece by piece of an ensemble.

Finding an architect equal to the project was no easy task at a time when taste was changing profoundly and the rising sense of modernity could easily demolish the very concept of the building and its historical references. The 19th century had seen the triumph of architecture 'de style', of gothic châteaux and churches, and Renaissance and Louis XIII mansions. At the beginning of the 20th century, theatrical Romanticism was already a thing of the past, and the sumptuous papier-mâché decors that Henri Duponchel had concocted for James de Rothschild's mansion in rue Laffitte (1836) had long fallen out of fashion. Over half a century had passed, in which 17th- and 18th-century classicism had triumphed over the art of the Middle Ages and the Early Renaissance. The genealogy of the 'grand style' thus had its forebears, from Armand Berthelin, architect of the Louis XIV-style Château de Boulogne in 1850,[32] to Charles Questel, Honoré Daumet, Félix Langlais, Alfred Aldrophe, Jules Reboul and Charles Mewès, among others.[33]

However, the best-known of these classical historicists were Henri Parent and Hippolyte Destailleur. In 1876, Parent brilliantly refurbished the Hôtel de Boisgelin for the La Rochefoucauld-Doudeauvilles, having made a name for himself with his mansions around the Parc Monceau. Destailleur, apart from his mansions for the Rothschilds,[34] built the gigantic Château de Franconville (1876–82),[35] an almost exact copy of François Mansart's Maisons-Laffitte, at a time when the art of the early 17th century was no longer fashionable.

Another generation had taken over from these masters, whose work dated back to the end of the Second Empire or the beginning of the Third Republic. At the turn of the century, the most prominent was undeniably Ernest Sanson, who had trained under Destors and then Questel before working for Bailly, from whom he took over. He built so many prestigious mansions that he alone came to epitomize the 18th-century French taste that Parent and Destailleur had revived before him.[36] Louis Parent,[37] nephew of Henri, Walter-André Destailleur,[38] son of Hippolyte, and Maurice Sanson, Ernest's son, soon joined him, along with René Sergent, who had worked at the office for a long time before starting his own practice in 1902. Of all the architects of their generation, they were the most capable of designing a prestige mansion. Indeed, it is hard to imagine official architects such as Charles Girault, Victor Laloux, Paul Nénot, Joseph Cassien-Bernard and Jean-Camille Formigé being interested in this type of project, which they did not habitually undertake. Of course the modern architects rejected any reference to period architecture and were more used to designing residential buildings and villas than mansions.[39]

The architect René Sergent.
Photograph reproduced in René
Bétourné, *René Sergent, architecte.
1865–1927* (Paris, Horizons de
France, 1931).

► Staircase of the Hôtel Otto
Bemberg, 28 rue Émile-Menier,
Paris XVI, 1911.
Reproduced from Bétourné, p. 27.
René Sergent limited his
repertoire to a few models, which
he transposed in different ways
from building to building. This
was the case with the conjunction
of the large staircase with central
well and wrought-iron balustrade
and the colonnade inspired by
Gabriel. For the Hôtel Bemberg,
he offset them with the lightness
of a suspended staircase, on a
reduced scale, going up to the
bedroom floor.

An exceptional architect

Being in regular contact with the Duveens and
especially the Seligmanns, Moïse de Camondo
probably did not waste much time when choosing
an architect. René Sergent had just built these two
dealers' 'exhibition mansions', in place Vendôme
(1907) and in rue de Talleyrand on the esplanade
des Invalides (1910).[40] For one of them he had
adopted an almost literal interpretation of Gabriel's
Petit Trianon, rather strangely set at the back of a
courtyard behind the majestic, ordered façade on
the square itself. For the other he designed an
austere elevation whose large, arched first-floor
windows rested on a double base formed by a
supporting pedestal course and an extremely low
mezzanine floor. This highly personal vision, as
faithful to the great examples of French classicism
as it was original in its way of implementing them,
was not that of a mere imitator, even a virtuoso
one, as Sanson and Destailleur could be. In his
mature work René Sergent proved himself an
inventive artist capable of breathing new life into
the most conventional repertoires. It was this rather
odd ability that persuaded Moïse de Camondo.
Despite his extremely precise brief – the creation
of a permanent setting for the display of his
collections – he allowed his architect great freedom,
trusting in his competence and not seeking to
dominate the project.[41]

He was right to do so. Sergent was a brilliant architect at the height of his artistic powers. His career was no less unusual. Instead of attending the École des Beaux-Arts, he enrolled at the École Spéciale d'Architecture, founded in 1865 by the engineer Émile Trélat to free the professional training of architects from the academic drawing practised in rue Bonaparte.[42] Run by a director who had graduated from the École centrale and also held a chair in civil construction at the Conservatoire des arts et métiers, the curriculum was largely professional: the study of techniques and materials, and the knowledge indispensable for the liberal exercise of the architect's profession ranked among the foremost preoccupations of a school that was also closely involved in training engineers. He graduated first in his year in 1884 when he was still only twenty and immediately went to work for Ernest Sanson, with whom he stayed for over fifteen years. There he benefited from an exceptional professional structure in an office which had its own library and considered the cultural knowledge of its associates to be indispensable. Very quickly, Sergent began both practising and teaching architecture, giving courses in construction at the École Spéciale. At the same time, he took an interest in architectural criticism, writing for two professional journals before editing *Le Moniteur des architectes* from 1894 to 1900. His former colleague René Bétourné was right when he remarked: 'He studied the works of

Although at first sight Sergent's façades may appear to be pastiches, to consider them as no better than imitations does not do them justice. Pushing the rules of classicism to their limits, the architect refined his references, playing on the relationship between their organization and the mass or space with which he balanced them to produce original, artistically inventive solutions.

▲ 'Hôtel de Messieurs Duveen Brothers', 20 place Vendôme, Paris I, 1907.

Reproduced from Bétourné, p. 33.

▼ The Champ-de-Mars façade of Jean-Philippe Worth's mansion at 4 avenue Émile-Deschanel, Paris VII, 1909.

Reproduced from Bétourné, p. 19.

► Courtyard façade of Otto Bemberg's mansion at 28 rue Émile-Menier, Paris XVI, 1911.

Reproduced from Bétourné, p. 25.

Mansard [*sic*], Delafosse, Daviler, Gabriel, Blondel, Brongniart, Ledoux and Chalgrin with intelligence and passion. He steeped himself in the beauty of the proportions of their buildings, in the colouring and scale of their profiles, in the elegance and charm of their decoration. Then, once he was sure he understood their grammar and orthography, he began creating.'[43]

The linguistic metaphor perfectly conveys the level of assimilation necessary for the practice of imitation – a far cry from the vision of the Romantic generation,[44] for whom imitation had become pastiche, a highly fashionable exercise during the 1910s.[45] Yet it is still true that the literal reproduction of referential models could be seen

as a kind of liberation, as intellectual detachment from them.[46] It is clear that the exercise of style now went hand in hand with an intellectual challenge whose aim was as much to check the accuracy of the reference as to express a profound understanding of its meaning. Sergent, like his master Sanson, was no mere imitator. He set out to imbue his models with a personal interpretation which revealed their profound meaning, if not on a historical level (with which he was not concerned), then at least in his generation's aesthetic understanding of them.[47] In other words, he looked to the past with the eyes of his own time whilst demanding the utmost faithfulness to the model he was using – a difficult, even daring exercise, since

▼ Elevation of the Hôtel de
Camondo, courtyard façade.
Reproduced from Bétourné, p. 22.

The rather dry elegance of this
elevation is entirely calculated.
Not a detail of the virtuoso
drawing, heightened with
45 degree shadows, is left out.
The precision of the engineer is
well demonstrated here.
The drawing is a necessary
intermediate step between
conception and execution, rather
than offering artistic 'effects' in
the manner of the École
des Beaux-Arts. The different
approach is all the more striking
with the house itself, shaped by
distortions of perspective and
changing viewpoint.

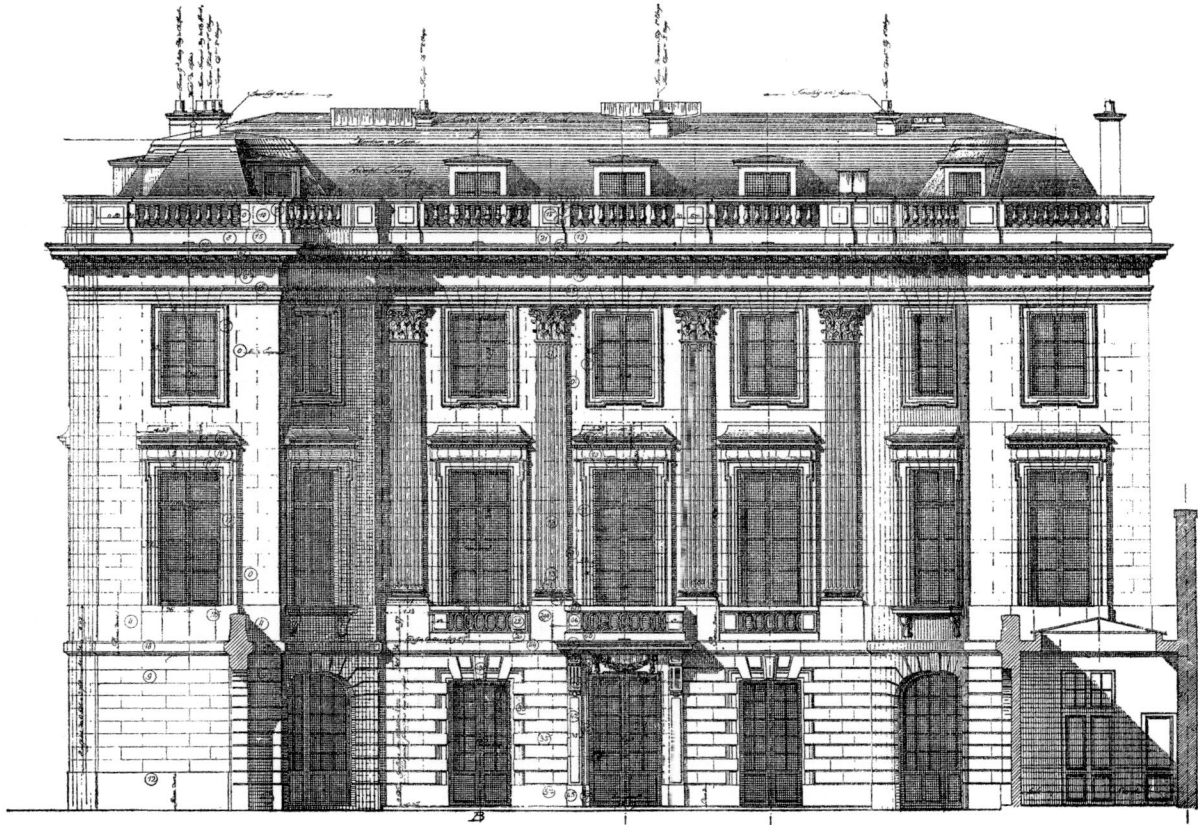

Façade sur Cour d'Honneur

he could easily have settled for sterile imitation. The art and manner of achieving this demands a capacity to combine references, to challenge or juxtapose them in a way that remakes them without weakening or caricaturing them, a task very different from that of the set designer. The architect's position is that of an intellectual who seeks to derive meaning from the handling of forms. Nothing could be more conceptual than this approach to creation.

In this respect, René Sergent belonged neither to the 19th century nor to its theatrical recreations. His works are not stage sets but meditations on a world which he sought to bring back to life by remaining faithful to it. He wanted to bring about a veritable 'renaissance' of 18th-century art, not merely its evocation. It is therefore not hard to understand his profound empathy with his aristocratic client, whose collection was the reflection of his inner world and culture. It was not a question of appearing but of actually being oneself, completely. This moral challenge was shared by the first generation of modernists, who no longer put up with convention unless it could be associated with total commitment. The second half of the 19th century had handled period architecture with a loquaciousness that turned it into an almost redundant costume. It practised the flaunting of luxury remorselessly, even to the point of vulgarity; Art Nouveau was

The courtyard façade of the
Hôtel de Camondo, 1936.
To give the cubic space of the
courtyard perfect proportions,
Sergent brought either end of the
façade round in a 90 degree
curve, a device freely inspired by
Gabriel's Petit Trianon. The eye
is drawn to the axial lines above
the pedestal course marking out
the perimeter. This arrangement
masks the volume of the attic
floor behind the Italian style
balustrade, and allows oblique
views of the neighbouring plots.

This geometrical projection does
not show that the wings on either
side of the rotunda are
perpendicular to one another, a
rare arrangement justified here
by the need to create views over
the park. An obvious comparison

is the Château de Montmusard,
designed in 1764 by Charles de
Wailly, whose surviving elements
form the inverted, concave figure
of a rotunda set between two
wings at right angles.

Façade sur Jardin

seen, in many respects, as the final testament to
this.[48] Not all of René Sergent's generation saw
things in the same way. Using the rationalist
tradition for one's own ends demanded efficiency
and restraint, not the pomposity of the Beaux-Arts
tradition. To do so was to rebel against the volu-
bility of decorative expression, to subject it to the
demands of architecture.[49] The classical grandeur
Sergent sought in Gabriel primarily reflected the
latter's mastery in the use of the ornamental repertoire.[50] The classical culture to which he aspired
was therefore not expansive but demanding, and its
complexity often eludes present-day visitors, who
see only clichés instead of his elaborate handling
of references.

The new building

The mansion's overall conception is a dazzling
demonstration. Reusing one of the key ideas of
Gabriel's Petit Trianon, Sergent exploited the
difference in level between street and park to create a
change that is imperceptible from the outside.
Without noticing, the visitor is led from courtyard
level on one side to the first floor reception rooms,
which open at the garden level on the other side.[51]
The consequences of this are visible in the façades,
whose treatment powerfully reflects the urban setting.
Pushing the differentiation Gabriel adopted for the
Petit Trianon to the extreme, Sergent modified the
volumes, rhythms and even materials of each façade

The difference in ground level between the street and the park was exploited by the architect to enhance the autonomy of the two façades, set back-to-back, using a principle borrowed directly from the Petit Trianon. Its transposition within the constraints of an urban environment is particularly skilful, especially since it frees itself from the conventions of the centred ground plan and its play of cross-axes to express the difference in relationships of scale and function between the courtyard and the garden.

to render their status more comprehensible.[52] He set them in such strong opposition to one another that one can no longer even associate them: the expressive schema of the two façades back-to-back, which Palladio had used in his renowned Malcontenta, here becomes confrontation.[53] The visitor is left without a reference point, in a 'conversion zone' that surpasses one's capacities for observation. The interior layout contributes to this disorientation. The public area on the ground floor, divided by a long transverse supporting wall, is limited to the hall and adjoining corridors, dominated by the wide main staircase which is set against the façade and invisible from the outside.[54] The rest is taken up by service rooms, hidden behind the doors leading to them: two worlds side by side, both unaware of one another and complementing one another.[55] Closer observation of the corridors reveals two concurrent circuits. One begins by following the building's axis from the entrance, soberly marked by the first-floor balcony, its consoles and stone balustrade, and ends in the middle of the main hall. But this trajectory culminates in a dead end, in the form of a shallow gallery, whose walls, complete with full decorative trappings, are hung with landscape paintings above slender wrought-iron consoles.[56] A second path follows a line independent of the main axis. Intended for motor cars, it turns towards the corner of the courtyard to pass through a porch into a covered entrance.[57] The entrance is set diagonally to the

▲ The staircase seen
from the upper ground floor.
From Bétourné, p. 23.

◄ The foot of the staircase
in the main hall on the lower
ground floor.

The monumental stone staircase,
an obligatory feature of any
mansion, is inspired by illustrious
18th-century models, including
the wrought-iron balustrade
(an exact copy by the Parisian
craftsman Baguès of the
balustrade Joseph Bosc made
for the Hôtel Dassier in Toulouse
in 1780). But the staircase's
incorporation into the space of
the vaulted hall on the lower

ground floor, and its arrival
on a wide landing, strangely
associated with a portico
colonnade creating an inner
gallery, break all the conventions
of period architecture.
The fluidity of the spaces and
their interpenetration belongs to
a modern vision of architecture,
in many respects foreshadowing
that of the interwar period.

▲ At the end of the gallery behind the main hall, this door leads to the covered motor car entrance, where guests would arrive for receptions.

ground plan, behind a large wrought-iron gate. It opens onto a rotunda dominated by an enormous marble nymphaeum set against a mirror.[58] The visitor must then decide which direction to take. The long gallery on the left leads back towards the hall and the main entrance. This unexpected 'spiral' trajectory is the main element of an arrangement based on the contrast between the main axis and a very unclassical diagonal arrangement. One has to look at several well-known examples of modern thought in the 19th century to understand its origin: from the house Hector Horeau built near Primrose Hill in London in 1855 to several variations proposed by Viollet-le-Duc and his disciple Anatole de Baudot.[59]

▼ Entering from the covered motor car entrance, opposite the nymphaeum fountain, the eye is drawn towards the gallery behind the hall and the main staircase opposite the door from the courtyard.

The angle in the y-shaped ground plan, repeated in the corridors on each floor, enables the articulation of the alignment of the rooms overlooking the courtyard with the L-shaped plan on the garden side.[60] The ensemble therefore obeys logic whilst keeping the surprises that give the building its character.[61] There is nothing ordinary about this arrangement: it breaks the conventions of the axis and the ground plan to create a dynamic all the more surprising in the contrast between the fluidity and interpenetration of the circulation spaces and the stable volumes and ordered decoration of the rooms. Everything is organized around constant tension. Views recede from the interior spaces; rooms follow one another in irregular succession, leaving strange residual spaces where they meet; outside and inside no longer correspond; spaces interlock or dilate in the most unexpected ways. These arrangements should not be considered in isolation, but as a means of creating an architectural 'narrative' that unifies the whole. Well before Le Corbusier, Sergent handled a series of architectural moods in a symphonic manner, yet still managing to introduce dissonances that lend vigour.

Gabriel would certainly have been surprised by the freedom with which Sergent both reused his vocabulary to the letter and succeeded in updating it. Without doubt, Sergent borrowed from the early baroque architects, especially from François Mansart, but he also drew inspiration from the manner in which the post-Revolution architects Ledoux and Boullée recreated Androuet de Cerceau's formal Renaissance exercises. Comparisons can instantly be drawn with the approach of Edwin Lutyens, Josef Hoffmann and even Adolf Loos, who practised the same calculated dissonances, challenges and interlocking techniques to break the conventions of academic order.

Underlying the conflicting styles and references used in the first decade of the 20th century there is a shared modernist language. In this respect, the use of the 18th-century style in the Hôtel Camondo remains surprisingly contemporary artistically, in a period tempted by nostalgia. At the very least it denotes great freedom of spirit, off the beaten paths of tradition. It is this freedom behind the mask of appearances that must be understood if one is fully to grasp its conceptual power and originality, which – for anyone who does not appreciate the subtle distinction – can still be just as disconcerting almost a century later.

► René Sergent, plan of the upper ground floor. Reproduced from Bétourné, p. 20. The L-shaped ground plan conceals a diagonal set around a star-shaped hall. The upward spiral passes from one staircase to the other, changing floor and orientation in the most unexpected way. There is the same subtlety in the organization of the rooms, which are autonomous yet whose forms flow into one another in unconventional symmetry.

p. 80
The staircase leading up to the private apartments.

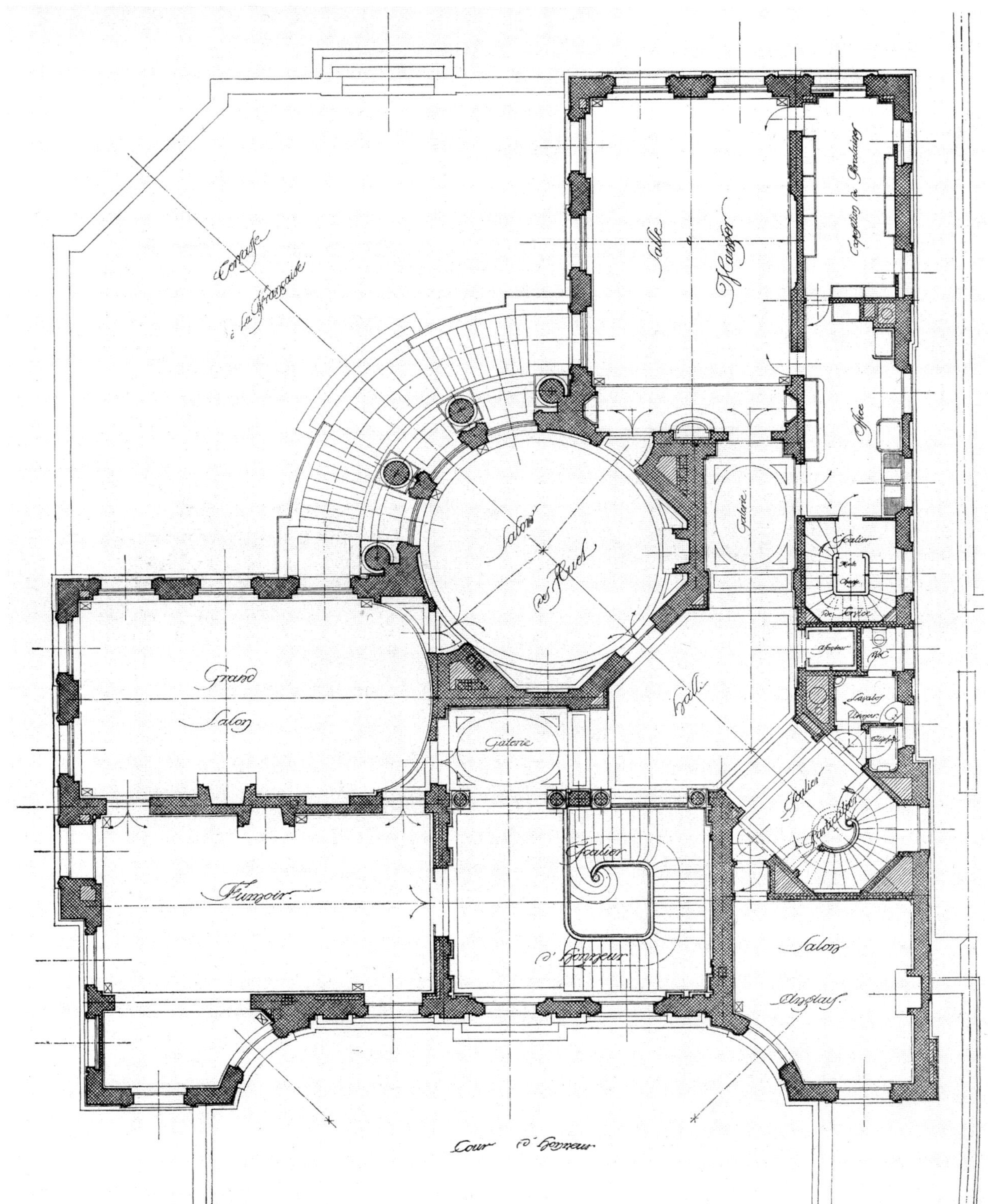

Terrasse
à la Française

Salle
à Manger

Carpeting de Bendings

Office

Galerie

Salon
de Rivol

Escalier

Grand
Salon

Galerie

Hall

Escalier
Particulier

Fumoir

Escalier
d'Honneur

Salon
Anglais

Cour d'Honneur

Building a collection *Bertrand Rondot*

The acquisition of taste

Arriving from Istanbul in early adolescence, Moïse was immersed in the opulence of the house on the edge of the Parc Monceau that the architect Denis-Louis Destors had refurbished for his father Nissim. One can easily imagine him as a child being initially impressed and very probably delighted, but then later, perhaps unconsciously and prompted by not always well-meaning comments, becoming aware of the vanity of these overbearing drawing rooms furnished in the styles of several centuries but lacking authenticity. Reserved as a young man, as he was as an adult, Moïse's character was incompatible with so much ostentation. What did he dream about in his bedroom with its 'red grained' wall hangings and Italian, certosina[1] bone marquetried furniture, sitting on a day-bed with Japanese embroideries on yellow silk?[2] How would the young man's taste develop and the collector in him emerge?

Moïse de Camondo's cousin Isaac undoubtedly played a role as mentor. The two men were very similar, in their lifelong passion for collecting and also in their eventual boredom with the world of finance. Isaac guided Moïse's first steps as a collector, and his ease and eclecticism probably fascinated him. It was also Isaac who introduced Moïse to one of the Paris art world's outstanding personalities, Charles Ephrussi, co-owner of the *Gazette des Beaux-Arts*. This 'awakener of minds' seems to have been the young collector's guiding angel, appearing at every important moment in his life. His society contacts (he was a member of Princess Mathilde's circle) and support for the arts of his time (he launched the Impressionists, and he appears prominently in Renoir's famous *Luncheon of the Boating Party*) made him the ideal person to introduce Moïse into the world of collectors and artists, and to the many pleasures of scholarly curiosity.[3]

Moïse de Camondo probably owed his first genuine initiation to his father. Count Nissim de Camondo was the indirect master of the pavilion that Claude-Nicolas Ledoux built for Madame Du Barry at Louveciennes and that was now the property of his mistress, the wealthy American Alice Tahl, Countess de Lancey.[4] Edmond de Goncourt wrote scathingly of 'the ironic interior of Louveciennes, where Mme Du Barry once lived and where Mme de Lancey now lives, and where the banker Camondo replaces Louis XV'.[5] It is not hard to imagine the young man gaining a lasting impression of this residence, steeped in history and the absolute quintessence of what he would later most admire. Could it have been, perhaps unconsciously, the model for his great labour of love, the '18th-century artistic residence' that he was to build later in life?

In 1889, Moïse de Camondo lost his father when he was only thirty. But as his heir, the collector in him was able to flourish. He merely had to choose a domain in which to excel. The realization that his life could be devoted to collecting began to take root properly when his family circle grew. When he married Irène Cahen d'Anvers in 1891 he joined a family of serious collectors and connoisseurs of the great styles of the *Ancien Régime*. The Cahen d'Anvers played an active role in the rediscovery of the 18th century that had begun in the middle of the following century, prompted not only by the writings of the Goncourt brothers but also by the hammers of both demolition men and auctioneers. Theirs was an authentic 18th century – not badly copied or reinterpreted, but restored and recreated as far as was possible. The panelling from the Hôtel de Mayenne[6] had been fitted in the Cahen d'Anvers' mansion in rue de Bassano, built in 1881 by the architect Hippolyte Destailleur, but their great achievement was the restoration of the Château de Champs-sur-Marne, acquired in a dilapidated state

Isaac de Camondo bequeathed mainly 18th-century works to his cousin Moïse, but also left a series of watercolours by Jongkind, which he had displayed in the 'Cézanne room' in his residence on the Champs-Élysées, alongside pictures by Renoir and Monet. Moïse eventually hung them in the Blue Drawing Room in rue de Monceau (see p. 114).

The two interiors, though both graced by the same mahogany table, are strikingly different. Isaac de Camondo's dining room is furnished with little concern for decoration: his faience is arranged in display cases that stand on plain, wall-to-wall carpeting, whereas Moïse's dining room, in which the table is shown with its semicircular extensions fitted, is a harmonious ensemble corresponding to a historical style.

in 1895.[7] As a privileged and attentive observer Moïse was able to follow this process and learn much from it. But the pupil would go further than the teacher, as revealed by two details in particular: the Cahen d'Anvers hung their large portraits by Bonnat and Carolus-Duran in the music room at Champs,[8] and thought nothing of decorating the staircase's new balustrade with their monogram. Moïse de Camondo would never have allowed himself such social anachronisms; he hung the few family portraits he owned in his mansion's private apartments.

As his father and uncle had been before him, Moïse was profoundly influenced by the aura of the Rothschilds, with whom the Camondos eventually became distantly related by marriage.[9] Adolphe de Rothschild – who transformed his house into a veritable museum – and then Maurice were their neighbours in rue de Monceau.[10] Isaac was a close friend of the famous scientist Henri de Rothschild, and both were passionate music lovers; Moïse was an acquaintance of his cousin Robert, a keen collector of Art Deco.[11] Nonetheless, he set himself apart from this prestigious model, espousing neither the eclecticism of the preceding generation nor the often extreme specialization of his own. He was more akin to the Baron Ferdinand de Rothschild. The builder of Waddesdon Manor in the 1870s and '80s summed up his family's contribution to this renewal of interest in the century of the Enlightenment in his

▼ As with the other rooms in the Château de Champs, the Cahen d'Anvers furnished the music room in the 18th-century style, matching the decoration of the walls, but they also hung their portraits by the society painters Carolus-Duran and Bonnat.
From the *Gazette illustrée des amateurs de jardins*, 1933.

◄ The Hôtel Cahen d'Anvers, which Moïse de Camondo's parents-in-law had built on the corner of rue de Bassano and place des États-Unis, was inspired by 17th-century architecture, particularly the extraordinary Hôtel de Beauvais in the Marais district. It immediately became quite well known, after it was featured in *La Semaine des constructeurs* in 1883 (no. 16, 20 October 1883, pp. 186–88), as shown here.

▲ *Carle Dreyfus* by Aaron Bilis, charcoal, 1935, Paris, Musée du Louvre.
Carle Dreyfus, a curator at the Louvre and a close friend, shared Moïse de Camondo's passion for the 18th-century decorative arts.

memoirs: 'Whether it is to the credit of my family or not may be a matter of opinion, but the fact remains that they first revived the decoration of the 18th century in its purity, reconstructing their rooms out of old material, reproducing them as they had been during the reigns of the Louis, while at the same time adapting them to modern requirements'.[12]

Moïse de Camondo, then still a debutant collector, was introduced into museum circles by Isaac, one of the founder members of the Société des Amis du Louvre in 1896, and by his neighbours, the Dreyfus. His very close but much younger friend Carle Dreyfus – they saw each other almost daily – spent his entire career in the Louvre's Department of Objets d'Art,[13] and his father, the great collector Gustave Dreyfus, must certainly have made an impression on Moïse.[14] He also had contacts among the curators of the Musée des Arts Décoratifs, Jacques Guérin, Paul Alfassa and particularly Louis Metman, and established increasingly close relations with the Union Centrale des Arts Décoratifs. Gradually, he built up a solid network of contacts, many of whom attended the famous 'Louvre' and 'Marsan' lunches he hosted in his later years, which also drew other Parisian museums. His friend David David-Weill went alternately to both, as did his dear friend Carle Dreyfus. Curators at the Musée Carnavalet – François Boucher and Adrien Fauchier-Magnan – were also invited to the Marsan lunches, while the curators of Versailles, Gaston

Brière, and Malmaison, Jean Bourguignon, went to the Louvre lunches. The eclectic collector Raymond Koechlin, also president of the Conseil des Musées Nationaux, was a regular guest at these functions. Other great collectors were also invited: Carlos de Beistegui, Jean Bloch, Count Arnauld Doria and Marquis Hubert de Ganay. Some of Moïse de Camondo acquisitions were suggested by his curator friends: the bronze bust of Mme Le Comte by Guillaume II Coustou was bought in Berlin via the intermediary of Paul Vitry, a curator at the Louvre,[15] and Carle Dreyfus bid for him at the Doucet auction in 1912.[16]

The young collector underwent his initiation patiently; a few decades later he had become a much-consulted authority. Moïse de Camondo naturally succeeded his cousin in his main responsibilities in the museums, notably on the board of trustees of the Union Centrale des Arts Décoratifs.[17]

The world of collecting would be nothing without a profession which developed so spectacularly in the 19th century: antique dealing.[18] Although Moïse de Camondo sometimes patronized traditional family sources such as Siegfried Bing and Auguste Sichel,[19] who sold antique furniture but also Oriental art, he mainly frequented the great dealers specializing in 18th-century furniture – Larcade, Wildenstein, Kraemer, Fabre, among others[20] – and to a lesser extent Duveen, who catered chiefly for the American market.[21] With the Seligmann brothers, these professional relations

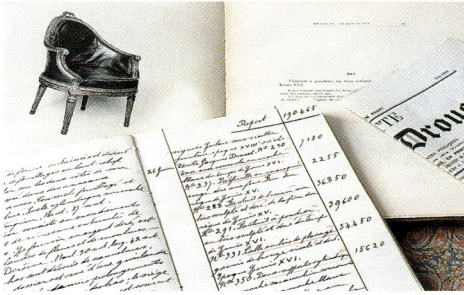

► Moïse de Camondo seems to have been especially fond of this commode, since he put it in his bedroom in rue de Monceau. It was his first major purchase from Seligmann, in 1912. An elegant Transition period work by Martin-Guillaume Cramer, it has the cabinetmaker's characteristic interlaced marquetry.

developed into a friendship that would survive crises, payments by instalment over several years and political and economic upheavals. Jacques Seligmann was two years older than Moïse and Arnold was ten years younger. Their brilliant career as antique dealers developed alongside Moïse's equally brilliant one as a collector. From them, he purchased his very first works, most of them minor and modestly priced[22] and not all of them antique.[23] The collector had not yet emerged from behind the wealthy client, despite the antique dealers themselves indicating his errors.[24] The young Moïse progressively acquired a sharper eye. A first important purchase stood out, and foreshadowed both the direction and quality of his future collection. On 11 July 1892, Moïse de

Camondo bought a commode in the transitional style stamped by Cramer, which he eventually put in the bedroom of his mansion in rue de Monceau.[25]

He sold most of his early purchases within a few years, sometimes only months later,[26] and built up a collection by replacing less interesting pieces with new acquisitions. The Seligmann brothers willingly agreed to exchanges, thereby enabling him rapidly to raise the quality of his collection to a level more in keeping with their reputation.

Although he frequently went to Galerie Charpentier and the Hôtel Drouot, Moïse de Camondo rarely bid for works in person, preferring to do so via an antique dealer, as was customary at a time when competition between collectors

was fierce and secrecy often the key to success. His cousin Isaac, on the other hand, openly bid at auctions and became a prominent personality in the art world.

Moïse de Camondo was thus an important but discreet actor in the art market until the interwar period. He was discreet but methodical: he kept all his invoices and also a purchase ledger, begun in 1909, several of whose pages summarize his principal earlier acquisitions, gifts and inheritances.[27]

The early residences

Paradoxically, the first house Moïse de Camondo lived in after his marriage was fully furnished: 21 rue de Constantine, on the Esplanade des Invalides, sublet from M. and Mme Heimendahl, themselves the tenants of Princesse de Sagan.[28] Rodolphe Heimendahl was a close acquaintance of Irène de Camondo's father, Louis Cahen d'Anvers.[29] Obliged to leave Paris for several months, he suggested the young couple rent his residence in October 1891.[30]

The inventory gives a clear idea of the surroundings in which Moïse and Irène de Camondo lived for almost a year.[31] In a sober but monumental Neoclassical décor, Louis XVI furniture dominated

► This carpet is one of the ninety-three carpets woven at the Savonnerie manufactory between 1671 and 1688 for the Galerie du Bord de l'Eau in the Louvre. The fiftieth in the series, it is decorated with an allegory to Air, symbolized by the heads of the four winds blowing trumpets and complemented by two imitation bas-reliefs in blue monochrome depicting Aeolus and Juno. Actually, the carpet was originally longer – almost 10 metres – and one can see that the acanthus foliation on a black ground is now cut off by an added border. Despite this, it was one of Moïse de Camondo's most important acquisitions, and one which he had previously admired during his time living in the Heimendahl mansion in rue de Constantine.

an elegant, probably rather conventional interior, yet one that nevertheless contrasted completely with the pompous setting in which Moïse had grown up. The apartments had just been furnished and although one notes a few comfortable ottomans and sofas, the overall impression is of an interior of great clarity and stylistic unity.[32]

On the extremely well-furnished first floor, in the small drawing room, there was a 'large ancient carpet covering the room' and a 'large antique tapestry subject Fishing in [its] gilt frame'. How could one possibly tell from these terse inventory descriptions that the former was a Savonnerie carpet woven for the Grande Galerie in the Louvre and the latter a Beauvais tapestry from the *Amusements champêtres* series, after a cartoon by the painter François-Joseph Casanova? Moïse de Camondo greatly appreciated these exceptional works and when the Heimendahls were forced by financial difficulties to move house, he bought them via the intermediary of their mutual friend, Charles Ephrussi. They are now among the jewels of the museum's collection.[33]

The young couple had to leave the mansion in rue de Constantine in June 1892 and moved into an apartment placed at their disposal by the Ephrussi brothers, Ignace and Charles, in their mansion at 11 avenue d'Iéna.[34]

His time at this residence, only a short distance from the Musée Guimet, corresponded to a turbulent

The mansion at 19 rue Hamelin, built in 1898, was the first genuine showcase for Moïse de Camondo's growing collection. The façade, inspired by the Neoclassicism that emerged towards the end of Louis XV's reign, hints at the spirit of the treasures within.

Moïse de Camondo's taste for Neoclassicism was less marked in rue Hamelin than it would be in rue de Monceau. While he was here he acquired major objects in the rococo style, including in 1896 this large candelabrum with Meissen porcelain figures.

period in Moïse de Camondo's life: the birth of his two children was followed by Irène's totally unexpected departure. It was also a period of transition for the collector. After his formative but probably frustrating period in rue de Constantine there finally came a time when he had to furnish his home himself.[35]

However, it was when he moved into 19 rue Hamelin, a mansion built by the architect Paul Rouyrre,[36] that his collection truly began to take shape. Moïse, again advised by Charles Ephrussi,[37] began his tenancy in April 1899. It was not entirely finished, which gave Moïse the opportunity to complete the interior decoration himself.[38] He knew he would inherit the family mansion in rue de

Monceau one day, but the house that he was renting already had to be a public manifesto of his tastes and refinement. The façade itself, the most impressive in the street, had the sober elegance of Ange-Jacques Gabriel's French Pavilion at Trianon or the Ermitage at Fontainebleau, and the collector would remember this when he built his own house.

The vast first floor had an 'antechamber, large staircase and private staircase, large and small drawing rooms, smoking room, dining room and butlery', and the second floor had five bedrooms and a dining room with butlery[39] – a room plan heralding that of the future mansion in rue de Monceau. It is hard to gauge how much work Moïse de Camondo had done himself but he was certainly largely

◄ This candelabrum is one of a pair bought at the auction of the Duchess de Maillé's collection in 1900. They were in the large drawing room at rue Hamelin and are now in the Dining Room. The griffon and satyr-head decoration, in the arabesque style in vogue in the late 18th century, is reminiscent of the work of the famous bronze founder François Rémond, or more probably that of Pierre-Philippe Thomire.

◄ One of a series of seven canvases by Jean-Baptiste Huet, this *Shepherd Entrusting a Letter to a Dove* (detail) reflects Moïse de Camondo's interest in the charming decorative style of the 18th century epitomized by Boucher's pastoral scenes. Huet, however, was more restrained than his teacher. Moïse de Camondo hung the series in the small drawing room in rue Hamelin.

responsible for the interior decoration.[40] It was for this house that he acquired the *La Fontaine's Fables* tapestries, after Jean-Baptiste Oudry, from Seligmann in 1900, as well as the series of seven large pastoral pictures by Jean-Baptiste Huet that he set into the panelling of the small drawing room in their 'Louis XVI frames', and the marble chimney-pieces he had put into the main drawing rooms.[41] He bought first-rate furniture: the roll-top desk by Œben[42] (see p. 169), the *bonheur du jour* writing table decorated with Sèvres porcelain plaques by Martin Carlin, purchased from Seligmann in 1899 (see pp. 142–43),[43] and the commode with sliding panels by Riesener (see p. 147) from Wildenstein in 1909.[44] These acquisitions continue to set the collection's very

particular tone today and would govern the main architectural choices in his future residence.

It was during the years spent at rue Hamelin, from 1899 to July 1913[45] that the collector's taste became more refined and a far more ambitious project began to take shape in his mind, one which would not be subject to the vagaries of rented accommodation: the reconstruction of the family mansion.

Moïse de Camondo belonged to a dynasty known as 'the Rothschilds of the East'.[46] But this heritage was essentially professional and denominational, and the epithet referred above all to the family's banking and philanthropic activities. As a collector, he asserted himself not as an heir but as a

These six vegetable dishes were made in Paris in the early 1840s by the silversmith Pierre-François Queillé for the Turkish market. The lids have a characteristically convex form and bear the import stamp of the Ottoman Empire. Moïse de Camondo probably liked them more for their French provenance and classical purity than out of nostalgia for his family's history.

Moïse de Camondo parted with almost all of his father's painting collection, notably all the Orientalist pictures, including this painting by Alberto Pasini, *Entrance of a Mosque in Teheran*, lot number 31 at the auction of Count Nissim de Camondo's painting collection at the Hôtel Drouot on 18 November 1910.

Moïse de Camondo bought this vase (left) and its twin at the auction of his uncle Abraham Behor's collection in 1893 (nos 112 and 113 in the catalogue, above). He kept none of the furniture or paintings collected by the preceding generation, but did keep most of the Far Eastern porcelain. In the spirit of part of his collection, he had rococo gilt bronze mounts made for these early 18th-century Chinese porcelain 'rouleau' vases and placed them on the lacquer corner cabinets on the main staircase.

pioneer. When he inherited his father's collection in 1910, he had not the slightest nostalgic qualm about selling it off almost in its entirety at three auctions.[47] The oppressive furniture derived from historical styles, the 17th-century Dutch paintings, the 18th-century Venetian paintings, Courbet's *Hunters in a Forest*, it all went... The only pieces he kept were those that perfectly matched his vision as a collector. In the new mansion, the Gobelins and Beauvais tapestries would have surroundings more befitting their subtle refinement, as would the Chinese and Japanese porcelain, with or without gilt bronze mounts.[48]

There was nothing now that would recall the family's Ottoman past. The Orientalist pictures his father was so fond of, José Laguna y Perez's *Courtyard of an Arab House* and Alberto Pasini's *Entrance of a Mosque in Teheran*, were sold without regrets. Henri Léopold Lévy's *The Sack of Sancta Sophia in Constantinople*, despite its Istanbul subject, found no more favour in Moïse's eyes than the few mementoes of his youth.[49] His faithful secretary Léonce Tedeschi wrote: 'after two meetings at rue de Monceau yesterday and two more this morning, I've finished with the "Turqueries", having sold all the *tchibuks* [pipes] ...and everything that was on the dining room table.'[50] So it is curiously touching to note that he kept six vegetable dishes by the silversmith Pierre-François Queillé, made in Paris for the Turkish market in the early 1840s and which the

► Moïse de Camondo was familiar with Jacques Doucet's collection in his mansion in rue Spontini, including these doors from the Hôtel Dubarry in Toulouse, which inspired the design for the doors of the Salon des Huet. The thin-columned frame was copied quite freely, and the interior decorator Decour supplied two 'ancient subjects, in the Boucher style' for the overdoors. They were later replaced by canvases by Huet. Reproduced from Adrien Fauchier-Magnan, *Les Dubarry. Histoire d'une famille au XVIIIᵉ siècle* (Paris, Librairie Hachette, 1934) pl. 7, p. 144.

Camondos probably brought back to Paris with them from Istanbul when they moved in 1869.

Collector and decorator

Moïse de Camondo was fifty when he was finally able to embark on the project he had been nurturing for such a long time, the 'recreation of an 18th-century artistic residence'. From 1911, he worked in close consultation with the architect René Sergent on the design of the new mansion. The plans were drawn up to accommodate the works of art in his collection, the house's walls adapted to fit period panelling, and models were made to weigh up certain effects.[51]

That year, he sought out period panelling for the main rooms.[52] The panelling for the Large Drawing Room[53] was acquired from the interior decorators Lemoine and Leclerc. They had recently been removed from an apartment at 11 rue Royale, and their exact original arrangement was known. However, Moïse de Camondo did not attempt to reinstall them as they had been originally, nor did his architect wish to – neither was an art historian – and he had no qualms about stripping one of the five doors and using it for the entrance to the Large Study.[54] From Armand Sigwalt he bought the panelling for the Dining Room and the two mirrored niches to frame the entrance to the private staircase in the gallery.[55] The polished oak panelling

and marble chimney-piece purchased from Édouard Larcade were fitted in the library and dictated that floor's proportions.[56] The following year, for his bedroom, the same antique dealer sold him panelling from a residence in Cours du Chapeau-Rouge in Bordeaux,[57] illustrating not only the vitality of Neoclassicism in that city but also the scarcity of Parisian panelling of equivalent quality then on the market[58] (see p. 216). Additional panelling was ordered from the Decour company,[59] who produced panelling for other rooms from Sergent's drawings.[60]

Moïse de Camondo's prime concern was always overall harmony and if necessary he would complete an interior using copies. Formal coherence took precedence over authenticity. Thus, unable to find a period wrought iron balustrade suitable for the main staircase, he commissioned the Baguès company to make an exact copy of the wrought iron balustrade in the Dassier mansion in Toulouse, dating from 1780, and the masterpiece of the great craftsman of that city, Bosc (see p. 118).[61] Similarly, he had copies made of bronze window and door fittings that he had been unable to procure in sufficient quantities.[62]

His scholarly vision of the 18th century is clearly shown in his choice of colours. The Large Drawing Room is white and gold, the walls of the Library and Large Study, places of reflection, are oak-panelled,[63] the Dining Room is decorated in

The marble setter Gilis's estimate for the dresser in the dining room describes precisely how it was to be made with a combination of Campan and yellow Sienna marble: 'solid moulded top…with inlaid pilasters, backboard and four sculpted consoles, moulded back panel and base'. Prior to this, the interior decorator Decour had produced 'two different models of dresser for the marble carver, executed in pine with consoles cut out as requested'.

Photograph on the left taken *c.* 1936.

shades of green[64] and his bedroom in greys. Although the collector did not opt for the traditional 18th-century progression of rooms, he did preserve their relative levels of ornateness, unlike his contemporaries, who decorated all rooms with the same pomp.[65] Yet these colour choices are all closer to early 20th-century taste than that of the 18th century. Other aspects of the collection, such as the arrangement of the furniture, reveal this detachment from an idealized model. In this respect, in the Dining Room, the order for a 'Louis XVI dresser, …mixed Campan marbles and Sienna Yellow'[66] is instructive, and a noteworthy concession by the collector to contemporary taste in the great aristocratic residences during the Belle Époque.[67]

Moïse de Camondo gave shimmering fabrics a key role in the overall effect, a choice possibly related to his Levantine ancestry, but also reflecting his choice as a collector. But there was none of the deeply upholstered furniture laden with brocade and fringes that was then a stock feature of luxurious interiors. Shunning these facile comforts, he included strictly 18th-century seating only in his interiors.

Textiles also played a subtle role in the mural decoration. The pale limestone of the main staircase was offset by the warmth of a Gobelins chancellery tapestry[68] (**see p. 120**), while the simply moulded panelling in the gallery enhanced the Aubusson tapestries of the *Tenture chinoise,* inspired by

► In the Large Study, the *Fables of La Fontaine* tapestry series, woven for the Royal Military College at Sorèze, was inset in plain oak panelling. Particular care was taken over the curtains, 'in antique red lampas with yellow stripes [belonging] to Monsieur', which were 'lined with red sateen, cotton fleece and Marceline, silk fringe with migrets front and bottom, pleated heads...at the top a pelmet in the same lampas'. The upholsterer and interior decorator Decour made for 'the top of the large bay two curtains in the lampas with a red ground...and a large pelmet in the same lampas lined with red sateen'. Moïse de Camondo paid particular attention to the consoles supporting the architrave of the bay. 'Instead of what was proposed in the estimate, four clay studies, cast in plaster with three presentations' were submitted by the Decour company for Moïse to choose from.

Photograph taken *c*. 1936.

cartoons by Boucher (see p. 141). In the Large Drawing Room, an alcove was created specially for the Beauvais tapestry, *La Pêcheuse*, from the *Fêtes italiennes* set after Boucher (see p. 142), and in the Dining Room, *La Pêche au filet*, originally in the house in rue de Constantine, was hung above the large marble dresser.[69] The hanging of a single tapestry framed by panelling was a characteristic of the great early 20th-century decorators on both sides of the Atlantic[70] and Moïse de Camondo was obviously not averse to it. On the other hand, he adhered closely to the 18th-century tradition in the Large Study, whose panelling frames the *Fables of La Fontaine* tapestries, evoking their original position in the Royal Military College at Sorèze.[71]

◄ This large Savonnerie carpet, *c.* 1740, with 'trimmed' corners fell foul of the law banning feudal insignia during the Revolution: the fleur-de-lis on the royal coat of arms was removed and the shield left empty. Fortunately, the royal crown and collars of the orders were spared. This exceptional carpet, bought in September 1920, completes the decoration of the Salon des Huet and fits its octagonal shape.

The black marble and limestone chequerboard floor, like the 'Versailles' parquet flooring, is not hidden beneath the wall-to-wall carpet or Turkish rugs that Moïse had known in his youth, but laid with the finest examples of work from the royal manufactories. In the Large Drawing Room, he brought together an exceptional selection of the production of the Savonnerie manufactory during Louis XIV's reign,[72] each of these jewels being forays outside the 18th century.

The chairs are upholstered with Savonnerie, Beauvais and Aubusson tapestries, petit point embroidery and carefully preserved antique fabrics. The 'two Louis XVI *fumeuses* covered with worn antique velvet' were 'stripped and reupholstered to preserve the velvet'.[73] These were the two *voyeuse* chairs from Mme Elisabeth's Turkish drawing room at Montreuil, and which had long since lost their original *toile de Jouy* upholstery.[74]

Moïse took particular care with the choice of curtain fabrics. Eighteenth-century tapestry pelmets were placed on the main staircase, in the Small Study and the Porcelain Room, and in the Salon des Huet they echo the Gobelins door tapestries[75] (see pp. 160–61). Most of the textiles for the other rooms came from rue Hamelin.[76] Only the Dining Room was decorated more simply, where the windows were given a 'large folded blind in coarse silk, squared fringe at the bottom'.[77] The rods of the chandeliers were decorated with 'silk cabling, silk acorns at the

► Bearing Louis XIV's proud motto, *Nec pluribus impar*, this large Savonnerie point tapestry belongs to a set woven at the Hôtel des Invalides between 1678 and 1684 and intended for the central hall.

▼ This rare photograph, taken inside the house during the collector's lifetime, shows Moïse de Camondo's daughter Béatrice sitting on the *bergère* by Claude Chevigny inherited from Isaac de Camondo. Moïse de Camondo had the seat covered with embroidered silk, bought specially.

bottom, silk cartisane at the top', except in the Salon des Huet, where the rod of the chandelier is sheathed. Again, it was Decour who supplied the silk cabling for hanging the pictures.

A very personal 18th century

All in all, the house is less a collector's residence – in the manner of the Doucet[78] mansion and Cernuschi[79] mansion (which the Goncourt brothers described as a 'hôtel-musée', or 'mansion-museum') – and more that of a creator, the creator of the 'artistic residence' that Moïse de Camondo described in his will. The result was a house to which everything

and everyone else – Moïse before all others – had to comply.

The collector left no writings in which he expressed the taste and philosophy governing his choices. It is only in his letters to antique dealers that he clearly states what the collection suggests, although these peremptory remarks can give a caricatured impression of him. Modern art was of course excluded from the outset, not out of incomprehension but because it was illsuited to his project. He politely refused to allow his name to be associated with an exhibition Paul Vitry proposed to him: 'as you know, I am a collector solely of 18th-century art and it would be inconsistent of me to accept the patronage of modern art, to which

The simple moulded panelling of the upper ground-floor gallery serves as a showcase for the Aubusson tapestries from the *Tenture chinoise* series after François Boucher, two of which are hanging on the private staircase. The overall effect must have been considered too cold because Moïse de Camondo bought two Beauvais tapestry panels in 1927, which he used as overdoors. They were woven later but the colours match the Aubusson chinoiseries. The large tapestry from Les Invalides was placed on the floor. Was this because Moïse de Camondo was unaware that it had originally been hung, or a deliberate choice emphasizing his residence's luxury? It had already been laid on the floor in rue Hamelin. The gallery is furnished with an important set of chairs by Pierre Gillier, upholstered with Aubusson tapestries.

The consoles with high mirrored piers framing the door to the Salon des Huet come from Moïse de Camondo's first residence in rue de Constantine. On them are two Chinese porcelain vases inherited from his father Nissim. On the left of this picture, the bronze *Child with a Bird* by Pierre-Philippe Thomire, in the niche in the passage to the private staircase, is mounted, like its companion piece, on a Sarancolin and white marble column bought at the Doucet auction in 1912.

Photograph taken *c.* 1936.

◄ The decoration of the Small Study, particularly the Adam-style frieze, has an English feel to it, so much so that it is sometimes called the English Drawing Room. Furnished as a picture collector's study, it contains several of the collections masterpieces: the two views of Venice by Francesco Guardi, acquired in 1932, and the series of sketches by Jean-Baptiste Oudry for *The Hunts of Louis XV*. They are integrated into an extremely ordered display including small terracotta medallions by Jean-Baptiste Nini. Moïse de Camondo was unable to buy the sketch by Oudry at the top; separated from the other eight in the late 19th century, it was recently donated to the museum in lieu of tax to complete the series.

I have in no way had recourse in the house I have just had built'.[80] However, he was not insensitive to the art of his time and it was as an enlightened patron that he participated in the acquisition of Courbet's *Studio* in 1920.[81] Similarly, finding the frames of contemporary works mediocre, on the eve of the 1925 International Exhibition, he launched the Modern Frame competition.[82]

Earlier periods were also excluded. Declining an offer from an antique dealer, he wrote that he was 'not a buyer of Louis XIV furniture'.[83] Rococo, which had appealed to him in his younger days, was later given up: 'I am not a buyer of Louis XV pieces,' he declared in 1929;[84] he had already written to the London antique dealer

Leopold Davis[85] in 1922: 'I buy only Louis XVI furniture'.

With rare exceptions Moïse de Camondo concentrated exclusively on the last decades of the 18th century, those of the transition period and the reign of Louis XVI. This taste for pure, strict forms, which he shared with the modernists, was a reaction to the excesses of authentic rococo and the most unbridled versions being produced by Parisian workshops since the 1870s,[86] and to its ultimate incarnations in Art Nouveau. It may well have been Gustave Dreyfus, during one of young Moïse's visits to boulevard Malesherbes, who had first guided him towards this then-neglected period and encouraged him to explore it.[87] Although Moïse's will does not

► It was traditional in great houses built since the Second Empire to decorate the flights of the main staircase with vases or busts. Moïse de Camondo, disregarding convention, placed two of the most priceless pieces of furniture in his collection, the two corner cabinets with Japanese lacquer panels by the cabinetmaker Bernard Van Risenburgh, on the landings. Their richness and polychromy, if not style, perfectly match the gilt wrought-iron balustrade made by the Baguès company and they serve as bases for the cylindrical Chinese porcelain vases bought at the auction of Abraham Behor de Camondo's collection.

mention it, it reveals that this choice became a passion for 'this decorative art which has been one of France's glories, during the period I have loved above all others'. The Camondo 'taste' had become a point of reference.[88]

All the fields of the decorative arts were brought together in this residence, none taking precedence or given special conditions. Each element of the collection found its place entirely naturally in ensembles which, although not exact reconstructions, were credible evocations of an imagined 18th century, revealing the extraordinary talent of its cabinetmakers, bronze founders, weavers and all the other crafts to which the collector paid tribute.[89]

This concern for unity is shown even in the way the works are arranged and by the subtle links established between one wall and another, one room and another, not only by architectural details, but even more by the presence of objects, small pieces of furniture, pictures and wall clocks in the transitional spaces. Moïse de Camondo's conception was different to that of the Rothschilds, who often kept their artworks in rooms devoted to them, thereby emphasizing the clear demarcation between their collections and their social life. Each work was acquired as part of a whole, with perhaps two exceptions: the Small Study, hung with crimson pekin silk, is treated as a picture gallery, and the Porcelain Room (see p. 181), which is fitted out like a

► The picture collection is dominated by portraits of women and children, such as this *Page Boy* and its pendant *Young Timpanist*, portraits of the Marquis de Serent's children by François-Hubert Drouais, hanging in the Large Drawing Room above the petrified wood vases from Queen Marie-Antoinette's collection.

▼ Formerly in Count Nissim de Camondo's collection, this oil on marble *The Children of Murat, King of Naples*, by Jean-Baptiste Isabey, is one of the rare works of this type in the collection, as Moïse de Camondo was not a 'buyer of miniatures'.

small museum room, with display cases lined with watered silk for the Sèvres porcelain 'Buffon birds' service, one of the sources of the collector's greatest pride.[90]

But within the 18th century Moïse de Camondo so admired, there were fields he deliberately ignored. Some were rejected outright as they were ill-suited to the interior decoration he had in mind. He did not collect drawings, for instance, whose fragility necessitated their being kept in portfolios and whose appreciation was too fleeting.[91] Although he had already acquired two paintings by the Raguenets, he refused to buy two drawings by these artists, pointed out to him by François Boucher, a curator at the Musée Carnavalet: 'as you know, I do not buy

drawings, which do not suit the decoration of my house at all; this is a pity as they are charming'.[92] Yet a few drawings and watercolours graced the walls of his private rooms, such as the portrait of the Godefroy brothers and their tutor by Jean-Baptiste Massé in his bedroom.[93]

The 'fine arts' – painting and sculpture – are not given the usual preferential treatment, but are handled as elements of an ensemble as in an orchestra. Moïse de Camondo shunned the 'grand genre' (history painting), preferring a more approachable 18th century. There are few portraits of men in his collection, which is dominated by female figures by Houdon, Clodion and Marin, Schall, Danloux and Vigée-Lebrun, and depictions

102

► The sculptor Clodion has come to represent the anacreontic 18th century which Moïse de Camondo seems to be summing up by this terracotta group of bacchantes. Although signed by Clodion and dated 1770, it is in fact a virtuoso 19th-century pastiche, whose matching piece belonged to Abraham Behor de Camondo.

▼ In Moïse de Camondo's bedroom, partly hiding Jean-Jacques Bachelier's *Childhood Amusements* (*c.* 1761), several Sèvres biscuit sculpture groups, from models by Louis-Simon Boizot, show the collector's interest in this type of porcelain sculpture.

► Like the *marchands-merciers*, Moïse de Camondo appreciated Far Eastern porcelain set in ornate gilt bronze mounts, and usually gave these pieces pride of place in his drawing rooms. This Chinese porcelain vase, one of a pair, with a grey crackle glaze, dating from the reign of Qianlong (1736–95), was given this mount in Paris in about 1760.

of children. Instead of mythological paintings extolling heroic virtues, the panelled walls are enlivened by Jean-Baptiste Huet's graceful pastoral scenes. Another ensemble reinstated in a period setting around the same time, by Henry Clay Frick on the other side of the Atlantic, inevitably comes to mind: the series of decorative paintings Fragonard painted for Madame Du Barry's pavilion at Louveciennes.[94]

Yet Fragonard, like Boucher,[95] were excluded, probably because the collector considered them too affected. Like the man, the dignity of the ensemble never wavers and maintains a certain modesty. Moïse de Camondo developed a more austere vision than his contemporaries, in the more spiritual manner of

the Goncourt brothers, and of which the most assiduous example at the time was Ernest Cognacq.[96] The landscapes are a special case. Alongside the more conventional Guardis and Hubert Roberts, the remarkable series of sketches by Oudry for the *Hunts of Louis XV* tapestry set must have reminded Moïse de Camondo of his passion for this aristocratic pursuit when he was not on his estate at Aumont.[97]

The porcelain reflects the overlap between collection and decoration. Moïse de Camondo placed a great many of his Chinese and Japanese porcelain vases, often mounted as the *marchands-merciers* did, in *ormolu* (the 18th-century term for mercury-gilded bronze), on chests of drawers, on top of bookcases or

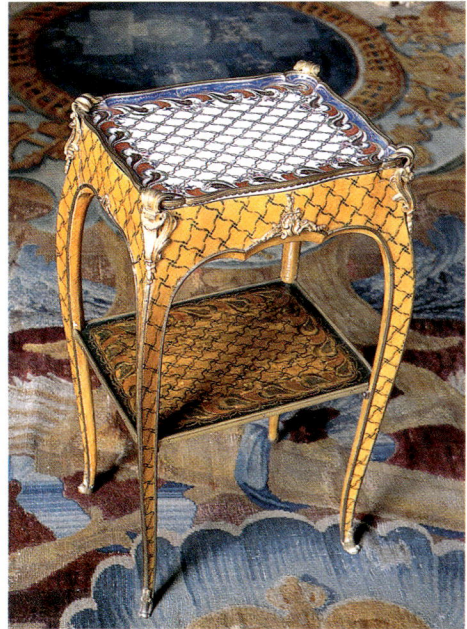

◄ A *bonheur du jour* writing table
by Martin Carlin, *c.* 1766.
The presence of this ladies' piece might seem
surprising in the home of a collector like Moïse
de Camondo, but it reveals his taste for the most
refined pieces with Sèvres porcelain plaques.

▼ A *table cabaret* with a Sèvres porcelain top
by RVLC, *c.* 1760.
The Martin varnish reproducing the trelliswork motif
on the Sèvres porcelain 'Courteille' top, originally also
reproduced its colours. The varnish has since yellowed;
Moïse de Camondo was attracted by this fine
'camomile-coloured' piece and bought it from the
antique dealer Bensimon in 1934.

on the stretchers of consoles. Strangely, he acquired
no Sèvres porcelain vases. Did this reflect their rarity
on the market or the discredit tainting them at the
time?[98] Neither the two trumpet-shaped vases with a
blue ground in the Small Study, nor the garniture of
Niderviller decorative porcelain vases[99] (see p. 132)
compensate for the fact that this most emblematic of
Sèvres creations is not present. He certainly tried to
reunite a large portion of the three exceptional
'Taillandier background Buffon birds' services. But
when Sèvres porcelain is integrated into furniture his
interest was unbridled and he proved to be a peerless
connoisseur, acquiring several pieces decorated with
Sèvres porcelain plaques, a *bonheur du jour* writing
table and a *table chiffonnière*, both by Carlin, a cabaret

table by RLVC and two cabinets with medallions in
the Wedgwood manner.[100] The Louvre did not yet
have any – the museum's first piece was a *table
chiffonnière* by Carlin, bequeathed by Baroness
Salomon de Rothschild in 1922 – and the taste for
these rarities seems to have taken refuge in Anglo-
Saxon surroundings.

An original vision

Like all collectors, Moïse de Camondo attached
great importance to the provenance of works he
sought to acquire.[101] The oldest were often the most
prestigious but also demanded more caution.[102]

◄ One of Moïse de Camondo's most distinguished acquisitions was a pair of vases in a particularly rare material, fossilized or petrified wood. The gilt bronze mounts, commissioned by the jeweller Joseph-Ange Aubert in 1784, are by François Rémond. Without knowing it, the collector reunited several other masterpieces by this famous bronze craftsman in the Large Drawing Room; as well as the mounts of these vases, they include one for Madame de Pompadour's lacquer vase, made for the *marchand-mercier* Dominique Daguerre in 1783, and the imposing arabesque chandelier.

Madame de Pompadour is a mythical figure for those rediscovering the 18th century. The *table chiffonnière* by Martin Carlin bought from S. Lion[103] (see p. 144) is flatteringly presented: 'the table I sold you … appears to have been given to Madame de Champeaux's ancestor by the Marquise de Pompadour'.[104] Yet the provenance claimed is chronologically impossible, as Madame de Pompadour died in 1764, before the cabinetmaker's admission to his guild and the piece's creation.[105] However, did Moïse de Camondo acquire this table because of its supposed prestigious provenance, in exchange for another very similar one that had formerly belonged to the humbler 'Madame de Croissilles'?[106] Queen Marie-Antoinette has

fascinated collectors even more than the king's mistress, and, unsurprisingly, certain pieces have this supremely attractive provenance. The *bonheur du jour* writing table by Carlin is one such piece.[107] Here again, the legend confounds the chronology. But the story is plausible since there were pieces like this at Versailles, although not in the queen's chambers.[108] One of Moïse de Camondo's most beautiful acquisitions, the pair of petrified wood vases, had regained this link with the queen lost since the late 18th century. Jean Seligmann, in the description attached to his invoice, notes: 'these vases, whose mounts are attributed to Gouthière … are believed to have been in Marie-Antoinette's boudoir at Trianon'.[109] The name of the piece's

▼ This table, made by the bronze craftsman J. Chauffette in Paris in 1925, is a steel and gilt bronze reproduction of the table Riesener delivered to Pierre-Élisabeth de Fontanieu in 1771. Although several marquetried copies of this piece were made in the late 19th century, this is the only one entirely in metal. This must have appealed to Moïse de Camondo, who placed it – masterpiece of both metalwork and forgery – in the middle of the Salon des Huet **(see p. 108)**.

► The arrangement of the furniture in the Large Study shows the strict symmetry Moïse de Camondo applied in his furniture arrangements, with the fireplace as the central axis. On either side are the *voyeuse* chairs formerly in the Turkish drawing room in the Château de Montreuil, in Versailles, the property of Madame Élisabeth, Louis XVI's sister. Photograph taken *c.* 1936.

▼ This ebony and pewter-veneered table (*c.* 1785–90), formerly in the Stroganoff collection in St Petersburg and stamped by Weisweiler, has a metallic appearance evoking Antiquity's furniture, as does the patinated bronze *œnochoe* (wine jug) on the stretchers.

supposed creator, a famous bronze founder, and of the queen's favourite residence, are erroneous, since the bronzes are in fact by François Rémond and the vases were in the queen's bathroom at Versailles.[110] But the name of the prestigious owner must have influenced Moïse de Camondo, who was above all attracted by the rarity of the material and the extraordinary quality of their bronzes. He acquired other pieces of furniture with royal provenance without their origin being known or even suspected, and so tribute must be paid to the clairvoyance of a collector who knew how to recognize first-rate works. The four-leaf screen by Jean-Baptiste Boulard in the Salon des Huet[111] had lost its Garde-Meuble (Royal Furniture Repository) number, but its characteristic wheat-ear decoration enabled it to be identified, later in the 20th century, with Louis XVI's commission for the Games Room at Versailles.[112]

Moïse de Camondo's fascination for furniture in metal can clearly be seen. As well as the two silvered bronze console tables in the Salon des Huet, in 1933 he bought a polished steel and gilt bronze table from Arnold Seligmann attributed to Riesener and 'believed to have been given to Vergennes by Louis XVI after the Treaty of Versailles'.[113] One assumes that the price paid, 250,000 francs, reflects both the originality of the material and the prestige of its supposed provenance. Unfortunately, neither stands up to scrutiny.[114] The piece is a copy of an authentic Riesener table delivered to the Royal

Furniture Repository for the personal use of Intendant Fontanieu, but which was thought to have come from Marie-Antoinette and which Empress Eugénie put in the Petit Trianon.[115] Some of the prestige of this table, one of the most famous pieces of 'royal' furniture since its rediscovery during the Second Empire, must have rubbed off onto the bronze and steel version.

Moïse de Camondo's prime and overriding concern in his collection was harmony. Perhaps he was unwittingly applying the rules for architects set out by Théodore Vacquer in his 'Principles of the Art of Building': 'Symmetry, which is one of the dependencies of regularity, dictates that all objects are placed with order and distinction, that they are well-aligned, and that their spacing be exact and regular...; that objects set on either side correspond exactly, either in their form and alignment in relation to the centre, or in their dimensions, and that the objects placed on them are along the same vertical lines. Symmetry does not exclude variety, as long as it is in accordance with the other principles'.[116]

The Salon des Huet epitomizes this extreme concern for equilibrium and symmetry more than any other room. The drawing room's axis, in line with the building's diagonal, seems to divide the space into two hemispheres that mirror one another, in which each object and piece of furniture has its counterpart in the other. Within this arrangement, Moïse de Camondo brings objects together that

◄ In 1927, Moïse added the
final touches to the Salon des
Huet. In March, he bought two
overdoors by Jean-Baptiste Huet
and a third in June of that year,
all from Wildenstein. This
enabled him to replace
the two overdoors depicting
'ancient subjects, in the Boucher
style' with compositions
analogous to the large mural
canvases and perfectly adapted
to the panelling.

The room's axis runs through
the central window and
the furniture arrangement by
pairs is organized around it.
A few unique works stand out,
notably the screen, by Boulard,
formerly in Louis XVI's Games
Room at Versailles and the
roll-top desk by Œben. In this
house no space is neglected:
the passageway leading to the
Large Drawing Room is furnished
with a small console, on which
a clock with a Chinese figure
once stood (it was later moved
due to its fragility; see p. 162).
A barometer hangs above it.
Photograph taken *c.* 1936.

others would have treated as unique masterpieces. This taste became, if not proverbial, then well-known. Antique dealers systematically offered him furniture and objects that they had in pairs. Gradually, he acquired the two corner cabinets by BVRB in 1911,[117] the two cabinets by Weisweiler with Japanese lacquer panels in the Large Drawing Room in 1921,[118] and in 1930 one of his most expensive purchases (for 800,000 francs), the two pieces decorated with porcelain plaques in the Large Drawing Room.[119] Sometimes, with the help of antique dealers, he would make great efforts to reunite pieces that had been separated for a long period. The cabinets by Leleu in the Large Study were both bought in 1922,[120] but Moïse de Camondo had to wait thirty years to reunite the two *commodes à l'anglaise* by Garnier in the Salon des Huet. With the help of the Seligmanns, who had sold him the first piece and acted as intermediary, Moïse de Camondo acquired the second one in 1928, from the antique dealer Leopold Davies in London, 'having seen a photograph'. Davies wrote to him: 'how pleased I am that Monsieur Arnold Seligmann and I have been able to reunite these two pieces in your very famous collection' – famous for its pairs, he seems to have implied.[121] The collector was sometimes blinded by this immoderate taste, despite friendly warnings. The two pieces bearing a spurious Carlin stamp and also the mark of the Château de Bizy at Vernon, were acquired from

▲   Moïse de Camondo was captivated by the discreet elegance of this panelling, acquired from the decorators Lemoine and Leclerc in 1911. It comes from the Count de Menou's first-floor drawing room at 11 rue Royale in Paris. The entrepreneur Louis Le Tellier commissioned his son, the architect Pierre-Louis Le Tellier, to build three luxury apartment buildings on three plots acquired in 1781, at 9, 11 and 13 rue Royale. To reduce the cost, the sculpted wood and stucco decoration, executed from 1783 to 1785 by Louis Fixon, sculptor to the King's Buildings, was identical in each building.

Its ornateness is concentrated on the door frames, while its large, simply moulded panels are ideal for an early 20th-century collector to hang pictures. Moïse de Camondo had no qualms about altering the panel's original arrangement by creating two cut-off sections, on which he placed two doors framing an alcove for the Beauvais tapestry *The Fisherwoman*, after François Boucher, acquired from Wildenstein in 1910.

The 'Le Tellier' sets of panelling were among the most sought-after ensembles of the time. The panelling from the Count de Menou's bedroom was installed in the Hôtel Errazuriz in Buenos Aires, built by Sergent between 1911 and 1917. Another set of panelling, from the drawing room at 13 rue Royale, acquired by Lemoine in 1924, was eventually installed in the Philadelphia Museum of Art in 1932.

Photograph taken *c*. 1935.

The marble bust of Mme Le Comte
by Guillaume II Coustou, bought in 1914,
was later joined by the patinated bronze version
(right). The two busts, bought with their
piedouches, were displayed on one of the many
marble and gilt bronze plinths that Moïse de
Camondo acquired. The marble bust was put in
the Small Study where it stands in the middle
of the arrangement, with the sketches by Oudry
and Nini's medallions. Perry & Co. in London
were consulted for the picture lighting used
throughout the house, as seen in this
photograph taken c. 1936, but which
unfortunately has since been removed.
The bronze bust can be found on the same
floor, in the Large Study.

The bust of Mme Le Comte,
photographed in 1914 when it
was acquired.

Larcade in 1907.[122] Doubts about their authenticity did not deter Moïse de Camondo from buying them. He may have been less convinced by the antique dealer's vehement reaction to this than the spectacular appearance of these two skilful 19th-century pastiches.[123]

Not content with owning pairs of objects, he was sometimes also interested in having the same objects in different media. The large collection of etchings he hung in the first-floor gallery in some cases echoes the pictures in the drawing rooms – the portrait of Necker by Joseph-Siffrein Duplessis, for instance, or Nicolas Lancret's *Les Rémois*. The marble bust of Madame Le Comte by Coustou, acquired in 1914, was joined later by the patinated bronze version.[124] Houdon's extraordinary bust, *Summer*, bought in 1912, was soon joined in 1918 by its pale plaster double.[125] Sometimes, this game led him to similarities of purely scholarly interest: the two sculpture groups in the niches in the Gallery, *Child with a Bird* and *Child with an Empty Nest*, cast by Thomire from models by the sculptor Bridan inspired by antique works in the Borghese collection, are echoed by two small bronzes in the Salon des Huet, after the same antique works and probably the work of Francesco Righetti's workshop in Rome.[126] More surprisingly, in the Salon des Huet, who now notices that the chubby children on the Gobelins tapestry with a yellow ground on the fire screen, are repeated above the overmantel, on a crimson ground?[127]

▲ Jean-Baptiste-André Gautier-Dagoty, *Portrait presumed to be of the Duke and the Duchess de Chartres with the Penthièvre and Conti families*, *c*. 1775–76.
Was it a premonition of his family's tragic end, or the realization of the inevitable disappearance of the family name after the death of his only son, which prompted Moïse de Camondo to buy this family portrait in 1932 to hang in the Blue Drawing Room?

This painting of a large group must have contrasted with the emptiness of his house where he now lived alone.
The identity of the family in this portrait, painted by one of Queen Marie-Antoinette's official painters, was unknown when Moïse de Camondo bought it, but he was not put off by this aristocratic anonymity.
He had sought refuge in the 18th century, fascinated by its vanities, and collected at first by convention, then by passion.

From residence to museum

The mansion and its collections were intended for Nissim, Moïse de Camondo's charming and promising only son. His death in 1917 shattered all these plans. Moïse's grief as a father was echoed by his confusion as a collector, and when his daughter Béatrice, now Madame Léon Reinach, left home in 1924, he was alone with his life's work. But his mind was made up: the house would one day be a museum, and his will clearly states this. Moïse de Camondo could now devote himself completely to this new mission, in which the passionate collector – as he continued to be for the rest of his life – also became a meticulous curator. His acquisitions reflec-

ted his pursuit of perfection, and the evolution of the art market after the First World War influenced his purchases. The sale of the former Russian Imperial collections brought him up against a redoubtable rival, Calouste Gulbenkian, but it was an opportunity to acquire, via the antique dealer Jacques Helft, specta-cular pieces of silverware – an area relatively neglected by Moïse de Camondo until then – by Robert-Joseph Auguste, and by Jacques-Nicolas Roettiers belonging to the famous Orloff service.[128]

For the Blue Room – the last room he refurnished and more intimate than the first floor reception rooms – he acquired a highly original painting: an ambitious group portrait, recently identified as the Duke of Chartres and his family.[129]

Could he have imagined that in doing so he was bringing the Duke back to the Monceau Estate that he had originally created, yet would hardly have recognized? In the rest of the house, little by little, the interiors were raised to a level of perfection no longer in keeping with the privacy of family life, but well suited to the public figure that he now wished to become. In 1935, the spectacular gilt and blue bronze chandelier[130] and the two petrified wood vases which had belonged to Queen Marie-Antoinette joined the finest furniture in his collection in the Large Drawing Room to put the finishing touch to his masterwork.

▲ This photograph of the Blue Drawing Room taken before Moïse's death shows a more comfortable, less formal room: there is a small Louis XV-style table for magazines, a lace cover on the back of the wing chair by Noël Poirier, and Chinese porcelain vases converted into lamps on the large writing table attributed to the cabinetmaker Claude-Charles Saunier. To the right of the fireplace hangs *The Gentlemen of the Duke d'Orléans in the uniform of the Château de Saint-Cloud* by Philippoteaux after Carmontelle, one of the works most strongly associated with the collection today.

p. 117
View of the Lower Ground Floor Gallery looking towards the doorway to the covered motor car entrance.

A Tour of the House

photographs by Jean-Marie del Moral

The Upper Ground Floor

The Large Study

A Tour of the House
The Reception Rooms

The Reception Rooms on the upper ground floor, overlooking the garden, might seem few in number for a residence such as this. Indeed, there is no gallery specifically for painting and sculpture nor any cabinet of curiosities; in this house, devoted as it is to the 18th-century French decorative arts, the collections themselves were always an integral part of the Camondo family's life.

Unlike mansions built during the Ancien Régime, with their conventional enfilade, the architect René Sergent opted for a 'fan-shaped' arrangement with all the rooms opening onto the L-shaped gallery, whose form shows the mansion's ground plan.

The Large Study, at the top of the main staircase, is the antechamber of the Large Drawing Room, traditionally the most luxurious room. The room in the central rotunda, the Salon des Huet, links the Large Drawing Room to the Dining Room, which in turn leads to the Porcelain Room. The more intimate Small Study is set apart from the other rooms.

The reception rooms

Upper Ground Floor

The Large Study [a], pp. 128–39

The room's name might seem misleading at first, since it looks more like a large oak-panelled drawing room hung with tapestries. It was sometimes called the smoking room ('fumoir'), and may also have been a music room, as suggested by the term 'tribune des musiciens' ('musician's gallery') that Sergent used in his original plans to refer to the curved part of the room that looks over the courtyard. It was here that Béatrice once played the piano, but the piano was moved after she left home and was replaced by the large mahogany roll-top desk by Claude-Charles Saunier. However, the description of this room on invoices during the house's construction hints at the rather austere personality of the master of the house: 'Monsieur le Comte's office.'

The Large Drawing Room [b], pp. 142–58

In this large room looking out over the garden, the elegant Neoclassical panelling that came from rue Royale provides the perfect setting for many of the collector's master-pieces. On the walls, apart from the portrait sketch of the Prince de Bauffremont by Adelaïde Labille-Guiard, all is feminine grace and youthful freshness. *Geneviève Le Couteulx du Molay* by Élisabeth-Louise Vigée-Lebrun dominates the group; *La Bohémienne*, the tapestry hanging opposite, owes her charms to François Boucher, author of the cartoon; and the Marquis de Serent's children, portrayed as *The Timpanist* and *Page Boy* by François-Hubert Drouais, add a juvenile touch (Moïse de Camondo was so fond of them he even preferred them to pictures by Fragonard). Instead of a clock, a marble bust of a young woman by Houdon, an allegory of Summer, graces the mantelpiece. But it is a king's mistress and a queen who are evoked by the most extraordinary objects: a Japanese lacquer bottle formerly in Madame de Pompadour's famous lacquer collection, and a pair of petrified wood vases once in Queen Marie-Antoinette's private rooms at Versailles.

The Salon des Huet [c], pp. 159–71

Originally planned to be oval, this drawing room was given its definitive shape – an octagon rounded by a curve on the garden side, with a circular cornice – in order to hang the series of pastoral scenes by Jean-Baptiste Huet.

Moïse de Camondo's taste for symmetry and balance is demonstrated by the presence of many pairs of pieces in the room. The room's three French windows look out over the box parterre, while through the door on the opposite side there is a view across the gallery to the elegant spiral of the private staircase.

The complex forms of each room and the changes in axis from one room to another were all opportunities for the architect to create skilfully shaped passages and circulation spaces in which the collector could also display his works.

The Dining Room [d], pp. 172–78, 180, 184–86

As in the Large Drawing Room, the room's rectangular volume is subtly enlivened by recesses: a shallow niche houses the large marble dresser, and the double doors giving on to the gallery and the Salon des Huet are set in a theatrical hemicycle clad with mirrors.

On the other hand, the door to the butlery is concealed in the panelling, as is the door to the adjoining Porcelain Room, an almost secret room which one can imagine the collector revealing to surprise his guests. Respecting the traditional hierarchy of rooms, this arrangement skilfully links the dining room to the reception rooms and adjoining service rooms.

As in the Large Drawing Room, one of the French windows opens on to the steps leading down to the garden. The furniture is arranged around a large mahogany table which can be enlarged to seat up to twenty guests by means of semicircular extensions or simple pine flaps concealed beneath a white tablecloth.

The Porcelain Room [e], pp. 179–83

The Porcelain Room, which has a lower ceiling, is the only room on the upper ground floor with a mezzanine above. It is also the only room containing display cases, but it has all the charm of a small library from the time of the Enlightenment. When he was on his own, Moïse de Camondo would take his meals in this more intimate and private room, where he could contemplate his little porcelain 'aviary'. Nearly all the pieces on the moiré silk shelves have ornithological subjects, including the hard-paste Meissen porcelain tea and coffee service and the three 'Buffon birds' services made at the royal manufactory at Sèvres.

The Small Study [f], pp. 189–205

Occupying a corner of the house, the Small Study is the only room that is not integrated into the suite of reception rooms. Its entrance, located behind the main staircase, can only be seen as one is about to go up the staircase leading to the private apartments on the first floor. Accentuating this deliberate intimacy, as though one has already reached part of the private upstairs world, the entrance is through a single rather than a double door.

It was called the 'English drawing room' because of the large frieze painted in gold monochrome beneath the cornice, evoking the work of the Adam brothers in England. It was also called the 'Directoire drawing room', at a time in the early 20th century when this sober and elegant style was coming back into fashion.

Unlike the other panelled rooms, the walls of the Small Study are covered with pekin silk, and several jewels from the paintings collection are hung here: Oudry's series of sketches for *The Hunts of Louis XV*, the views of Venice by Guardi and Paris by Hubert Robert. A portrait of a man dominates the room, that of the famous minister and financier Necker by Duplessis – no chance acquisition by the banker Camondo.

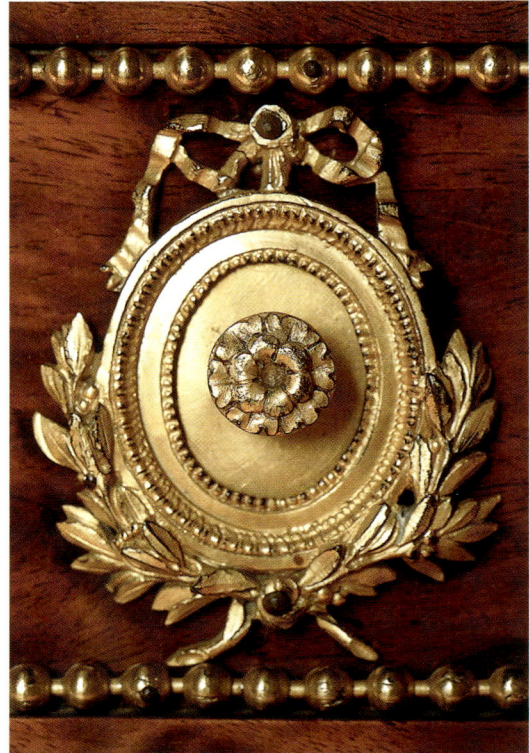

The Large Study

The Large Study

The Large Study

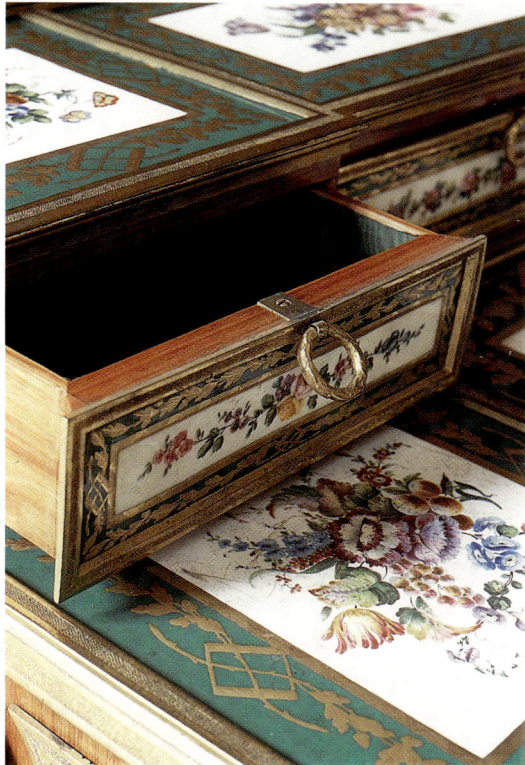

The Large Drawing Room

The Large Drawing Room

Looking from the Large Drawing Room to the Salon des Huet

The Salon des Huet

The Dining Room

The Dining Room

The Porcelain Room

The Porcelain Room

The Porcelain Room

The Dining Room

The Gallery, Upper Ground Floor

The Small Study

The Small Study

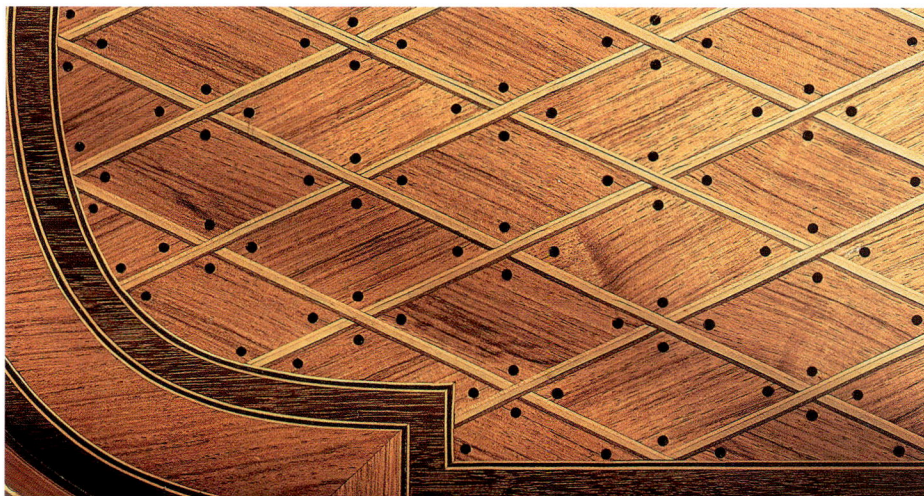

The Small Study

The Gallery, First Floor

A Tour of the House
The Private Apartments

The first floor – corresponding to the second floor on the courtyard side – is reached via the same type of small spiral staircase one finds in most of Sergent's mansions and which clearly marks the distinction between the reception rooms and the private rooms upstairs. As on the upper ground floor, the apartments of the master of the house and his children, Béatrice and Nissim, open onto a right-angled gallery, lit by skylights traversing the attic floor above, which was reserved for the servants' quarters and service rooms. The central library acts as the pivotal family meeting place. Each apartment has three main rooms: a bedroom, a dressing room and a bathroom.

Altered due to events – Nissim's tragic death and Béatrice's marriage – these apartments testify to Moïse de Camondo's solitude during his later years. Beatrice's apartment was converted into a comfortable drawing room and Nissim's became a memorial to a son who died before his time.

The Private Apartments

First Floor

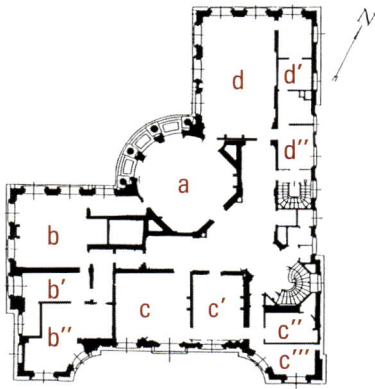

The Library [a], pp. 210–13

Located in the central rotunda above the Salon des Huet, the Library is the hub of the private apartments. Its shelves follow the curves of its walls and its oak panelling creates a warm atmosphere in a room conceived more as a drawing room than a study.

Eighteenth-century editions of the great Roman, Greek and classical authors, bound in calfskin or morocco, sit beside auction catalogues, history and art history books, many of whose authors were guests of the Camondos. Some of the books came from Moïse's father's library, notably *Histoire de la poésie des Hébreux* and *Les Illustres Français* by Nicolas Ponce, discreet reminders of the family's roots and the path of integration it chose. Moïse de Camondo also proudly kept the book he had been awarded in 1874, when he was a pupil of fourteen at the Lycée Fontanes (now Lycée Condorcet) for First Prize in History-Geography, and a certificate of merit for Greek and French grammar.

Moïse de Camondo was a member of several bibliophile circles, including the Société des Amis de la Bibliothèque Nationale and the Amis de la Bibliothèque Doucet. On the tea table by Bernard Molitor in the middle of the room were the most recent numbers of the *Gazette des Beaux-Arts*, edited by his friend Charles Ephrussi. Every year he had these reviews bound in red morocco in keeping with the rest of the room.

Moïse de Camondo's apartment [b], pp. 214–23

A door in the panelling opens from the Library on to a passageway that leads directly to Moïse de Camondo's bedroom. From the gallery end, one enters the apartment through two small antechambers, lit by a skylight.

The bedroom's elegant Neoclassical panelling came from a house in Cours du Chapeau Rouge in Bordeaux. A delightful allegory to Sleep, a painting of a sleeping nymph attributed to Hugues Taraval, kept watch over the count as he slept, with opaque blinds drawn down behind the curtains after nightfall.

It was in this room that Moïse de Camondo kept one of his earliest purchases, the commode by Mathieu-Guillaume Cramer, recalling his first loves as a collector. On the floor, a remarkable Savonnerie carpet demonstrates his passion for the work of this famous royal manufactory. There is a slightly melancholy overtone in the mixture of genre scenes and portraits on the walls, if only in their titles – *Bad News* by Jean-Baptiste Marie Pierre – and in the theme of the 'A la Douleur' clock on the mantelpiece.

What a striking contrast meets the eye in the bathroom [b']: it is tiled throughout in a modern idiom. The dressing room [b"], which follows the curve of the façade, breaks completely with the French flavour of the rest of the house: the ceiling decoration is freely inspired by English stucco motifs and is a rare example of Edwardian decoration in early 20th-century Paris. The mahogany panelling along the lower part of the wall was formerly in the Asian art gallery in Isaac de Camondo's apartment on the Champs-Élysées. Here, however, it emphasizes the room's resolutely British tone.

Nissim de Camondo's apartment [c], pp. 225–29

As things turned out, Moïse's only son Nissim hardly lived in his apartment. The family moved into the house on the eve of the First World War, and Nissim, who enlisted almost immediately in 1914, stayed there only briefly on leave before he was killed in action on 5 September 1917. His study [c], soberly decorated with Directoire panelling, was turned into a memorial room dedicated to Moïse's closest relations, whose memory he wished to preserve through the bequest of the house and the collections it contained. The presence of his father, Count Nissim, the icon of the family's success, presides over the room in the large portrait painted by Carolus-Duran in 1882, but his son's empty steel and gilt bronze bed is just as poignant. Nissim never had his portrait painted but everywhere there are photographs recalling his aristocratic presence.

The next room, originally Nissim's bedroom, is now devoted to the Camondo family's souvenirs. As in the other apartments, there is a bathroom [c"] and a dressing room [c'''], one of the only rooms in the house whose walls are papered above the lower panelling – in a house decorated throughout with panelling and wall fabrics – which is connected to the private staircase via a short passageway

The Blue Drawing Room [d], pp. 231–35

After Béatrice's marriage to Léon Reinach in 1924 and their move to Neuilly, Moïse de Camondo converted his daughter's boudoir and bedroom into one to create a large light drawing room-cum-study. It was called the Blue Drawing Room because of the colour of the panelling, which was originally peacock blue but has turned green with time. The writing table by Claude-Charles Saunier in the middle of the room is surrounded by less precious, more comfortable furniture, more informally arranged than on the upper ground floor, on a large carpet woven at the Beauvais manufactory.

Views of Paris in the 18th century – picturesque *vedute* by the Raguenets and imaginary landscapes by Pierre-Antoine Demachy – suggest Moïse de Camondo's fondness for the city. It was also here that he hung the Jongkind watercolours his cousin had bequeathed him. Béatrice's former dressing room [d'] and bathroom [d"] have been retained.

Moïse de Camondo's apartment

Nissim de Camondo's apartment

The Blue Drawing Room

The Blue Drawing Room

The Hall

The Gallery, Lower Ground Floor

Behind the scenes

Marie-Noël de Gary

Exploring behind closed doors often means having to break a taboo; but entering this secret realm also means running the risk of finding nothing more than the mediocre and obscure. In this house that is far from the case: the worlds of master and servants are outstanding in every respect. The owner's and architect's shared desire to employ the latest technology to improve efficiency and comfort, particularly using equipment from the luxury hotel industry, is plain to see. Yet the complexity and fragility of some of its equipment, still in the early stages of development, required considerable maintenance; the day-to-day running of the house and catering for the family's needs kept a staff of twenty busy. This contradiction between tradition and modernity at the dawn of the 20th century demands closer inspection.

Tradition and modernity

p. 244:

The kitchen (4) is located in the northeast corner of the building beneath the dining room. It is reached via the service corridor that also leads to the servants' dining room. As the kitchen is below the garden level at the back, the windows on that side are set high in the walls.

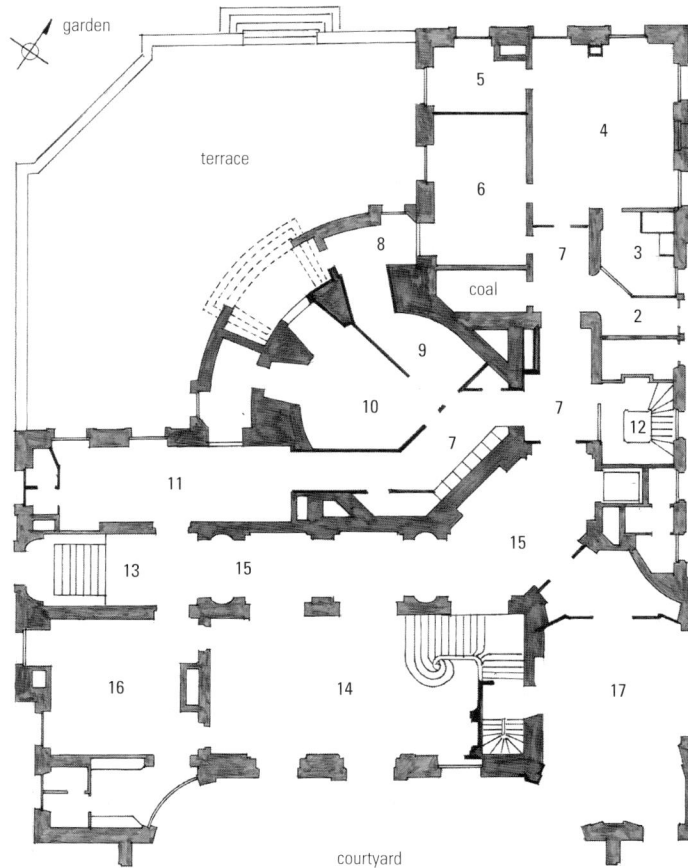

Plan of the lower ground floor. In the left wing, the footmen's waiting room; in the middle, the pantries and butler's pantry; in the right wing, the kitchen and adjoining rooms.

1. Service façade
2. Service or tradesmen's entrance
3. Chef's office
4. Kitchen
5. Scullery
6. Servants' dining room
7. Service corridor
8. Pantry
9. Cold room
10. Butler's office
11. Footmen's waiting room
12. Service lift and staircase
13. Garden hall
14. Hall
15. Gallery
16. Guests' cloakroom
17. Covered motor car entrance

The servants' quarters

At the beginning of the 20th century, the many tasks necessary for the smooth running of a private household and the comfort of its residents were performed in specific rooms on each floor. These areas occupied a considerable proportion of the building. In the Camondos' house, excluding the outbuildings, the service spaces occupy almost the same floor area as that of the apartments themselves.[1]

Combining efficiency and discretion, comfort and hygiene, the architect René Sergent took great care to integrate the building's functional systems with the residential rooms; equally he sought to equip its service rooms to ensure maximum efficiency. Having worked on the Savoy and Claridge's hotels in London, and having designed the Trianon-Palace Hotel at Versailles, he was well acquainted with the latest technology in providing modern comforts and worked with only the most advanced firms. The directors of the companies responsible for the main installations – Mildé (electricity), Kula (plumbing) and Cubain (ovens and ranges) – were all graduates of the École Centrale.[2]

The architect and his client were undoubtedly in agreement about the domestic installations, as they were on the historical reconstitution and arrangement of the collections, and it seems certain that Moïse de Camondo decided not to keep his

▼ The service façade (1) can be seen from the mews behind 105 boulevard Malesherbes. Other mansions in avenue Velasquez and the buildings in rue de Monceau also backed onto this mews used by tradesmen and servants. The five rows of windows correspond to the house's service floors. On the left, behind the railings, the gates lead into the covered motor car entrance (17).

▼ The ramp between the service façade of the building and the edge of the property rises 1.90 metres and provides easy access to the garden. The kitchen windows on the mews side are at the normal height.

parents' house not just because it was incompatible with his grand design as a collector, but also because it was ill-suited to the social life he wanted to lead, with all modern comforts. Exacting, even obsessive by nature, Moïse de Camondo ensured that the design of his house was rational and that everything in it worked perfectly. In the grand tradition of the aristocracy, for whom home economics was an integral part of managing of one's property, he took a direct interest in the daily running of his household. Léonce Tédeschi, a senior executive of Isaac de Camondo & Co. who had always managed the family's domestic affairs, looked after Moïse's private business. From his office on the first floor of the outbuildings, he took care of everyday matters and checked invoices, but the master of the house oversaw everything and made all the decisions.[3]

As in all private residences, staff and tradesmen did not use the front door in the main courtyard, but entered via the mews at 105 boulevard Malesherbes. The mansion's nondescript, east-facing service façade runs along one side of this cul-de-sac. The regular, linear arrangement of its windows reflects the purely functional nature of the rooms on this side of the building.

Delivery vehicles entered through the double gates at the end of the railings at the left hand end of this façade, and tradesmen on foot used the gate on the right. A narrow passageway running around

247

◄ The white faïence wall tiling inside the service entrance (2) indicates the functional nature of this part of the building. The chef's office is behind the glazed partition.

▲ The servants' clothes lockers opposite the butler's office in the long service corridor (7) that runs parallel to the gallery behind the hall.

▲ The pantry (8) is located beneath the flight of stairs leading from the dining room to the terrace. The hooks on the ceiling were for hanging meat and poultry.

▼ The chef's office (3) has a door into the kitchen and a hatch in the glass partition for checking food deliveries. Food was sent up to the butlery and upper floors in the dumb waiter on the left, operated by a pulley mechanism. The base and embrasure of the window are in painted wood-grain, as in the other ground floor rooms and the servants' dining room.

the house inside the railings provided direct access to the garden. Inside the tradesmen's entrance, a corridor leads to the ground-floor service rooms and the servant's staircase. The kitchen and its adjoining rooms were immediately on the right, and the butler's pantries and cold storage rooms on the left. The footmen's waiting room, opening directly onto the main hallway, was further along. For easy cleaning, the walls of the short hallway inside the tradesmen's entrance were tiled with white glazed earthenware tiles supplied by the Ebel company and painted with white Ripolin gloss further up.[4] The glazed partition allowed light into the chef's office. All the doors to the ground-floor service rooms have frosted glass panes for the same reason.

The food storage rooms are located in the rotunda in the middle of the ground floor. Fresh food was kept in the pantry or in the cold room, where the chef and the butler had refrigerated cupboards. These were replaced by a Frigidaire in 1929. The most spacious room was the butler's pantry, where groceries and prepared fruit and desserts were stored away from the heat of the kitchen.

In the kitchen (4), the rotisserie, 2.70 metres high and 2.55 metres wide, stands between the two large windows. Large joints of meat were roasted in the coal-fired oven in the middle. On the left is the wood-fired grill, and on the right, the gas-fired slow-combustion oven. The dome houses the smoke-jack that drove the spits until an electric motor was fitted in 1931. The kitchen floor is laid in glazed stoneware tiles with black cabochons with a double black and white border. The skirting is also in black stoneware and the same fillets are repeated on the wall tiles.

CUVES A LAVER IDÉAL GRANIT

The kitchen had two enamelled earthenware sinks for washing vegetables beneath the windows looking onto the garden. They were removed and have been temporarily replaced by similar sinks. Catalogue of the Kula company, 1912.

The kitchen

The kitchen is the most spectacular room, on account of its being entirely tiled in white faience, including the ceiling.[5] In the middle is a massive cast-iron and steel range, and on one side of the room, between the two large windows, stands an imposing rotisserie with two side ovens, both custom-made by Cubain. The firm, the official manufacturer for the French Army and Navy, had supplied several prestigious hotels and most of the royal courts of Europe, the Prince's Palace in Monaco, the Viceroy of India's residence in Calcutta and numerous châteaux and mansions.[6] The range was lit each morning by the kitchen boy, then the chef maintained its cast-iron plates at the required temperature with shovelfuls of coal as necessary. The heat from the range and ovens required a special ventilation system. Cool air was fed in via underfloor ducts from inlets beneath the garden terrace, and the cooking fumes were drawn out through a vent above. The system for letting out the steam from the sinks in the adjoining scullery, via ducts concealed in the kitchen's double ceiling, was more complex. The double ceiling also insulated the dining room above from the heat and especially the noise of the kitchen. For the same reason, none of the kitchen windows on the garden side could be opened. Only the large windows in the service façade, on either side of the rotisserie, could be used for ventilation.

The large cast-iron range (almost 3 metres long), coal-fired by two furnaces, one on either side, has four roasting ovens and two warming ovens with double doors at the ends. The rack, supported by columns with brackets, was used for utensils and dishes. The cast-iron plates in the floor provided access to the underfloor smoke flues. The walls and ceiling are tiled throughout for ease of cleaning, in conformity with the hygiene standards of the time. On the left is the open door of the chef's office, a little to the right is the door into the corridor and on the far right is the scullery door.

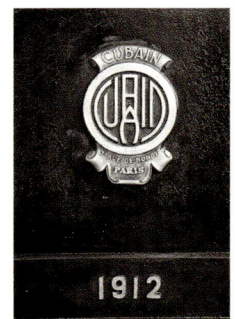

On each side of the range is the stamp of the maker, Cubain, and the date of its construction and installation, 1912.

▼ The double copper sink in the scullery (5) was designed for cleaning copper kitchen utensils while avoiding the effects of electrolysis. The right-hand sink has a lining enabling a constant flow of hot water around it, to maintain the dishwater at a high enough temperature to degrease the utensils. The unlined left-hand sink was used for rinsing. Both sinks are set in a cast-iron frame standing on legs concealed behind the sheet metal front. The sink's beech top protected dishwashers from the burning hot copper and prevented denting the utensils.

◄ As in the kitchen, the scullery walls are covered with cement tiles with flush joints for optimum durability and impermeability. The curved tiles where the walls and ceiling meet were designed to facilitate the flow of condensation. The ceiling tiles, laid diagonally, are kept in place by flat-headed nails whose hooked ends are held by a metal mesh.

▲ The scullery door's white ceramic knobs are grooved to provide a better grip.

If the kitchen facilities and equipment in the great mansions often remained archaic, this was partly because there was sufficient staff for the operation and upkeep of its ranges and ovens. There was also the entrenched culinary wisdom that cooking in copper saucepans on a cast-iron range was infinitely superior to gas-fired or electric cookers. Yet the patisserie was always done in a gas oven, until it was replaced in 1931, at the chef's request, by a white enamelled electric oven.

As can be seen from the imposing rotisserie and side ovens, spit-roasting was still highly favoured, but great chefs made their name cooking at the stove. Chefs were responsible for the constant improvement and variety of kitchen utensils. An impressive arsenal of thick copper pans was used; copper spreads heat evenly and helps to prevent sticking or burning. The inside of the pans was tinned to prevent oxidation, and to avoid damage to their precious lining by scouring they were soaked at length in a boiling hot solution of water and caustic soda.

To protect himself from the searing heat of the range and ovens, the chef wore the traditional thick white jacket, neckerchief, short bibless apron wound several times round the waist, lightweight trousers, and of course the heavily starched chef's hat. The chef was an important and respected household figure. He ruled over his domain, took orders from the master of the house, compiled

◄ ▼ One of the two oak dressers in the servants' dining room (6). It has fifteen numbered lockers in which members of staff kept their personal effects, napkins, bowls, medicines, etc.

▲ The serving hatch allowed dirty dishes to be passed directly from the servants' dining room into the scullery.

menus accordingly and procured and controlled all the ingredients used in their preparation. His expenses were reimbursed monthly with his wages. Count Moïse de Camondo, who led a far more withdrawn life after his son Nissim's death, rarely entertained. The family's daily meals therefore probably failed to satisfy his chefs' culinary aspirations and they never stayed for long at rue de Monceau.

The menus for those rare dinners between 1930 and 1935 are all extremely conventional in their succession of courses: a hot or cold hors d'oeuvre, fish, an entrée (meat or poultry), then the roast or a dish in aspic with a salad followed by vegetables. Chester cakes, ramekins, condés and parmesan paillettes were served instead of cheese, followed by a bombe glacée or a parfait, or more often than not, as in Turkey, a fruit granita (for an example of the menu, see p. 53).

The 'salle des gens' or servants' dining room next to the kitchen is directly connected with it via a serving hatch. Here, year in year out, twelve to fifteen servants ate their meals: the butler, the underbutler, one or two manservants, footmen, the chef, the chef's assistant, an odd-job man, a laundry maid, the gardener and the stoker in charge of the heating system. These posts were maintained until 1925, after which the footmen, maintenance workers, kitchen staff and dishwashers were gradually released from service.[7] The youngest employees

◄ The servants' dining room (6) is dimly lit by a high window and a glazed partition letting light in from the scullery. It is an austere room, painted plain white above the low oak-effect panelling. The long oval table is a replica made to the dimensions mentioned in archive documents.

▼ The service staircase (12)
has a central lift to all floors from
the basement to the attic floor.
The aerohydraulic piston lift was
powered by a water compressor,
operated by compressed air from
the Compagnie parisienne.

◄ The enamel plaque just
inside the service entrance,
showing the way to the service
staircase.

▲ The glazed oculus lets light
into the upper ground floor
gallery. The left part is in the
staircase and the right part in the
butlery on the mezzanine floor
(see p. 187).

lodged on the top floor of the outbuildings[8] and
all the other servants lived on the attic floor of the
mansion itself, in large rooms with ensuite toilets
and a communal bath. To carry out their respective
duties on all floors, servants used the service
staircase and lift.

The butler and his realm

The butler ruled over his own domain on the
ground floor, but it was upstairs that he exercised
his power to the full, mainly in the dining room,
where he was responsible for table service, and in
the butlery, where he presided over the care of the
porcelain, crystal and silver. The laundry maid
supplied him with tablecloths from the laundry on
the top floor; he would usually lay a Tournai
porcelain service.[9] He had two pantries, one next to
the dining room and another for the silverware on
the mezzanine, with its adjoining room lined with
cupboards, called the 'strong room', behind which
he had a small office.

The butlery is on the upper ground floor (see p. 126).
The walls are painted in white gloss and the panelling in wood-grain to match the furniture. The jointless 'porphyrolithic' floor covering was laid by Blanc et Cie and could be oiled or polished.

The table services and glasses were washed and put away in the butlery. On one side, between the windows, above the double zinc sink unit, is a water-sterilizing device that uses ultraviolet light. On the other are the oak dressers and a plate-warmer.

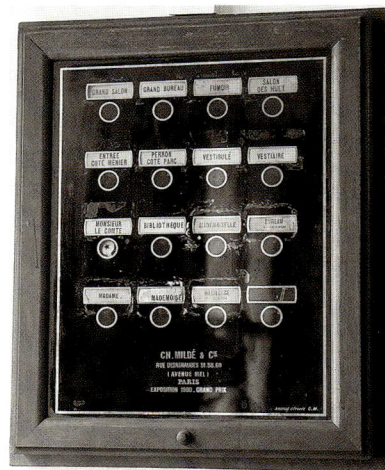

► The water sterilization unit above the sink used ultraviolet light emitted by a mercury vapour lamp. This system, devised by Dr Nogier, was manufactured by the Lacarrière company, which installed three machines in the butler's rooms and kitchen.

◄ When a bell was rung in a room in the apartments, a bell board in each of the main service rooms showed servants which room the call came from. They would simply press a button at the bottom of the frame to free a magnet which returned the marker to its place.

▲ The double moulded zinc sink unit sits between the two windows. At the end of the room is the dumb waiter shaft.

◄ The cast-iron plate-warmer opposite the dumb waiter was made by the Cubain company. It was also used to keep dishes warm when they came up from the kitchen. On the ground floor, plates that were ready to serve could wait on a steam-heated hot plate. On this floor, the plate warmer was heated by hot water circulating in coils beneath.

▲ The butler entered the dining room discreetly through a door concealed in the panelling.

Details of the cupboard handles: the same type was fitted on all the doors of the furniture in all the service rooms.

◄ *In the strong room for the silverware, the boxes and drawers in the four cupboards are lined with red cloth.*

The silverware was washed in a wooden tub and then treated with various products, usually whiting and an alcohol-based cleaner, but it was the knives that demanded the most care. After use, their blades were rubbed on a long, narrow board covered with leather and coated with red metal cleaner bought either as a powder or paste. Buhler paste and Goddard powder were bought at Brooker, a hardware shop at 135 boulevard Haussmann specializing in 'brushes, wooden utensils and English articles'.

► *The silverware was kept in the 'strong room' adjoining the second butlery on the mezzanine floor. Both rooms had the same oak dressers, dumb waiter shaft and double moulded zinc sink unit. The adjoining room has a reinforced door and custom-designed cupboards for storing silverware and cutlery. The butler's office is at the far end.*

Pierre Godefin entered the service of the Camondo family as butler to Abraham Behor in 1882 and remained at rue de Monceau until 1933.[10] He therefore had the complete confidence of the master of the house, who entrusted him with a variety of tasks. He oversaw the servants and the daily running of the house, called in firms to carry out repairs, placed orders and paid bills.

The butler was responsible for the purchase of household wares, mainly from Genestier, 'specialist in antique and modern stocks', who supplied all the china and glass for many years. In 1914 they received an order for '12 crystal glasses engraved with the count's coronet, replacements for broken items'; and in 1915 for 'a cut-glass fruit bowl made for its silver stand' and hand-painted cornflower blue coffee cups. He sent a set of salad spoons 'with ivory handles' to Odiot for repair; he ordered glasses from Perrier & fils and cups from Le Grand Dépôt.

He had English anthracite delivered for the heating and paid the bills for pest control, the telephone (Administration des postes et telephones), water (Compagnie générale des eaux), gas (Société du gaz, Paris City Council) electricity (Compagnie parisienne d'éléctricité) and compressed air (Compagnie parisienne de l'air comprimé). He ordered the staff's clothes and livery at La Belle Jardinière and their patent-leather shoes from Ch. Loula. He also paid the count's press subscriptions (*Le Figaro, Le Gaulois, L'Illustration, La Revue de l'art, La Gazette*

▼ The house's keys were also kept in this room, classified in rows corresponding to each floor of the building. Each key has a metal tag with the name of the room engraved on it.

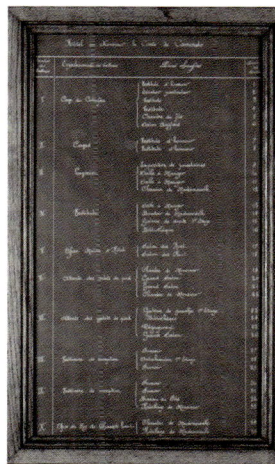

◄ The framed list of heated rooms shows the location of the ten hot air ducts that feed the 35 heating vents. To ensure the perfect preservation of his collection, the regulation of the heating system was one of Moïse de Camondo's major preoccupations. The heating distribution plans, always on view in this office, attest to another of the butler's responsibilities.

◄ The butler's office was the only servant's room with windows looking onto the garden. All the other service room windows were frosted. It was here that the butler dealt with daily business, placed orders and paid suppliers.

des Beaux-Arts, etc.), club membership fees (Touring Club and France-Amérique), the stationer, bookbinder, piano rental, fur storage,[11] pharmacy, doctor, vet, cooper, clockmaker and florist.

The butler's ledgers tell us much about the daily needs for food and household products. The hardware requirements of the mansion, stables and garage were met with frequent small orders specified by their uses or brand names: alkali, alcohol, spirits salt, turpentine, chamois leathers, whiting, tissue paper, horsehair brushes, feather dusters, crystals, bottles of bleach, Buhler paste, Goddard powder, knife powder, wire wool, tubs of soft soap, Kiwi polishes, Curémail, soft bristle brooms, straw brooms, sponges, green soap, Miror, polishers, floorcloths and all kinds of brushes (bath, sink, parquet, all-purpose).

Local shopkeepers delivered groceries, bread, dairy products and fruit, and renowned houses more exceptional delicacies: Boissier for petits fours, Hédiard for certain selected fruit, Fouquet for jams, etc. The caterer Rebattet was called upon for receptions. The count himself ordered from certain select merchants, especially wine, and also regularly had olive oil sent from Nice, olives and capers from Athens and boutargue[12] from Marseille.

► Swan's neck wall lamp with a tulip-shaped frosted glass shade made by Holophane, as installed throughout the servants' quarters and in Moïse de Camondo's dressing room (**see p. 264**).

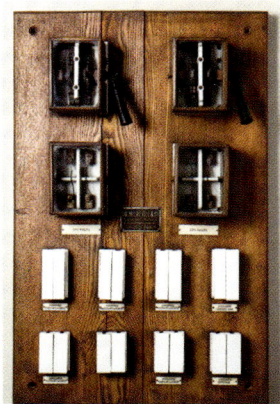

▲ The fuse and circuit breaker board by Mildé for the radiators and electrical appliances in the bedrooms.

▲ The rheostat is still in place in the butlery on the mezzanine floor. It enabled the concealed cornice lighting to be dimmed in the reception rooms.

▼ Invoice received from the Mildé company in August 1913.

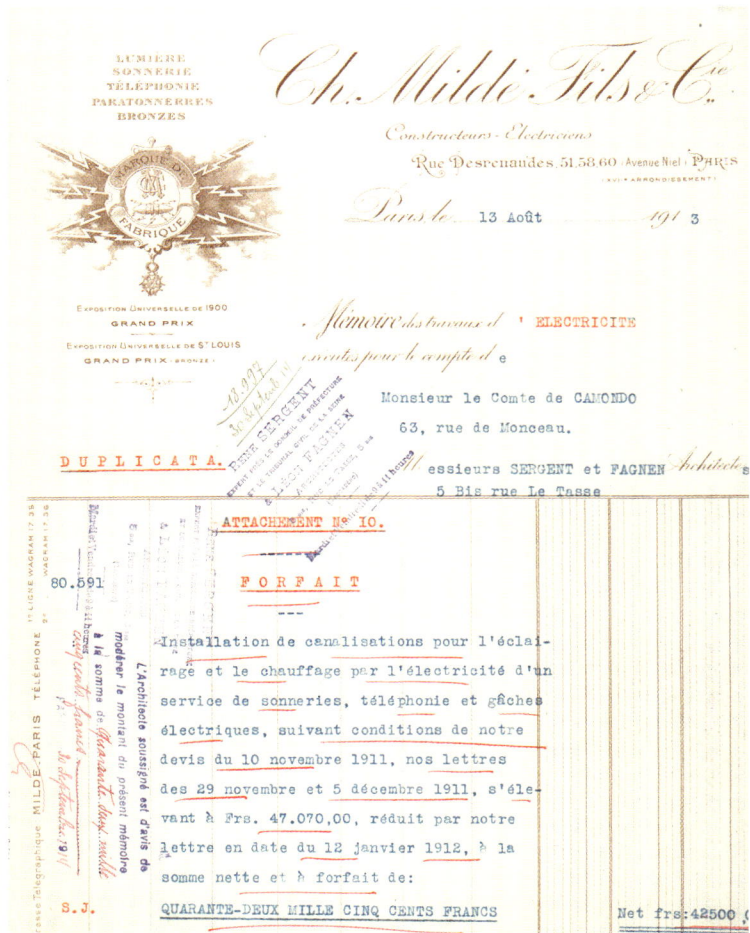

The electrical circuitry

The Mildé[13] company was responsible for the installation and maintenance of the electrical system. The maintenance contract covered lighting (circuit breakers, sockets, switches, plugs), bells and telephones and the recharging of their Leclanché batteries. The firm's reputation was such that Proust wrote: 'Talking of eyesight, have you heard that the new house Madame Verdurin has just bought is to be lighted by electricity? I didn't get that from my own little secret service, you know, but from quite a different source; it was the electrician himself, Mildé, who told me. ...Even the bedrooms, he says, are to have electric lamps with shades which will filter the light.'[14] In the early 20th century, incandescent light bulbs were constantly being improved, both for existing lamps or for new types of lighting.[15] Unlike Boni de Castellane, who could not bear electric lighting in living rooms,[16] Moïse de Camondo's chandeliers were lit by electric candles: the flame-shaped bulb was screwed into a porcelain socket in a wooden sheath imitating a candle. The form of the bulb differed depending on the lamp: flame-shaped, spherical, transparent or frosted for lamps, cylindrical for display cases and picture lighting (**see p. 112**) and semi-silvered for indirect cornice lighting in the reception rooms.[17]

The electrical system required regular maintenance but also constant repair, and memos

LAVABOS IDÉAL GRANIT

MONTAGES ATTENANTS AUX BAIGNOIRES

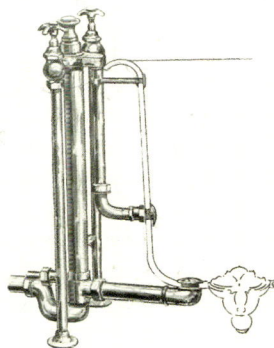

N° 104
1ᵐ25 - 0ᵐ62. Cuvette 0ᵐ56 - 0ᵐ36

Lavabo à une place en "IDEAL GRANIT" monté sur piètement fonte laqué blanc uni maintenant le Lavabo à 5 centimètres du mur, robinets eau chaude, eau froide, vidage "Sanitas".

	Superchoix	Choix A	Choix B
Complet, cuivrerie nickelée, série courante	Frs. 336	Frs. 304	Frs. 261

	Superchoix	Choix A	Choix B
Complet, cuivrerie nickelée, série lourde et de précision spécialement recommandée	Frs. 355	Frs. 323	Frs. 280

En plus, pour siphon cuivre nickelé. Série courante	Frs. 11
En plus, pour siphon cuivre nickelé. Série lourde	Frs. 15
En plus, pour piètement cuivre nickelé au lieu de fonte laquée	Frs. 30
En plus, pour tuyaux d'alimentation et de vidange descendant jusqu'au sol avec raccords et rosaces de fixage en cuivre nickelé	Frs. 40

70

MONTAGE E
Recommandé

Fourniture et ajustage d'une robinetterie attenante, eau chaude, eau froide, alimentation par macaron intérieur évitant le bruit et la buée, vidage américain à trop-plein combiné, siphon ; le tout en cuivre nickelé, série lourde et de précision.

Pour baignoires fonte émaillée Frs. 140
Pour baignoires Idéal Granit Frs. 150
En plus pour tuyaux d'alimentation descendant jusqu'au sol, avec raccords et rosaces de fixage, le tout en cuivre nickelé. Frs. 20

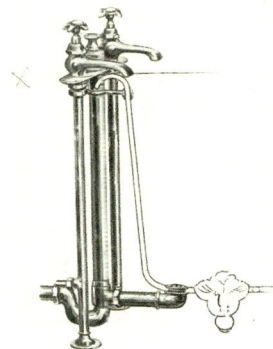

MONTAGE F
Recommandé

Fourniture et ajustage d'une robinetterie attenante, eau chaude, eau froide, avec robinets se déversant par dessus la gorge, vidage américain à trop-plein combiné, siphon, le tout en cuivre nickelé, série lourde et de précision.

Pour baignoires fonte émaillée. Frs. 155
Pour baignoires Idéal Granit. Frs. 165
En plus, pour tuyaux d'alimentation descendant jusqu'au sol, avec raccords et rosaces de fixage, le tout en cuivre nickelé. Frs. 20

34

concerning payments to Mildé contain detailed descriptions that allow a precise idea of the house's very comprehensive electrical installation. In the bedrooms, there were electric bed warmers and additional electric radiators when needed, and the bathrooms had sockets for hair dryers. Electric hotplates, toasters and irons were used daily, and the candelabra on the dining room table were plugged into sockets beneath the carpet.[18]

Electricity was needed to power the vacuum pump;[19] then in 1929 the Frigidaire and lift, previously powered by compressed air, also used electricity. In 1931, the spits of the rotisserie and the ignition of the new oil-fired boiler were converted to electricity. The same year, with a view to replacing the gas cooker with an electric cooker, Count de Camondo and his cook went to Baron de Rothschild's mansion at 2 rue Saint-Florentin to see how one worked, then to the sales office of the Compagnie Parisienne d'Électricité to enquire about consumption rates at different times of day. As ever, the count was interested in progress, but measured efficiency against cost.

◄ In Moïse de Camondo's bathroom, the white and blue wall tiling has a simple basketwork pattern bordered with friezes. The grey and white stoneware floor tiling is also bordered with a faience frieze. The door opens into the bedroom.

► Next to the bath in Nissim de Camondo's bathroom, there is a footbath with long pivoting shower pipes specially fitted to the taps. Against the back wall is the heated towel rail. On the walls is a frieze of square motifs in two tones of green above the white hexagonal wall tiles, in turn surmounted by a green fillet similar to the one decorating the skirting.

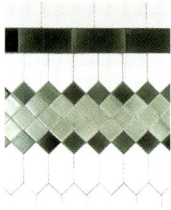

Nissim de Camondo's bathroom. The white wall has a two tone green border.

In Béatrice de Camondo's bathroom, the bath is set in an alcove. The yellow and white wall tiling has a frieze of small Delft landscape tiles between two yellow fillets.

Modern bathrooms

Each family member had his or her self-contained suite with bathroom and dressing room. Moïse's was the largest of the three bathrooms but its design and fittings were similar to Nissim's and Béatrice's. Like ancient Roman baths, they have a vaulted, gloss-painted ceiling to facilitate the flow of condensation down the walls. The glazed earthenware wall tiles and stoneware floor tiles are white, with a single colour for borders and friezes – blue for Moïse, green for Nissim, yellow for Béatrice. Their two-tone geometric decoration is extremely sober yet beautiful.

The bathrooms' ultra-modern decoration was complemented by the latest bathroom equipment,

supplied by Kula.[20] This company, which also installed the plumbing throughout the mansion, was the exclusive importer for two English manu-facturers of porcelain and glazed earthenware. Kula sold a model called 'Ideal granit', which it described as 'perfection in sanitary ceramics and whose superiority over comparable products has been acknowledged by a number of architects'. To cater for the luxury hotels' American clientele and to meet more modern hygienic standards, manufacturers ceased production of wooden bathroom furniture with porcelain bowls and zinc or copper bathtubs. This new type of installation was still rare in private homes but became more widespread in the 1920s, yet many Parisian apartments, even the most

luxurious, did not change their bathroom fittings until the 1950s.

In 1912, the year the Camondo mansion was commissioned, Kula published its complete catalogue[21] with illustrations of all models. Not all the original pieces in the bathrooms are still in situ, but this invaluable document enables us to identify them precisely: bath, footbath, bidet, washbasin, dressing table and toilet, and the nickel-plate brass taps and fittings: heated towel rack, clothes hangers, towel rails, soap dishes, carafe and glass holders.[22] Strangely, none of the shower systems in the catalogue were ordered.

The bathrooms' unostentatious luxury and uncompromisingly modern decoration is a fine example of the collaboration between architect and client. Only the Delft faience frieze of landscape tiles in Béatrice's bathroom, probably added at her request, slightly disrupts their geometric decoration.

After washing, Moïse would retire to the adjoining dressing room, where he could rest on a comfortable bench upholstered with broad-striped silk fabric. The low gu (Brazilian long-veined mahogany) panelling in this room comes from the Oriental gallery of Isaac de Camondo's apartment on the Champs-Élysées. Dismantling and reinstalling the panelling was an extremely costly undertaking, and in the end Moïse almost regretted reusing it. The upper parts of the walls are hung with watered silk fabric, and a large sliding mirror could be used to

◄ To reach the wardrobe room on the attic floor, Moïse de Camondo's valet went up the inner staircase from the antechamber. The bracket under the stairs was for a fire hose.

► Nissim de Camondo's dressing room and the corridor leading to his apartment are hung with the same striped floral wallpaper. The orange-coloured glass ceiling lamp is suspended by a cord decorated with silk acorns.

► In Nissim de Camondo's dressing room, the light switch was painted in trompe-l'œil to blend in with the wallpaper. Wooden studs conceal the screws fixing the panelling to the wall.

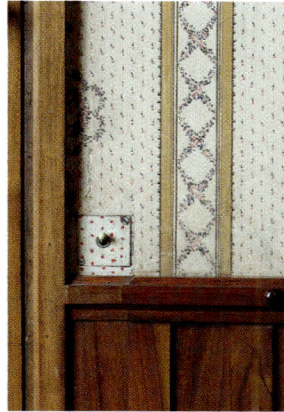

► In Béatrice de Camondo's dressing room, the walls are hung with fabric block-printed with stylized blue-green flowers and stripes on a white ground. As in all the rooms in the house, the light switch is brass, here inset in the wood panelling.

close off the window. The elegant network of circles and diamonds on the stucco ceiling, lit by small frosted glass tulip lamps, is reminiscent of Robert Adam. The walls of Nissim's dressing room are hung with wallpaper and Béatrice's with printed fabric.

On the floor above, Moïse and Nissim each had a room with numerous unvarnished oak wardrobes and Béatrice had a 'roberie'. Moïse's valet used a small inner staircase leading up to his wardrobes and another room for cleaning his shoes and caring for his morning coats, overcoats, etc. Shirts and their starched collars and cuffs were sent out to a laundry for washing. As a rule, all the house's linen was sent out for cleaning by specialized firms who delivered it back.[23]

The hallway leading to the garden **(13)** is located at the end of the lower ground floor corridor, next to the guests' cloakroom **(16)**. As the garden is higher than the courtyard on this side of the building, a flight of steps leads up to the glazed door opening to the west, opposite the mansion built for Abraham Behor de Camondo.

▼ Achille Duchêne's design for the garden, in black pencil, undated, from the Duchêne collection, Musée des Arts Décoratifs. At the foot of the terrace, the lawn ends in a semicircle facing the Parc Monceau. The fountain and statues were never installed. In period photographs, there is only a plane tree in the middle of the lawn, which, like the large ones bordering the garden, had to be pruned in 1917 and 1924.

The master's touch in the garden and courtyard

The garden and plants provide a good example of the demands Moïse de Camondo made on his suppliers. To transform the garden of the former mansion and design the terrace, he enlisted the services of Achille Duchêne,[24] probably on René Sergent's advice. The Duchênes, the famous father-and-son team of landscape gardeners, had forged an exceptional reputation for the restoration and creation of the gardens of historic residences, and Achille Duchêne was also a talented designer of small urban gardens. From September 1912 to May 1913, he produced three estimates, all accepted, for levelling the plot and creating a raised embankment, lawns, flowerbeds and paths.[25] A new entrance, no longer opening directly onto the Parc Monceau but onto avenue Vélasquez, was created to enable free access outside the public garden's opening hours. Moïse was not satisfied with all the preliminary work: 'I expressed my surprise at not having once seen Monsieur Duchêne supervise the work of his contractor at the habitual meeting, which would have enabled us to exchange our impressions on the result which, for my part, did not fill me with enthusiasm in the slightest. M. Sergent and I therefore asked M. Collin to inform M. Duchêne that we wished to see him at the very next meeting on site.'[26] However, Moïse did not hold Duchêne's

► An ink drawing of the first design for the box parterres for the terrace, in their state before 1920. This plan, annotated 'project 2' and two variations annotated 'project 1' and 'project 3', were signed by Sergent, Fagnien and Bétourné. There is a photograph of this state in the Archives Duchêne.

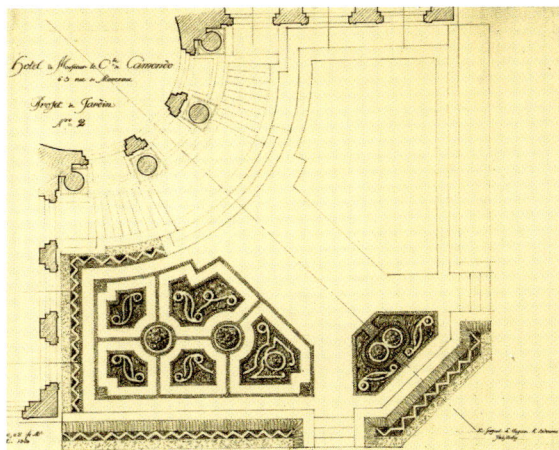

▼ The terrace parterre in an autochrome photograph, c. 1920–28, planted with pink begonias, blue ageratums, coleus and houseleek. There are red geraniums in the Medici vases placed around the edge of the terrace in 1920, and in the pink marble basin at the foot of the steps. This arrangement was published in 1930 in 'Un jardin sur le Parc Monceau chez le Cte de Camondo', *Art et industrie*, October 1930, pp. 7–8.

▲ A watercolour design for the box parterres on the terrace, 1928. This final alteration, carried out at Moïse de Camondo's request, is still in situ, although the box hedges have developed considerably.

absences against him and recommended him 'with pleasure' to Henri Menier, who had just acquired the Château de Chenonceaux.

When the work was finished, Collin delivered a wide variety of plants for the lawns and flowerbeds: four very large, well-developed rhododendrons, twelve medium-sized rhododendrons, seven azaleas, four Chinese peonies, six pink althaeas and to go around the tree trunks polygonum, clematis, honeysuckle and Dorothy Perkins roses. There was also room for three maples, including a laciniate, a Lombardy poplar, an American walnut, two negundo maples, an acacia and five *Prunus pissardi*, and twelve large Chinese privets were planted to conceal the park keeper's kiosk in the Parc Monceau.[27]

On the terrace, there were low box hedge parterres with planted areas infilled with red and white brick gravel chippings. In the autumn of 1913, 2,400 different-coloured pansies, tufted pansies and yellow and brown wallflowers were planted, and the following spring, a mixture of double-flowered yellow marigolds, 'Zurich' sage and stock (*Matthiola incana*), large-flowered pelargoniums, four different types of geranium and eight varieties of begonia. During the war, certain orders were cancelled 'due to circumstances', but the will to maintain a vividly coloured flowered carpet in front of the windows in all seasons never waned. Having admired the parterres in the French-style garden at Vichy in 1917, Moïse

► The garden
as it looks today
from the terrace.

► In this photograph of the terrace in 1918, one can clearly make out the box hedge borders of the parterres, the box hedges close to the house itself and around the edge of the terrace.
The windows had been filled up with sandbags in case Paris was bombed. See *L'Illustration*, 4 January 1919.

► In January 1928, the pyramid-shaped laurel trees in the courtyard were moved to the sides to make room for four stone vases purchased by Moïse de Camondo. These vases were formerly in the niches in the façade of the Château de Liancourt in the Oise. The courtyard is gravelled, with sandstone paving at the foot of the mansion itself. The terraces are emphasized with a box border and hemispherical box trees. The trelliswork above the stable courtyard, erected in 1919, was designed by Achille Duchêne and raised in height in 1929. It was restored in 2003.

◄ The pyramid-shaped laurel trees between the windows. On the left, on top of the wall enclosing the courtyard, is a band with a scrolled frieze that was removed in 1922. This band is similar to the one on the wall enclosing the courtyard of the Petit Trianon at Versailles.

widened his choices and in 1919 desired a 'mosaic of succulent plants': 'during to a trip to Strasbourg this summer, I saw mosaic patterned plantations which pleased me greatly and of which I brought back photographs.'[28] Several horticultural firms were involved in this delicate undertaking in 1920, in finalizing the design, producing plans[29] and carrying them out. The round flowerbed, which still had its box hedge border, kept the same form for around ten years, with various planting schemes.

The invoices for the ensuing years show deliveries of daisies, box, ivy, heather and geraniums, and the annual 'lawn grass' for resowing the lawn. The correspondence with suppliers in Paris and Versailles[30] indicates Moïse's constant attention to his garden, but it was the annual delivery of rhododendrons which regularly prompted the most criticism on his part: they were never delivered early enough, and never in good enough condition. In 1925, the Moser company finally lost patience: 'We regret to inform you that we are unable to continue the subscription consented to you by Monsieur Vilette. We have taken this decision due to the difficulty which occurs each year in finding robust plants likely to meet with your satisfaction.'[31]

Moïse de Camondo finally gave up planting flowering plants. In 1926, he signed a contract with a new supplier, Toutin et Roussel,[32] who created a parterre in 1928 composed solely of box. The flowering border at the base of the terrace was also

done away with and the geraniums in the Medici vases were replaced with box globes and aucubas. Although the box on the terrace has since grown out of all proportion, the original design still remains.

Floral decoration is also present in the courtyard where the terraces of the outbuildings were originally bordered with stone troughs planted with box plants and wooden containers were ordered for laurels. Following the fashion since 1870, at the foot of the mansion itself Moïse de Camondo placed laurels procured from a renowned nursery in Ghent. The Belgian horticulturalist J.P. Hartmann supplied six spherically trimmed plants, then four pyramidal ones, which were placed between the windows.

To give the courtyard additional intimacy, in 1919 a well-known specialist in 'artistic trelliswork', H. Bocquet,[33] created a screen above the grooming courtyard, which was raised in 1929 when a storey was added to the building next door.[34] In 1913, Moïse also had a trellis built to conceal the motor car courtyard from the garden. It is visible on the right of a photograph of the mansion taken from the garden in 1936.

A 'House-Museum'

The Large Drawing Room as it was when the museum was opened, reproduced in *L'Illustration*, 26 December 1936.

Opening to the public

The terms of Moïse de Camondo's will, drawn up in 1924 (**see p. 3**), were very precise. They included the inalienability of his collections and the organization of the future museum: the collections could not be added to, except for the books in the library; the furniture had to stay in its original place; and his *Instructions and advice for the curators of the Musée Nissim de Camondo* were carefully set out. Finally, in a codicil dated 1932,[35] he added: 'It is to be understood that no object in my collection should leave my mansion to be loaned for exhibitions.' He lent works during his lifetime but never the jewels of his collection, which he

allowed only appointed visitors to view in his mansion.[36] Faithful to the family tradition of handing down and the educational mission pursued by his ancestors, he bequeathed his life's work to everyone. The museum was inaugurated on 21 December 1936, only a year after his death – barely enough time in which to draw up an inventory, compile a catalogue and photograph the collections.[37]

The opening was a major event and the colour photographs published in *L'Illustration* provide a priceless record of the arrangement of the main rooms.[38] The museum had relatively few visitors but soon became an obligatory pilgrimage for students, collectors and art lovers eager to visit this

Instructions and advice for the curators of the Musée Nissim de Camondo

As I stated in my will, I wish this museum to be admirably maintained and kept meticulously clean. The task is not an easy one, even with first-class staff, of whom there must be a sufficient number for this job; but the work is made easier by a complete vacuum cleaning system which works cheaply and marvellously well. Due to its powerful operation, this method of cleaning should not be used for antique carpets, tapestries and silks but it is of great benefit. Furthermore, it is essential that the draught excluders should always be kept in perfect condition, since they not only retain the heat inside the house but also prevent a good deal of dust from entering the rooms.

The heating system consists of two boilers which work separately, the large one during severe cold, the small one for normal temperatures. I have almost always used the small boiler and I consider that for a museum, which should not be overheated, and since visitors usually keep their coats on, only this one should be used, especially as it is much more economical. Central heating is unfortunately very bad for veneered furniture, panelling and even parquet floors, so the heating vents must be closed as soon as an adequate temperature is obtained, and must be closed especially after the public leave, on non-visiting days and at night; the heat retained by the walls is sufficient to maintain a pleasant temperature in the mansion; this is how I have always proceeded. Any negligence in this respect would incur damage to a piece of furniture or a picture....

In the same way, one should turn off any water pipes that are not necessary, such as those in the bathrooms, which will avoid the need for extremely difficult and expensive repairs. In case of frost, turn off the pipes to the garden to prevent them from bursting. In short, turn off all pipes that are not necessary for an uninhabited house.

The floors in the hallways near the stairs have to be cleaned specially and with great care. Please ask my staff how to do this.

All the windows have metal shutters with security bars which ensure good security against burglaries, but it is important to check that all the shutters are closed and that the bars are in place as the risk of theft from the Parc Monceau side is high. A good night security guard service is also necessary, especially when people realize that the museum is not inhabited.

All the windows have exterior awnings to protect against the sun Make sure that they are put to good use.

On rainy days, the public should enter via the wrought-iron doors from the covered motor car entrance linking the courtyard to the mews that leads to boulevard Malesherbes. This door is approached via a wide paved area which could be covered with matting and where one could place umbrella stands.

Fire prevention is ensured by Harden extinguishers but it is essential that these are maintained in good working order.

My friend Carle Dreyfus will be able to provide invaluable information for compiling the catalogue. He knows all my pieces and everything that I know about them myself. I also have a small notebook in which I have listed all my purchases, unfortunately not from my earliest days as a collector but for some twelve years or so, and it contains useful information from which you may benefit if my heirs consent to let you have access to it.

The courtyard is decorated with wooden planters containing trimmed laurels. These trees do not withstand frost and must be taken inside before the winter. This may easily be done using a small cart easily handled by two men. The planters should be stored in the glazed tack room of the stables, where they have daylight and a suitable temperature. On fine days they should be aired by leaving the doors open.

Finally, I would like to express the desire that my servants who so wish should be kept on as keepers, especially the concierge, as they are good servants who are very familiar with the building's upkeep. But this is by no means an obligation and does not apply to the kitchen staff and mechanics.

Paris, 20 January 1924. M. de Camondo

◄ Restoration of the silk fabric of the screen in Moïse de Camondo's bedroom, chain-stitch embroidered with polychrome bouquets.

private residence that was now open to the public, a 'house-museum' whose guests' cloakroom had become the visitors' cloakroom.[39]

Preserving, restoring, protecting

By the 1970s, the state of the house had begun to give cause for worry. The roof, heating and electrical systems needed repeated repairs (financed by the state), and major refurbishment work was carried out in the 1980s.[40]

The same was true of the collections and, in order to restore them, the Union Centrale des Arts Décoratifs had to appeal to donors and corporate sponsors. In 1985, the Comité pour Camondo was set up to liaise with donors and succeeded in raising more than 10 million francs over the next ten years.[41] The panelling, furniture, paintings and textiles in each of the reception rooms, and then the private apartments, were gradually restored. Their reopening was a major event and an opportunity to rekindle public interest in a museum that had gradually been forgotten.

But a judicious compromise still had to be struck both to preserve the collections and to respect Moïse de Camondo's express wishes. The chairs in the visitors' corridors, for instance, were removed, as were objects considered too fragile. The carpets in place, protected by carpet underlay

▼ Removing dust from a carpet. Since the museum's opening, this large Beauvais carpet, which Moïse de Camondo had originally placed on the landing of the staircase on the upper ground floor, had been in the hall. To protect it from light and dust, it was temporarily put into storage in 2003.

▼ Taking down a tapestry. Moïse de Camondo had originally placed this tapestry panel, depicting a war trophy, on the floor of the upper ground floor corridor (see pp. 97, 98–99). When the museum was opened in 1936, it was hung over one of the corridor's mirrored doors for the sake of preservation. In 2000, to respect the corridor's architectural unity, it was taken down and temporarily put in store.

pathways, were rolled up and those in the galleries removed. The museum is currently studying the possibility of placing dust covers on certain chairs whose period upholstery has to be preserved.

To apply current preventive conservation standards is even more difficult here. With regular attention and meticulous care we are daily attempting to follow the constraints imposed by the upkeep of a mansion.

New spaces opened to the public

In spring 1995, the final phase of the Comité pour Camondo's ten-year restoration campaign centred on Moïse de Camondo's apartment. The bathroom was a revelation: the private apartments were designed in the most modern and functional manner. Opening it to the public revealed a facet of the house that its owner had deliberately concealed. His recreation of 'an 18th-century artistic residence' had hidden the private living spaces and even the work of the architect.

Following this first incursion into the private domain, a refurbishment programme was established for the entire mansion, including the outbuildings. The situation rapidly proved promising and study of the records of the original installation work and the house's upkeep were an invaluable source of information.

Restoration of the former bedroom in Nissim de Camondo's apartment.

► Cleaning the marble bust of Abraham Salomon de Camondo.

► The original pelmet by the interior decorator Decour.

► Installating the new pelmet. The watered silk mural fabric and curtains were rewoven by the Prelle company, supplier of the original order in 1912.

▼ Since 2003, the family's mementos have been on display in the former bedroom of Nissim de Camondo's apartment: objects, photographs and busts of ancestors. Above the commode, the portrait of Abraham Behor de Camondo by Léon Bonnat, 1882; on the left, a marble bust of Abraham Salomon, and on the right, of Count Nissim de Camondo by R. Hertz.

The restoration work carried out in 2003 concentrated on Nissim's apartment. Only one room had previously been open to the public. The former bedroom, dressing room and bathroom were now restored to their original state. In the absence of large available spaces, the bedroom, the last room in the museum visit, was devoted to the history of the Camondo family (portrait paintings and busts of members of the family, archive documents and photographs).[42] Acquisitions have complemented this collection, notably the prayer books belonging to Abraham Salomon[43] and pieces from the porcelain dinner service formerly in Count Nissim's *yali* on the Bosporus.[44] The ivory toilet case that belonged to Élise, Count Nissim de Camondo's[45] wife, is on display with her husband's collection of tie-pins, donated by Moïse to the Musée des Arts Décoratifs.[46]

The opening of some of the mansion's service rooms, especially the kitchen in 1999, was perhaps the boldest innovation. The urgent restoration of the service façade, funded by the state and contributions from private donors, were two crucial factors in achieving this.[47]

Recent studies of private life and customs have emphasized the importance of revealing the functional aspect of one of the few Parisian residences not to have undergone irreversible alterations.[48] The current public interest in the art of cooking is very strong. There have never been so

Restoration of the servants' quarters between 1997 and 1999.

► Polishing the rotisserie in the kitchen (see p. 249).

▼ Preparing the wood-grain decoration above the dresser in the servants' dining room (see p. 254).

► Detail of the 'three-tone speckled granite decoration', obtained by stippling two tones of brown and white on a grey ground (see p. 254).

► Restoring the panelling in the service corridors (see p. 248).

many recipe books, publications on the decoration and history of the kitchen, and such intense media interest as there is today, and exhibitions on the art of entertaining and gastronomy are on the increase.[49] In the film *Babette's Feast*, Stéphane Audran, playing the former cook of the Café Anglais, recreates a famous menu in exile culminating with *cailles en sarcophage* (quails in pastry cases) – this famous Parisian restaurant was one of the favourite haunts of two generations of the Camondo family (see p. 44).[50]

In France, visitors flocked to visit the period kitchens of the châteaux, but rarely had access to the adjoining rooms. They therefore had only a very incomplete idea of how the house's service was organized and of the parallel world of its servants.[51] It was in the United Kingdom that these hidden aspects of historic monuments were first revealed and several remarkable publications bear testimony to this, notably the work done by the National Trust since the early 1970s.[52]

The modernity of the Hôtel de Camondo's kitchen is comparable to that of the great luxury hotels, yet its arrangement and details are typical of the residences in the Monceau district.[53] Missing items of furniture were replaced, as was some of its equipment, based on the cook's purchases, lists of kitchen utensils sent to the tinsmith and the books of the great chefs, especially Urbain Dubois and Auguste Escoffier. It is not a full reconstruction but

◄ The covered motor car entrance beneath the staircase in the mansion itself (17).

▼ The garage, restored in 2003, now has its original decoration. The large sound-insulating acoustic panels on the walls are the only addition.
The floor is cement and the panelling is polished cement. The walls were originally painted with a Ripolin industrial gloss paint mentioned in the memos of the interior decorator Feist concerning the painting of the outbuildings and servant quarters. The earlier, metallic structure was originally painted grey-green, with a double red-brown fillet around the ceiling caissons.

▲ The capital of one of the iron pillars in the garage.

a partial recreation, stirring memories and the imagination.[54] And to complement one's visit, Jean Renoir's *La Règle du jeu*, James Ivory's *The Remains of the Day* or Robert Altman's *Gosford Park* may be thoroughly recommended. Their period reconstructions and portrayals of the relationships between master and servant are exemplary.[55]

The restoration of the outbuildings

In 1944, the Centre d'Art et de Technique, later renamed the École Camondo, taught its first courses in the outbuildings.[56] As the school developed, it took over both wings, gradually stripping them of some of their original fittings.[57] There are no period photographs of the outbuildings, but what has survived of the original interiors and study of the archives have provided the necessary information for their restoration.

The garage was in the left wing. The way in was through a wide gateway between the caretaker's lodgings on the right and the staircase leading to the chauffeur-mechanics' lodgings on the left.[58] The garage's metallic architecture is part of the construction work Destors did for Count Nissim (see p. 31). The work carried out by Sergent centred on the windows, the sliding door on the courtyard side and the mural decoration. The cars were washed beneath the glazed awning in the courtyard

Top to bottom:

—The specially designed gnaw-proof door handles used in the stables. The ring is engraved with the name of the supplier, Mouton H. Oranger.

—The horses' enamelled cast-iron name plaques were fixed above their fodder racks. This one, 'Gisbon', is painted in two tones of blue and heightened with gold. There was also 'Jumbo', 'Stewball' and others whose names have been forgotten.

—The two tones of blue of the Camondo livery is repeated on the border of the enamelled bricks and beneath the adjoining enamelled cast iron rim preventing the wood panelling from being gnawed by the horses.

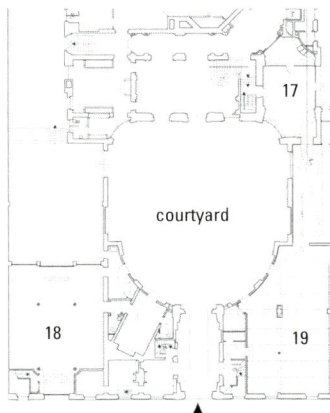

Plan of the outbuildings.
17. Covered motor car entrance
18. Garage
19. Former stables

Dismantling the cladding in the former stables revealed the original oak wall panelling and white glazed bricks on the back and side walls.
The glazed partition let in light from the tack room next door.

and the maintenance workshop was in the basement.[59] Moïse de Camondo had a life-long love of high-performance cars and the garage housed a succession of them (see pp. 47–48). Restored in 2003, it is now used for receptions.[60]

In the right wing, the fitting out of stables for nine horses was entrusted to the Mouton H. Oranger company.[61] The space is lit by two windows on the rue de Monceau side and by a fanlight above the door into the glass-roofed grooming room. Horses went in or out of the courtyard through the grooming room and there was an ingenious system for removing straw and manure into the passageway adjoining the mews via a narrow corridor beside the covered vehicle entrance.

Despite his growing interest in automobiles, Moïse still kept horses for the last of the horse-drawn carriages, and so that his children could go riding in the Bois de Boulogne. After Nissim died, only Béatrice continued to cross the Parc Monceau and take avenue Hoche to Étoile and the avenue du Bois.[62] By 1917 one of the tack rooms and the coachman's apartment had already been converted into the offices of Isaac Camondo & Co., which had just closed definitively.[63]

To continue the house's complete restoration and improve the museum's reception facilities, it was now necessary to restore the covered motor car entrance, located in the mansion itself, at the inner end of the right wing of the outbuildings, beneath

◄ Schoolchildren drawing in the hall.

the first flight of the main staircase. This entrance provided sheltered access to the hall in all weathers, and so it was logical that it should reclaim its original purpose by becoming the visitors' entrance (see p. 278).

Moïse de Camondo had an educational purpose in bequeathing his mansion and collections. His life's work has now been fulfilled beyond his wildest dreams. Far more than a lesson in decorative art, his vision of an art of living at the dawn of the 20th century remains. His house-museum continues to be, in its full respect for its collector-founder, a testament to the customs of the aristocratic bourgeoisie between the wars, when the world was affected by profound upheavals. One of

the last mansions to be built in Paris, it is now gradually coming back to life again and revealing the full diversity of the life of its occupants. The preservation of this house in its entirety enables each visitor to consider it his or her own residence during their visit.

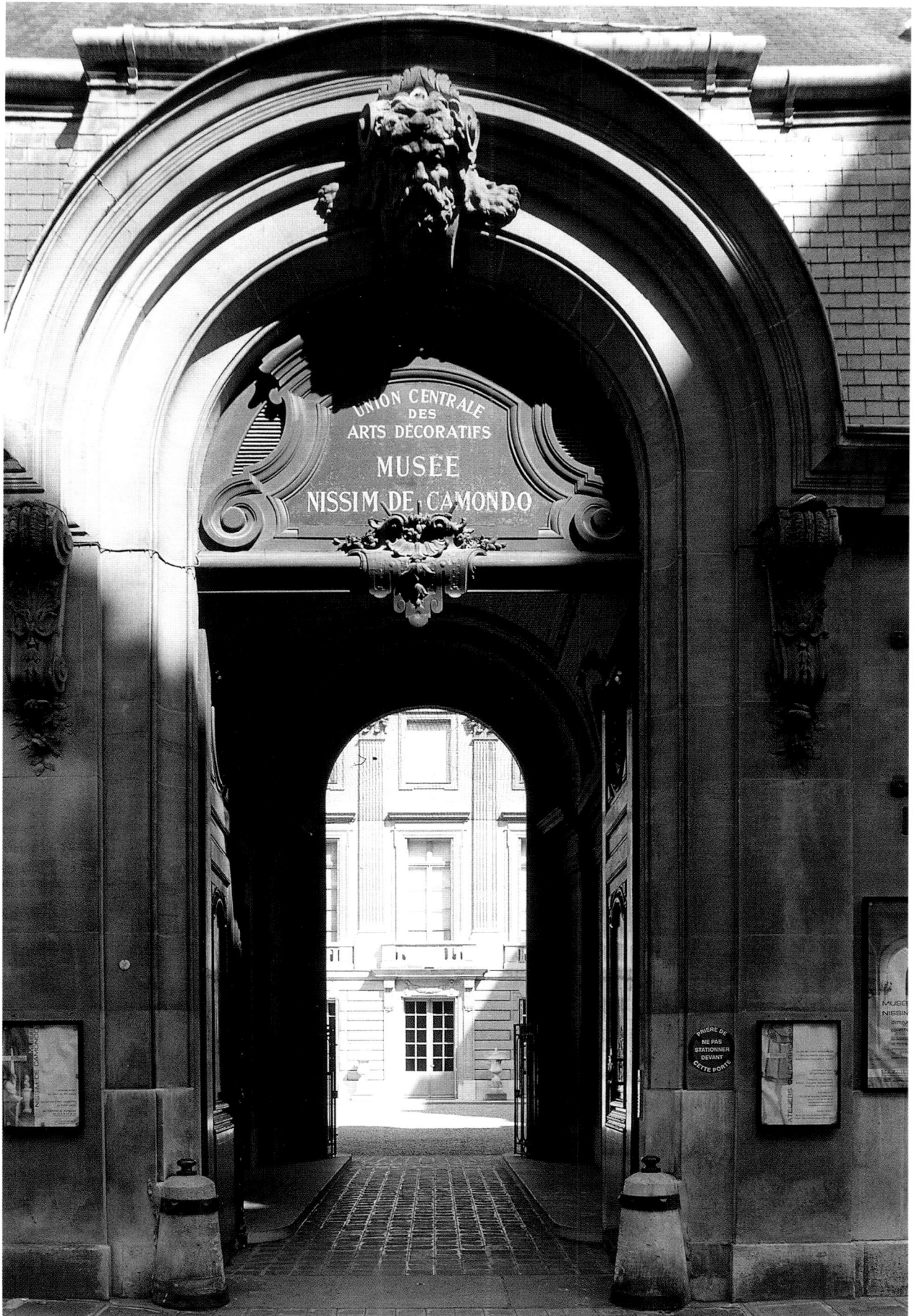

► The carriage
entrance.

Commentaries *by Bertrand Rondot and Mathieu Rousset-Perrier*

p. 117 *The Lower Ground Floor Gallery*
Large decorative landscapes by Hubert Robert hang on either side of a longcase regulator clock signed 'Lepaute, Hger du roi' (a company active from 1776 to 1792), in an ornate mahogany and gilt bronze case. The gallery is lit by rock crystal and amethyst chandeliers. At the end, the wrought-iron doors lead to the covered motor car entrance **(see also pp. 76, 242).**

pp. 118–19 *The Main Staircase*
At the foot of the main staircase visitors are welcomed by the white marble *Venus and Cupid*. In front of the niche with a palotte limestone vase, an armchair, probably Italian, that belonged to Isaac de Camondo. On the landing can just be seen one of the two Japanese lacquer corner-cupboards by BVRB.

p. 120 *Upper landing of the Main Staircase*
A Gobelins chancellery tapestry with the coat of arms of the Marquis d'Argenson occupies the whole of the staircase wall, well lit by two windows hung with Beauvais tapestry pelmets. The plaster statue, probably originally a torch bearer, was placed in 1923 in the niche that had been left empty by Sergent.

p. 121 *Armchair by the door to the Large Study*
Carved walnut; Savonnerie tapestry upholstery, with bouquets of polychrome flowers on a yellow ground.
c. 1720–30
H. 109, W. 70, D. 63 cm
Inv. CAM 38

One of Moïse de Camondo's last acquisitions in 1935, this armchair and its companion belonged to a set of ten. They come from the large drawing room in the Château de la Roche-Guyon, property of the La Rochefoucauld family.

p. 122 left *Lantern* (detail)
Chased and gilt bronze
c. 1780
H. 130, diameter 60 cm
Inv. CAM 39

As was customary in the 18th century, Moïse de Camondo lit the main staircase with a large eight-candle lantern, adapted for use with electric candle bulbs.
See also p. 120.

p. 122 right *Wall-light* (detail)
Attributed to Jean-Louis Prieur (master founder in 1769)
Chased and gilt bronze
c. 1780–81
H. 72; W. 55 cm
Inv. CAM 12 and CAM 40

Twenty of these wall-lights were ordered in 1779 from the Parisian sculptor and chaser Jean-Louis Prieur. They were for the Large Assembly Room in the royal castle in Warsaw, which had been refurnished by the French architect Victor Louis at the request of Stanislas August Poniatowski, king of Poland. The vagaries of Polish his-

tory have shrouded much of their past in mystery, but we know that in the 19th century they were in the collection of Prince Anatole Demidoff in Wisniowiec Castle in Poland. Moïse de Camondo bought eight from his decorator, M. Decour, for the Hall on the lower ground floor and the Gallery on the upper ground floor.
See also p. 121.

p. 123 *Athénienne, one of a pair* (details)
Carved, painted and gilt oak, chased and gilt bronze, patinated bronze
c. 1775
H. 105; diameter 42 cm
Inv. CAM 37

The *athénienne*, a bowl or dish on a tripod pedestal stand, first appeared in the 1760s. It could be used as a brazier – as this one was – or as a perfume burner or even a fish bowl. It is the piece that is most emblematic of the return to Antiquity. Although its form was directly inspired by the discoveries at Herculaneum and Pompeii, its name does not date from Antiquity. It was coined by the banker and collector Jean-Henri Eberts and refers to the picture by Joseph-Marie Vien, *La Vertueuse Athénienne*, shown at the 1763 Salon, a version of which Eberts owned. When Moïse de Camondo bought this pair formerly in the Burat collection in 1926, it was believed to have been given by Madame Du Barry to the church of Saint-Jérôme in Toulouse.
See also p. 121.

The reception rooms
See plan on p. 126.

The Large Study **pp. 124, 128–37**

p. 124 *Doorway onto the main staircase:*
'The Wolf and the Stork'
Aubusson manufactory tapestry, after Jean-Baptiste Oudry
De Menou workshop
c. 1775–80
H. 295, W. 124 cm
Inv. CAM 114

When the Collège de Sorèze in the former province of Languedoc was converted into a military school in 1776, the central drawing room was decorated with a set of eight Aubusson tapestry after Oudry depicting La Fontaine's fables. Moïse de Camondo acquired six, and the last two went to his friend Jules Ephrussi. Although made at the Aubusson manufactory, the set was inspired by the palm-leaf and flower garland frames of the *Pastorales à draperies bleues* woven at Beauvais from cartoons by Jean-Baptiste Huet.

p. 128–29 *Roll-top desk*
Stamped by Claude-Charles Saunier (master in 1752)
Oak, plum pudding mahogany veneer, chased and gilt
bronze, veined white marble top
c. 1780
H. 123, W. 133, D. 68 cm
Inv. CAM 55

p. 130 *Candelabrum, one of a pair* (detail)
Chased, patinated and gilt bronze, red Griotte marble
c. 1780–90
H. 117 cm
Inv. CAM 86
Full view p. 129, detail p. 133

p. 131 *Candlestick, one of a pair* (detail)
Chased and gilt bronze
c. 1770–80
H. 15 cm
Inv. CAM 91
Full view p. 129 and p. 132

p. 132 *Clock and candlesticks on the roll-top desk*
Inv. CAM 100
Inv. CAM 91

The mechanism of the clock with horizontal revolving
face is concealed in a Niderviller porcelain vase, part of
a garniture with two smaller accompanying vases.

p. 133 left *Candelabrum, one of pair* (detail)
Chased, patinated and gilt bronze, red Griotte marble
c. 1780–90
H. 117 cm
Inv. CAM 86
Full view p. 129, detail p. 130

p. 133 right *Clock, part of mantel set* (detail)
Niderviller manufactory
Hard-paste porcelain with gold
c. 1785
H. 36 cm
Inscription on face: *Arnould Pere A NANCY*
(Nicolas Arnould, clockmaker in Nancy in the second
half of the 18th century)
Inv. CAM 100

The clock is in the form of a vase, the porcelain bearing
the mark of the Count of Custine (two crowned *Cs*),
owner of the Niderviller manufactory 1770–93.
Full view p. 129 and p. 132

p. 134 *'The Wolf, the Mother and her Child'* (detail)
Aubusson manufactory tapestry
after Jean-Baptiste Oudry
De Menou workshop
c. 1775–80
H. 295, W. 229 cm
Inv. CAM 114

p. 135 *The fireplace and pier glass*
Reflected in the overmantel mirror, *The Fish and the
Shepherd Playing the Flute* tapestry. The clock and two
candelabra with Bacchic figures are displayed on the
mantelpiece that was formerly in a mansion in Bordeaux.
The two porphyry vases were previously in the Stroganoff
collection in St Petersburg.

p. 136 *'Bacchante Carrying a Satyr Child'* clock
Bronze by François Rémond, mechanism by
Charles-Guillaume Manière
Chased, patinated and gilt bronze, red Griotte marble
c. 1796
H. 75, W. 50, D. 21 cm
Inv. CAM 93

In 1796, François Rémond produced three bronzes for
three clocks with mechanisms by Manière, after a model
by Louis-Simon Boizot shown at the 1795 Salon.

p. 137 *'Bacchante'*
Élisabeth-Louise Vigée-Lebrun
Oil on oak
1785
H. 109, W. 88 cm
Inv. CAM 113

This delightful scantily clad bacchante, a creature belonging to the lofty genre of history painting and a rare
subject for Mme Vigée-Lebrun, was basically an excuse
to paint a female nude. It echoes the Bacchic figures on
the clock and candelabra on the mantelpiece, the vine
branches on the wall lights and the group by Foggini
portraying Bacchus and Ariadne on the console on the
opposite wall.

The Upper Ground Floor Gallery pp. 138–41

p. 138–39 *The gallery and staircase*
In a subtle interplay of space and architecture, the light
crosses the stairwell and illuminates the gallery, reflected
by the honey-coloured limestone and mirrored doors.

p. 140 top *Armchair, one of a pair* (detail)
Inv. CAM 38
Full view p. 121.

p. 140 bottom *Armchair, one of a set of eight, and a settee*
(detail)
Stamped by Pierre Gillier (master in 1749)
Carved and varnished beech, tapestry
c. 1750–55
H. 104, W. 73, D. 59 cm
Inv. CAM 312
Full view p. 141.

p. 141 *'The Chinese Garden'*
Aubusson manufactory tapestry
Wool and silk
Jean-François Picon workshop
c. 1750–70
H. 245, W. 340 cm
Inv. CAM 330

This tapestry, formerly in Count Nissim de Camondo's
collection, was woven at Aubusson, from compositions
by Jean-Joseph Dumons, painter at the manufactory
from 1731 to 1755. These compositions were adapted
from the *Tenture Chinoise* cartoons delivered to the
Beauvais manufactory by François Boucher in 1742.
The large carpet on the floor was woven in Poland and
is a rare example of the production of the country's
workshops in the first half of the 18th century.

p. 142 *Corner of the Large Drawing Room*
On either side of the alcove created for *The Fisherwoman*, the fourth tapestry in the *Italian Festivities* set woven at the Beauvais manufactory from cartoons by François Boucher, an angled corner doorway leads into the next room: the doorway shown here leads to the Gallery on the left and the Large Study on the right, visible through the open door.

p. 143 *'Bonheur du jour' writing table* (details)
Stamped by Martin Carlin (master in 1766)
Oak, tulipwood veneer, chased and gilt bronze, soft-paste Sèvres porcelain.
c. 1766
H. 81, W. 67, D. 42 cm
Inv. CAM 126

In the mid-18th century the *marchand-mercier* Simon-Philippe Poirier had the idea of decorating furniture with porcelain plaques, and supplied cabinetmakers in his employ with the precious materials necessary to make them. Martin Carlin was one of them, and made a speciality of these small luxurious pieces, in particular the ladies' writing tables known as *bonheurs du jour*. They were produced from 1765 to 1774. The letter-date *n*, painted by the Sèvres manufactory on nine of the plaques and corresponding to the year 1766, enables this piece's precise dating. Mme Du Barry owned a similar writing table. As soft-paste porcelain's fragility prohibits writing on paper placed directly on the plaques, the drawer opens to form a writing surface (right). Although it was made for a lady's room, Moïse de Camondo placed this desk in the Large Drawing Room.
Full view p. 142.

p. 144 *Round cabaret table*
Attributed to Martin Carlin (master in 1766)
Oak veneered with tulipwood, sycamore, box and mahogany, soft-paste Sèvres porcelain
c. 1770
H. 73, diameter 41 cm
Inv. CAM 133

p. 145 *Desk chair*
Attributed to Jean-René Nadal the Elder (master in 1756)
Carved and gilt walnut, leather
1775
Branded with the *CDT* surmounted by a closed crown of the Count d'Artois
H. 98, W. 66, D. 50 cm
Inv. CAM 136

In 1912, when Moïse de Camondo bought this desk chair at the auction of the Jacques Doucet collection, he was unaware of its prestigious provenance. Pierre Verlet had not yet discovered the meaning of the brands on numerous pieces of furniture, including this one, *CDT* surmounted by a closed crown. We now know that it indicates that it is the property of the Count d'Artois, Louis XVI's brother and the future Charles X. Moïse de Camondo acquired a royal piece without knowing it, formerly in the prince's rooms at Versailles and still with its original blue leather upholstery.

p. 146 *Window looking towards 61 rue de Monceau*
The portrait by Élisabeth Vigée-Lebrun dominates the Large Drawing Room. This feminine presence is echoed by the many tables in the room, as was customary in the 18th century, such as the *table en chiffonnière*, on which the collector placed an inkstand-cum-candlestick.

p. 147 *Commode with sliding panels*
Stamped by Jean-Henri Riesener (master in 1768)
Oak, veneered with amaranth, sycamore, burr maple, bloodwood, holly, hornbeam, hawthorn, maple, barberry, bois de féréol, chased and gilt bronze, violet Breccia marble
c. 1775–80
H. 94, W. 137, D. 60 cm
Inv. CAM 120

The original feature of this chest of drawers by Jean-Henri Riesener, the panels concealing the drawers, make it look like a cabinet. It has some of this cabinetmaker's hallmarks, however: the central bouquet of flowers in 'element by element' marquetry, and the diamond-patterned frisage on the sides. Riesener, who had inherited Œben's workshop, was renowned for the finesse of his marquetry, as demonstrated by the sliding panels of this commode, the division of whose slats does not disturb the continuity of the design of the bouquet.
See also p. 146.

p. 148 *'Geneviève-Sophie Le Couteulx du Molay'*
Élisabeth-Louise Vigée-Lebrun
Oil on canvas
1788
H. 100, W. 79 cm
Inv. CAM 172

Mme du Molay had her portrait painted by her friend Élisabeth-Louise Vigée-Lebrun. Born Sophie Le Couteulx de la Noray, in 1769 she married her cousin Jean Le Couteulx du Molay, owner of the Château de Malmaison from 1771 to 1799, when it was sold to Napoleon Bonaparte, then First Consul. It was at Malmaison, where the artist stayed many times, that she painted this portrait of the woman she considered one of the most elegant ladies in Paris.
See also p. 147

p. 149 *'Prince Charles-Roger de Bauffremont'*
Adélaïde Labille-Guiard
Oil on canvas
1791
H. 34, W. 23 cm
Inv. CAM 169

This small preparatory painting for the monumental portrait now in the Château de Versailles is one of the rare sketches in the collection. Although highly appreciated as a genre in the 18th century, Moïse de Camondo seems not to have particularly favoured it.

p. 150–51 *The fireplace and the door to the Large Study*
The lacquer bottle belonging to Madame de Pompadour dominates the middle of the room on a gilt bronze pedestal table, surrounded by furniture upholstered with tapestry, some of which bears the

stamp of Georges Jacob. Beneath François-Hubert Drouais' portraits of Sigismond and Armand de Serent as a page boy and a timpanist stand two petrified wood vases, formerly owned by Queen Marie-Antoinette, on cabinets with Japanese lacquer panels by Adam Weisweiler.

p. 152 left *Lidded vase, one of a pair* (detail)
Petrified wood, chased and gilt bronze
c. 1784
H. 43, W. 18 cm
Inv. CAM 153

For a long time the mounts of these priceless petrified wood vases were attributed to Pierre Gouthière due to the exceptional quality of the chasing of the intertwined snakes motif, but they have since been linked with a delivery made by François Rémond to the jeweller Aubert on 7 August 1784. The two vases were in Marie-Antoinette's collection at Versailles among other precious objects in petrified wood given to her by her family.

p. 152 right *'Hu' vase, one of a pair* (detail)
Porcelain with grey Guan crackle glaze
China, Qianlong Period (1736–95), *c.* 1740–50
Chased and gilt bronze mount, Paris, *c.* 1755–65
H. 49, W. 30 cm
Inv. CAM 157

The dragon was just as emblematic of the Far East in the 18th century as it is now. Shown here is one of the dragon handles of this *hu* vase, an extremely popular type from the 1720s to the 1750s. The *rocaille* period was also the high point of the craze for *lachine (chinoiserie)*. Monochrome crackle glazed or *truitée* porcelain was particularly appreciated, which the *marchands-merciers* mounted in gilt bronze.

p. 153 *Summer*
Jean-Antoine Houdon
White marble, gilt bronze pearls on the base
c. 1785, signed
H. 47 cm
Inv. CAM 165

In 1781, Jean-Antoine Houdon showed the terracotta models for his *Winter* and *Summer* statues at the Salon. Two years later, he showed his famous marble of *Winter*, known as *La Frileuse*, followed in 1785 by the marble of *Summer*. After these original full-length statues, he also sculpted several busts, including this one in marble. Like most of the busts in the collection, it is of a woman, and was thought to be the daughter of the painter Hubert Robert, when Moïse de Camondo bought it from Eugène Kraemer in 1912.
See also pp. 150–51.

p. 154 *Sake bottle* (detail)
Lacquered bronze
Japan, 16th century
Chased and gilt bronze mount by François Rémond (master in 1774)
1783
H. 47, diameter 28 cm
Inv. CAM 144

In the 18th-century collectors appreciated lacquer as much as they did porcelain. This rare type of sake bottle and its pendant once belonged to Madame de Pompadour, the greatest lacquer collector of her time. It was bought, without a mount, at the auction held after her death, by the great collector Randon de Boisset, and later by the *marchand-mercier* Dominique Daguerre. He commissioned François Rémond to make this beautiful mount with sphinxes and vine branches, whose refinement and chasing are the equal of the work of the greatest jewellers.
See also pp. 150–51.

p. 155 *Tea table* (detail)
Chased and gilt bronze, Sarrancolin marble
Late 18th century
H. 79, diameter 65 cm
Inv. CAM 134

The new attitude to antiquity in the late 18th century led to the creation of new forms of furniture, such as the tripod, but also prompted a renewal of ornamental vocabulary. Griffons, sirens and sphinxes became the favourite motifs of this new return to antiquity.
See also pp. 150–51.

p. 156–57 *Six-leaf screen* (details)
Savonnerie manufactory
Wool, oak frame
c. 1735–40
Each leaf: H. 137, W. 63 cm
Inv. CAM 141

Some of the most luxurious pieces produced at the Savonnerie manufactory were screen panels. Between 1707 and 1744, the manufactory offered eight different designs including this one from 1718 to 1738, woven from designs by François Desportes. This folding screen belonged to the descendants of Charles Duvivier, director of the manufactory in the 18th century.
See also p. 147.

p. 158 *Doorway into the Salon des Huet*
In the alcove in the Large Drawing Room, on either side of one of the settees, is a pair of delicate corner cabinets painted in blue and white monochrome bearing the stamp of Joseph Feurstein. The Salon des Huet can be seen through a hexagonal passageway that has a small oval cupola.

The Salon des Huet pp. 159–71

p. 159 *Console table, one of a pair*
Silvered and gilt bronze, green Egyptian marble
Model c. 1766
H. 92, W. 127, D. 50 cm
Inv. CAM 190

Like the wall-lights in the hall and upper ground floor gallery (**see pp. 121–22**), this console table and its pendant are reminiscent of the work done by the architect Victor Louis for the royal palace in Warsaw. A similar table in this palace, intended for the Portraits Room, had the royal monogram in the middle of the rim, whereas these console tables are decorated with female masks with

plaits and vine-leaf crowns. This model was created in 1763 by the locksmith and metalsmith Pierre Deumier. There are versions in steel and gilt bronze, and others, like this one, in silvered bronze and gilt bronze.
See also p. 161.

p. 160–61 *Two views of the Salon des Huet*
The Savonnerie carpet with bevelled corners, bearing the royal coat of arms and woven for Louis XV, is ideally suited to the Salon des Huet's hexagonal shape. The drawing room's three doors are hung with Gobelins door tapestries with a 'crimson damask' ground. They were delivered in 1775 to the Marquis de Marigny, Madame de Pompadour's brother. Two wall-lights in Sèvres porcelain with a lapis lazuli blue ground hang on either side of one of Huet's paintings, curiously set between two tall mirrored panels. A pair of *rocaille* candelabra stands on one of the Neoclassical silvered bronze console tables.

p. 162 *Clock with a Chinaman*
Chased, gilt and patinated bronze, onyx, white marble
c. 1785
H. 55, W. 30, D. 20 cm
Inscription on the face: *Sotiau* (Nicolas Sotiau, master clockmaker in 1782)
Inv. CAM 182

The taste for *chinoiserie* in the 18th century far surpassed the mere reuse of Chinese and Japanese lacquer and porcelain. Small oriental figures, known as *magots*, also became popular in the decorative arts, in bronze, lacquer and porcelain, on candlesticks, lamps and, as here, on clocks. This model enjoyed some success; the *marchand-mercier* Daguerre supplied a similar one in 1787 to the Prince Regent, the future George IV of England, for the study of his London residence, Carlton House.
See also p. 160.

p. 163 left *Hexagonal bottle, one of a set of three* (detail)
Turquoise-glazed porcelain
China, Qing dynasty (1644–1911), 18th century
Chased and gilt bronze mount, *c.* 1780
One: H. 34, the others: H. 31 cm
Inv. CAM 225

Turquoise-glazed Chinese porcelain was extremely popular during Louis XVI's reign and was often mounted in gilt bronze.
See also p. 160.

p. 163 right *Console table* (detail)
Inv. CAM 190
See also pp. 159, 161.

pp. 164–65 *'Pastorale'* (detail)
Jean-Baptiste Huet
Oil on canvas
c. 1775
H. 217, W. 158 cm
Inv. CAM 186

This dreamy shepherdess, surrounded by her favourite animals, is a detail of one of the seven pictures by Jean-Baptiste Huet that Moïse de Camondo bought from

Arnold Seligmann in 1900. The series is a testimony to the popularity of the theme of the stages of love, depicted here in a pastoral setting. Fragonard's masterful depiction of the theme, painted for Madame Du Barry's pavilion at Louveciennes in 1771, was installed by the great American collector Henry Clay Frick in his mansion on 5th Avenue in New York in 1915.
See also p. 161.

p. 166 *Pelmet* (detail)
Beauvais manufactory
Wool and silk
c. 1785
H. 410, D. 30 cm
Inv. CAM 233

The three windows have a pelmet and imitation leopard-skin curtains held by flower garlands on a light blue ground. Moïse de Camondo had them assembled by his upholsterer and decorator Decour. On the main staircase, in the Porcelain Room and the Small Study, the windows are also hung with similar Beauvais and Aubusson tapestry curtains and pelmets.

p. 167 *Table 'en chiffonnière'* (detail of tray)
Stamp of Roger Vandercruse, known as Lacroix (master in 1755)
Varnished oak and limewood, chased and gilt bronze, Sèvres soft-paste porcelain
c. 1760
H. 69, W. 33, D. 27 cm
Period label inside the side drawer: *806; table en chiffonnier*
Inv. CAM 194

Before they began ordering plaques from the Sèvres manufactory specifically for decorating furniture, the Parisian *marchands-merciers* used certain existing pieces such as the 'Courteille' top on this small *table en cabaret* in the Salon des Huet. Indeed, it was this tray, part of a 'déjeuner' or tea service, which was the first shape to be regularly mounted in furniture; since these small tables for ladies' work were also known as 'tables en chiffonnière', the trays were soon named 'plateaux de chiffonnière' at the Sèvres manufactory. Stamped by Roger Vandercruse, known as Lacroix (RVLC), it is similar to a series of pieces made from 1758 and bearing the stamp of Bernard van Risenburgh (BVRB). The refinement of these tables consists not merely in the integration of the Sèvres porcelain tray but also in the harmony between its decoration and the varnishing of the table itself. Here it is varnished with green and gold motifs on a white ground which, like the porcelain, has since yellowed, and this was how Moïse de Camondo always knew it.
See also pp. 104, 161.

pp. 168–69 *Roll-top desk*
Stamped by Jean-François Œben (master in 1761)
Oak and sycamore veneered with tulipwood, sycamore; amaranth marquetried with holly, service tree, maple, barberry, burr ash, burr maple and amaranth; chased and gilt bronze
c. 1760
H. 98, W. 82, D. 52 cm
Inv. CAM 191

Jean-François Œben, who invented the roll-top desk in the early 1760s, received an order for an exceptionally large and luxurious one from Louis XV in 1761. It was unfinished when the cabinetmaker died on 21 January

1763, and was completed and delivered to the king in 1769 by Riesener. Œben was also Madame de Pompadour's favourite cabinetmaker, and she commissioned a small roll-top desk very similar to this one but with a shelf between the legs. Œben's workshop, then the foremost in Paris, was renowned for its floral compositions with subtle trompe-l'oeil effects, a tradition which Riesener worthily pursued. The roll-top desk was very fashionable in the second half of the 18th century, and the initially slatted tops were replaced by rigid cylinders.

p. 170 *Bergère from a drawing room suite* (detail)
Stamped by Jean-Baptiste-Claude Sené (master in 1769)
Carved and gilt walnut and beech
c. 1770–80
H. 103, W. 68, D. 57 cm
Inv. CAM 198

This chair's exceptional ornateness and highly original carved decoration are hallmarks of Sené's work. He became the Crown's principal supplier of furniture from 1785, which suggests that this chair may have been part of a prestigious order. The frame-mounted upholstery of the suite's armchairs, enabling it to be changed from season to season, is another indication of the furniture's prestigious provenance. Unfortunately, only the two armchairs still have their original petit-point tapestry upholstery, visible in this detail. The other chairs are covered with modern silk fabric.

p. 171 *Twelve-candle chandelier* (detail)
Chased and gilt bronze, rock crystal, amethyst and smoked quartz
c. 1745–55
H. 137, diameter 110 cm
Inv. CAM. 206

From the second half of the 17th century, silvered or gilt metal-framed chandeliers with rock-crystal pendants were among the most valuable ornaments in a French interior, and they could cost several thousand pounds. This particularly ornate example is exceptional not only for its size but also for its gilt bronze *rocaille* candle cups and rings and the chromatic interplay of its rock crystal, amethyst and smoked quartz pendants.

The Dining Room and Porcelain Room
pp. 172–86

p. 172 *View over the garden*
The Dining Room, facing southwest, has five full-length windows, one of which opens onto a flight of steps leading down to the garden.

p. 173 *The table laid in the Dining Room*
The dining-room table is shown here laid with Chantilly soft-paste porcelain plates made around 1770. In the middle is a silver tureen by Auguste **(see pp. 174–75)**. The crystal glasses and silver flatware are contemporary Saint-Louis and Puiforcat replicas of period originals, and the tablecloth is by Porthault.

pp. 174–75 *Pot à oille* (detail)
Stamp of Robert-Joseph Auguste (master in 1757)
Silver
1784–85
H. 31, diameter 38 cm
Inv. CAM 254

The boar's head was one of the ornaments most frequently used by French silversmiths in the 18th-century, when hunting motifs were very popular. It particularly suited the *pot à oille*, a dish for a spicy stew introduced into France during Louis XIV's reign. This one is by Robert-Joseph Auguste, a member of a great family of silversmiths and principal supplier to Louis XV at the end of his reign, and then to Louis XVI. It was he who made the crown for the latter's coronation.

pp. 176 and p. 177 *Pot à oille, one of a pair, and wine cooler, one of a set of four*
Stamp of Jacques-Nicolas Roettiers (master in 1765)
Silver
1770–71
Pot à oille: H. 27, diameter 30 cm
Tray: D. 49 cm
Cooler: H. 24, diameter 25 cm
Inv. CAM 253–55

This service, ordered by Catherine II of Russia in 1770 for her lover Gregory Orloff and named after him, is often considered to be one of the finest examples of Neoclassical silver. Its pieces show that the Neoclassical style then emerging drew its inspiration as much from the Grand Siècle as it did from Antiquity. The memory of the extraordinary silver service commissioned by Louis XIV was still vivid – although it had been melted down by the king after 1689, it was still known from drawings and several tapestries. The scrolled console feet and pilasters on the *pot à oille* are direct references to the dishes created by Claude Ballin in 1670. The wine coolers are influenced by the orange-tree vases delivered to the Grand Appartement at Versailles between 1666 and 1669. Roettiers' models proved popular and in 1775 he delivered two similar *pots à oille* to Mesdames, Louis XV's daughters. Silversmith to the king, with his father, Roettiers had previously made a large service for the monarch. He was also the principal supplier of silverware to the king's mistress, Madame Du Barry, for whom he made a very famous gold service. The Orloff service was bought by the empress when her lover died in 1783 and remained in the Imperial collection until the 1917 Revolution. Part of it was later sold by the Soviets in the 1930s.

p. 178 *Pieces from the Orloff service and the door into the Porcelain Room*
Pieces from the Orloff service are arranged on a console table. On the shelf between the legs is a jardinière in varnished metal imitating Japanese lacquer. The petit-point embroidery inset in the panelling belonged to Moïse's father, Count Nissim de Camondo. On the door to the Porcelain Room, made to be concealed in the panelling when shut, hangs a Savonnerie tapestry picture.

p. 179 *The Porcelain Room*
When he was alone, Moïse de Camondo sometimes had his meals served in the intimacy of the Porcelain Room, surrounded by his finest Sèvres, Meissen and Chantilly pieces. The window of this room, which has a lower ceiling due to the mezzanine floor above, is hung with an Aubusson tapestry pelmet imitating drapery with a braided border.

p. 180 *'The Brioche' and 'The Cream Service'*
Gobelins manufactory
Wool
1811
Carved and gilt wood frame
H. 58, W. 66 cm
Inv. CAM 265

Woven at the Gobelins manufactory in 1811 after two still lifes by Anne Vallayer-Coster, *Lunch* and *Dessert*, painted in 1766, these small tapestry pictures were kept in store for three years before they were offered to the Duchess d'Angoulême in 1814, at the time of the first Restoration period.

p. 181 *Pieces from one of the 'Buffon' services, known as the Le Fevre service*
Soft-paste Sèvres porcelain with a dotted green ground, 'Buffon birds' and antique heads Marks: two crossed L and the letter-dates *gg* (1784), *ii* (1786) and *M. Imple de Sèvres* in red (1804–9)
Inv. CAM 293

Moïse de Camondo reunited an exceptional ensemble of Sèvres porcelain decorated with birds. They belonged to several services, including the one delivered by the royal manufactory in December 1784 to the Amsterdam merchant Le Fevre (or Lefebure), decorated with 'Buffon birds' and antique medallions. It was added to by Mme Le Fevre after her husband's death and Moïse was able to buy it almost complete. Catering for the 18th-century interest in nature, from 1779 the Sèvres manufactory reproduced François-Nicolas Martinet's illustrations for Buffon's *L'Histoire naturelle des oiseaux*, published in ten volumes between 1771 and 1786. Numerous services with ornithological decorations bear testament to the theme's popularity, such as the one offered to William Eden, ambassador of the king of England, a large part of which is in the museum

(inv. CAM 292). The 'Buffon birds' were combined in the 1780s with a very refined dotted ground with a 'partridge-eye' motif called 'Taillandier ground' after the painter who invented it. The antique medallions, however, are peculiar to the Le Fevre service.

p. 182 *Fruit dish from the Le Fevre service* (detail)
Soft-paste Sèvres porcelain with dotted green ground, 'Buffon birds' and antique heads
H. 21.5, W. 21.5 cm
Marks: two crossed *L*s and the letter date *gg* (1784)
Inv. CAM 293

p. 183 *Bowl on legs*
Soft-paste Sèvres porcelain with dotted green ground and 'Buffon birds'
Marks: *M. Imple de Sèvres* in red (1804–9)
21.5 x 21.5 cm
Inv. CAM 258

p. 184 *Pieces from a 'Buffon birds' service on the serving table in the Dining Room*
– *Serving table:*
Stamped by Adam Weisweiler (master in 1778)
Oak veneered with mahogany, chased and gilt bronze, white marble
c. 1780–90
H. 100, W. 190, D. 55 cm
Inv. CAM 238
– *'Buffon birds' service:*
Soft-paste Sèvres porcelain
Marks: two crossed *L*s, the letter-dates *pp* (1792), *qq* (1793) and *M. Imple de Sèvres* in red (1804–9)
Inv. CAM 258

Mahogany-veneered console tables with fluted column legs were among Adam Weisweiler's specialities. This one is remarkable both for its large size and curved edges. The design for the gilt bronze frieze with interlacing, arrows, roses and sunflowers, commonly found on Weisweiler's furniture, was probably provided by Dominique Daguerre. The same design also appears in pieces by Saunier and Riesener, who also worked for the same *marchand-mercier*.

p. 185 *Bust of a Negress*
Signed by Pierre-Philippe Thomire, after Jean-Antoine Houdon
Patinated and gilt bronze
H. 80 cm
Inscription on the bust: *fondu Ciselé par thomire*, and on the base: *RENDUE A LA LIBERTE ET A L'EGALITE PAR LA CONVENTION NATIONALE LE 16 PLUVIOSE DEUXIEME DE LA REPUBLIQUE FRANÇAISE UNE ET INDIVISIBLE*
Inv. CAM 259

The Folie de Chartres, the future Parc Monceau, was laid out for the Duke of Chartres from 1769 by Carmontelle, then by the Scotsman Thomas Blaikie, who decorated it in the English style with groves and gazebos. These included a fountain with a sculpture group by Houdon depicting a black servant woman (in lead) pouring water over her mistress (in white marble), first shown at the 1783 Salon. The marble figure is now in the Metropolitan Museum of Art in New York; the lead one has disappeared. This bust, cast in bronze, partially recalls it.

The inscription on the base is an allusion to the abolition of slavery, decreed by the Convention on 4 February 1794. **See also p. 186.**

p. 186 *Looking towards the Gallery*
The bust of a Negress after Houdon is flanked by two Portor marble urns. The Beauvais tapestry, *Fishing with a Net*, one of the *Pastoral Amusements* series woven after François-Joseph Casanova, hangs in the shallow niche framing the dresser.

p. 187 *Upper Ground Floor Gallery: display cabinet*
Oak, mahogany veneer, chased and gilt bronze, glass
François Rémond (master in 1774) and Étienne Maclard
H. 214, W. 239, D. 28 cm
Inv. CAM 308

This cabinet, now used to display Chantilly porcelain plates, was delivered to the Count d'Artois in 1786, for his natural history collection in the Palais du Tèmple in Paris. The oculus above the door to the butlery allows light in from the service rooms. **(see p. 255).**

p. 188 *In the Gallery: 'Child with an Empty Nest'*
Bronze, brown-black patina
Cast by Pierre Philippe Thomire
c. 1825
H. 77 cm
Inscription on the base: *PIGALE FCIT 1768. BRONZE PAR THOMIRE*
Inv. CAM 325

Despite the inscriptions on their bases attributing them to Jean-Baptiste Pigalle, *Child with an Empty Nest* and its pendant *Child with a Bird* were cast after terracotta models by Charles-Antoine Bridan, now in the Musée des Beaux-Arts, Chartres, and inspired by antique sculptures in the Borghese collection.

The Small Study pp. 189–205

p. 189 *The Small Study: table chiffonnière en auge*
Stamped by Jean-Henri Riesener (master in 1768)
Oak, veneered with tulipwood, sycamore, amaranth, pear, holly, ebony, chased and gilt bronze
1788
H. 78, W. 77, D. 35 cm
Label inside the drawer: *StC. no 56*
Inv. CAM 347

Riesener, Queen Marie-Antoinette's favourite cabinet-maker, delivered this *table chiffonnière en auge* (literally 'trough-shaped') for her private study in the Château de Saint-Cloud in 1788. It has the same *mosaïque et poids* marquetry motif (diamonds surrounded by filets with dots at each corner) as the lacquer writing table delivered four years earlier by Weisweiler and eventually placed in the same room. The finest example of this type of decoration is undoubtedly the mother-of-pearl and silvered bronze marquetry on the roll-top desk and another *table chiffonnière*, delivered for the queen's private study at Fontainebleau in 1786. This table, however, is an example of Riesener's sober style in the years leading up to the Revolution.

pp. 190–93 *Sketches for the cartoons for 'The Hunts of Louis XV'* (details)
Jean-Baptiste Oudry
Oil on canvas
Inv. CAM 440

Rekindling an ancient tradition, Louis XV commissioned the Gobelins manufactory to weave a set of tapestries for his chambers in the Château de Compiègne, entrusting their cartoons to Jean-Baptiste Oudry in 1733. Their number was increased from three to nine in 1738, and Oudry did not finish the cartoons until 1746. The Château de Compiègne was one of the king's hunting lodges and the tapestries depict the successive phases of his favourite sport. The pictures in the museum are sketches for the full-size cartoons, now at the Château de Fontainebleau. Moïse de Camondo acquired eight, to which the ninth has recently been added through a donation to the Musée des Arts Décoratifs in lieu of tax.

p. 190 *'Louis XV setting out with a bloodhound from Puits Solitaire in Compiègne Forest'*
1737
H. 45, W. 35 cm

p. 191 *'Le Forthu after the Kill'*
1745
H. 44, W. 34 cm

pp. 192–93 *'Rendezvous at the Puits du Roi crossroads in Compiègne Forest'*
1733
H. 45, W. 82 cm

p. 194 top *Mechanical 'à la Bourgogne' table* (details)
Inv. CAM 345
See also p. 195.

p. 194 bottom *Table chiffonnière en auge* (detail)
Inv. CAM 347
See also p. 189.

p. 195 *Mechanical 'à la Bourgogne' table*
Stamped by Roger Vandercruse, known as Lacroix (master in 1755)
Oak and walnut veneered with bloodwood, amaranth, tulipwood and holly, chased and gilt bronze
c. 1760
H. 72, W. 65, D. 46 cm
Inv. CAM 345

The 18th-century quest for comfort led to the development of furniture with increasingly elaborate mechanisms. One of the most sophisticated is the 'à la Bourgogne' table, named after the Duke of Burgundy, Louis XV's eldest grandson, born infirm. A lever or a button activates an elaborate spring mechanism which raises the chest of drawers at the back of the table-top. Jean-François Œben, who had received extensive mechanical instruction, was the leading specialist, but it was his brother-in-law, Roger Vandercruse, known as Lacroix, who trained in his workshop, who made this one. The inscription in ink 'trois piece argente', followed by the name Poirier, on the underside of the lower drawer in the stepped back, indicates that he delivered this writing table to the *marchand-mercier* Simon-Philippe Poirier, for whom he worked regularly.

pp. 196–97 *The Small Study, looking towards the fireplace*
Tables of various kinds stand on the Beauvais carpet, notably a small writing table by Boudin (master in 1761), near the *table chiffonnière en auge* by Riesener. On either side of the fireplace are two display cabinets stamped by RVLC, containing Vincennes, Meissen and Oriental porcelain and small terracottas by Clodion and Marin. A portrait of Jacques Necker by Joseph-Siffred Duplessis (1725–1802), painted *c.* 1781, hangs on the overmantel mirror.

p. 198 *Clock on the mantelpiece*
Chased and gilt bronze, marble
c. 1770–80
H. 57, W. 34 cm
Inscription on the face: *Ch. Dutertre à Paris* (Charles Dutertre, master clockmaker in 1758)
Inv. CAM 365
See also pp. 196–97.

p. 199 *'The Prince of Beauvau'*
Terracotta medallion, sculpted and gilt wood frame
Jean-Baptiste Nini, signed and dated 1767
diameter 15.5 cm
Inv. CAM 427

Jean-Baptiste Nini, born in Urbino and the son of a faience manufacturer, perfected the production of these small terracotta portrait medallions made in moulds using a very fine clay to reproduce the tiniest detail. He made portraits both of Parisian society and the inhabitants of the Chaumont area, where he lived and worked. There are sixteen of his portrait medallions in the Small Study.
See also p. 189.

p. 200 *'San Giorgio Maggiore and the Dogana'*
Francesco Guardi
Oil on canvas
H. 68, W. 101 cm
Inv. CAM 437

p. 201 *'The Piazzetta and the Riva degli Schiavoni'*
Francesco Guardi
Oil on canvas
H. 68, W. 101 cm
Inv. CAM 437

pp. 202–3 *'The Piazzetta and the Riva degli Schiavoni'* (detail)

p. 204 *'A Meal During the Hunt'*
François Boucher
Oil on canvas
H. 53, W. 36 cm
Inv. CAM 441

p. 205 *'The Porte Saint-Denis'* (detail)
Hubert Robert
Oil on canvas
c. 1770
H. 45, W. 33 cm
Inv. CAM 442

The private apartments
See plan on p. 208.

p. 206 *The landing on the private staircase*
Mounted on grey granite columns, a pair of patinated and gilt bronze candelabra formerly in Count Nissim de Camondo's collection greet visitors in the first-floor gallery. In this gallery, Moïse de Camondo hung his collection of engravings after pictures by Jean-Baptiste Siméon Chardin (1699–1779), including his self-portrait and *Woman Peeling Vegetables*. This 33-piece collection includes famous works such as *Boy with a Top*, *The House of Cards* and *Saying Grace*.

The Library **pp. 210–13**

pp. 210–11 *General view*
The Library is located in the middle of the private apartments, above the Salon des Huet. A Beauvais tapestry, *The Stopover*, from the *Bohemians* series, is set into the panelling above a drop-front secrétaire by Leleu, facing the fireplace. Around the tea table attributed to Bernard Molitor are drawing room chairs in sculpted and polished walnut.

p. 212 *Clock in the form of an obelisk*
Chased, gilt and silvered bronze, yellow antique, blue Turquin, red Griotte and sea-green marble
c. 1780
H. 81, W. 23, D. 23 cm
Inscription on the face: *Crosnier à Paris* (Antoine Crosnier, master in Paris in 1763)
Inv. CAM 606

On an obelisk, a symbol of eternity, Iris, messenger of the gods, is travelling between the earthly world, symbolized by Neptune, god of the Sea, and the celestial world, symbolized by the sphere at the top. This clock may have had an accompanying barometer, on which Ceres and her lions replaced Neptune and his dolphins.

p. 213 *Drop-front secrétaire*
Stamped by Jean-François Leleu (master in 1764)
Oak veneered with amaranth, sycamore, ebony, barberry, burr maple, box, kingwood, tulipwood, holly, chased and gilt bronze, white marble
c. 1770–80
H. 106, W. 143, D. 44 cm
Inv. CAM 584

Despite its unusual shape – wider than it is high – this drop-front secrétaire is entirely representative of the work of Jean-François Leleu. Its monumental form is one of this cabinetmaker's hallmarks, as is the 'à la reine' trompe-l'oeil marquetry with flowerets in hexagons, reserved for his most luxurious pieces. On the marble top, Moïse de Camondo placed the patinated plaster version of Houdon's *Summer* (**see p. 153**).

p. 214 *Corridor leading to Moïse de Camondo's apartment*
The small gallery leading from the Library to Moïse de Camondo's apartment is soberly furnished with a semi-circular console table bearing a Chinese vase. On the panelling above hang two watercolours of the Château de Chantilly and the Palais de Justice in Paris, the latter by Jean-Baptiste-Antoine Hanet, called Cléry, 1788.

Moïse de Camondo's apartment
pp. 215–23

p. 215 *'Mlle Duthé'*
Henri-Pierre Danloux
Oil on canvas
H. 72, W. 58 cm
Inv. CAM 700

Catherine-Rosalie Gérard, better known by her stage name, Mlle Duthé, was one of the most famous Parisian actresses in the late 18th century, as her many portraits suggest. The composition of this portrait is particularly original. The young woman is shown about to hang a picture on the wall in what could be her own home. But the scene is in fact taking place in the painter's studio. The actress offered this portrait to her lover, the banker Jean-Frédéric Perrégaux.
See also p. 216.

p. 216 *The bedroom*
On the marble-topped commode stamped by Mathieu-Guillaume Cramer (master in 1771) are three Sèvres biscuit sculpture groups after Louis-Simon Boizot, *The Marriage Offering* in the middle and *The Newlyweds* and *Discreet Love*, and two gilt bronze candlesticks. Hanging on the mirrored overmantel are *Les Frères Godefroy et leur précepteur*, a red chalk drawing by Jean-Baptiste Massé, and *Les Amusements de l'enfance*, an oil painting on copper by Jean-Jacques Bachelier. Bachelier's picture, painted in 1761, is a preparatory sketch for a tapestry cartoon. The commode is flanked by two armchairs by Georges Jacob (master in 1765).

p. 217 *The bedroom, near the fireplace*
The ornately sculpted six-leaf screen, dating from the 1780s, is by Louis Falconet (master in 1743). The clock on the mantelpiece is flanked by a pair of white marble, silvered bronze and paste candlesticks and two white marble figures of children. The two drawings above are *Flowers in a Vase* by Jacques-André Portail and *The Singing Lesson* by Nicolas Lavreince.

p. 218 *'A la Douleur' clock*
Chased and gilt bronze, white and blue Turquin marble
c. 1780
Model by François Vion (master founder in 1764)
H. 36, W. 26, D. 14 cm
Inv. CAM 671
See also p. 217.

p. 219 *'Bad News'*
Jean-Baptiste-Marie Pierre
Oil on canvas
H. 23.5, W. 18.5 cm
Inv. CAM 706

In the 18th century, man rediscovered himself and his sensibility and strove to represent the torments of the soul. Love, with its joys and sorrows, naturally had a special place in this. The theme of the 'à la Douleur' clock, the lost and found bird, whose symbolism can be interpreted in several ways, was extremely popular in the late 18th century. Marie-Antoinette herself had such a clock. In *Bad News*, the despair overwhelming the young woman reading the letter is echoed by her cumbersome dress.

p. 220 *Savonnerie carpet* (detail)
Savonnerie manufactory
Wool
1760
L. 478, W. 337 cm
Inv. CAM 721

A detail of the palm leaf decoration on one of the finest carpets in Moïse de Camondo's collection, which he put in his bedroom. It was woven at the Savonnerie manufactory after a model dating from 1745 by Pierre-Josse Perrot, its principal designer, and was delivered in 1760 to Mesdames, Louis XV's daughters, for the chapel at Versailles.

p. 221 *Candelabrum* (detail)
Chased, patinated and gilt bronze, Meissen hard-paste porcelain
c. 1740–50
H. 50, W. 44, D. 42 cm
Inv. CAM 666

This Meissen hard-paste porcelain figure of Juno and its pendant were incorporated into this gilt bronze candelabrum in Paris, a piece that exemplifies the taste of the *marchands-merciers* in the mid-18th century and is exceptional both in size and its bold design.
See also p. 216.

p. 222 *Alcove bed* (details)
Sculpted and painted beech
c. 1765–75
Red damask counterpane and upholstery with white embroidery
H. 163, L. 217, W. 153 cm
Inv. CAM 644

The extraordinary quality and ornateness of the sculpted wheatear and wild flower decoration of Moïse de Camondo's 'à la turque' bed are exceptional.

p. 223 *The alcove and, above the bed, 'Sleep'*
Attributed to Hugues Taraval
Oil on canvas
H. 70, W. 90 cm
Inv. CAM 704

Moïse de Camondo hung this allegory of sleep, now attributed to Hugues Taraval and one of the few female nudes in his collection, above his bed.

p. 224 *The Gallery, looking towards Moïse and Nissim de Camondo's apartments*
The gallery's south wing leads to Moïse's and Nissim's apartments. Nissim's former study is entered via the door on the left. The glazed door opens on to the first antechamber of Moïse's apartment.

Nissim de Camondo's apartment pp. 225–29

p. 225 *The mantelpiece in the bedroom:*
– *Clock*
White marble, chased and gilt bronze
c. 1790
H. 48, W. 34, D. 12 cm
Inscription: *Autray A PARIS* (Claude Autray, master clockmaker in 1784)
Inv. CAM 777
– *Pair of candelabra*
Patinated and gilt bronze
c. 1800
H. 52 cm
Mark: *LP/N 21044* and label written in ink: *Provient du/palais Royal/Cabinet Travail/du prince Royal/1er Etage Villier*
Inv. CAM 775

pp. 226–27 *Nissim de Camondo's bedroom*
Moïse de Camondo converted his son Nissim's study into a memorial room. Above the steel and gilt bronze bed is Carolus-Duran's portrait of Nissim's grandfather, Count Nissim de Camondo. Hunting and equestrian scenes recalling Nissim's leisure pursuits hang on the Directoire-style panelling. The figure of *Fidelity* is a plaster copy of the marble by Caffiéri in the Large Drawing Room.

p. 228 top *'Hunting Scene'* (detail)
William Shayer the Elder
Oil on card
H. 12, W. 11 cm
Inv. CAM 788

p. 228 bottom *'The Kill'* (detail)
Jean-François Demay, signed and dated 1837
Oil on canvas
H. 26, W. 34 cm
Inv. CAM 786

'A fine huntsman, and an elegant and bold horseman', Nissim de Camondo shared his family's love of hunting, and so his apartment contained numerous hunting and equestrian scenes.

p. 229 *View of Nissim de Camondo's bedroom between the two windows*
Above the desk by Feurstein hang two pictures by the most famous painter of hunting scenes of his time, Alfred de Dreux. On the desk is an oval oak inkwell stand veneered with ebony and decorated with gilt bronze vitruvian scrolls, and an imitation-wallet writing case, veneered with burred Burmese rosewood with a faceted steel frame attributed to Maire, a maker of game boards and inlaid pieces active during the Empire and the Restauration periods. The swivelling chair is upholstered in green morocco leather.

p. 230 *The Gallery, looking towards the staircase*
There are fourteen armchairs and a settee with caned backs and seats and cushions, by the Lyon chairmaker Pierre Nogaret (master in 1745), in the Gallery. The axis of each of the gallery's wings is marked by a cabinet. The rugs on the parquet floor were brought from Turkey.

The Blue Drawing Room pp. 231–35

p. 231 *'The Gentlemen of the Duke of Orléans in the livery of the Château de Saint-Cloud'*
Félix Philippoteaux
After a gouache by Louis Carrogis, known as Carmontelle
c. 1839
Oil on canvas
H. 59, W. 91 cm
Inv. CAM 568

pp. 232–33 *The Blue Drawing Room*
The Blue Drawing Room was created after Béatrice de Camondo's departure, by converting her bedroom and boudoir into a single room. Instead of trying to recreate an 18th-century atmosphere, Moïse de Camondo furnished it with comfortable chairs, including a bergère, a marquise, a duchesse brisée and a couch, arranged around the desk attributed to Saunier. The desk chair has kingwood veneering, rare on a chair. On the walls are views of Paris in the 18th century, a pastel portrait of an artist and the family reunion by Gautier-Dagoty.

p. 234 *Portrait presumed to be of the Duke and Duchess of Chartres with the Penthièvre and Conti Families* (detail)
Jean-Baptiste-André Gautier-Dagoty, signed
Oil on canvas
c. 1775–76
H. 130, W. 194 cm
Inv. CAM 567

The identity of the central couple seems finally to have been established. It appears to be a portrait of the Duke and Duchess of Chartres and their families **(see p. 114)** and, if so, represents a veritable dynastic manifesto to the glory of Louis XVI's plotting cousin.
See also pp. 232–33

p. 235 top *'The Samaritaine and the Pont-Neuf'*
Nicolas-Jean-Baptiste Raguenet, signed and dated 1755
Oil on canvas
H. 46, W. 85 cm
Inv. CAM 570

p. 235 bottom *'The Seine by the Louvre'* (detail)
Joseph Canella, signed and dated 1830
Oil on canvas
H. 35, W. 71 cm
Inv. CAM 564

From the First Floor Gallery down to the Ground Floor

p. 236 *In the first floor gallery*
A Qianlong Period (1736–95) *hu* vase with a lavender-blue ground and stag's head handles stands on the marble top of a sculpted and gilt wood console table. Above are two engravings after Chardin, *The House of Cards* and *The Moment of Meditation*. Both are part of Moïse de Camondo's collection of thirty-three engravings hanging in the first floor gallery, after the painter's masterpieces.

p. 237 *The first floor landing*
The open door leads to Nissim de Camondo's apartment. A short passageway leads to the bedroom, the dressing room and the bathroom **(see pp. 263–65)**. His valet used this passageway on his way to bring him clothes from his wardrobe on the floor above.

p. 238 *The spiral staircase*
At the bottom of the spiral staircase leading up to the private apartments is a terracotta statue, formerly in the Marquis de Biron collection, of three children leaning against a tree trunk and holding a garland of flowers. This sculpture group is a pastiche in the 18th-century rococo style.

pp. 239, 240 *Bottle vase, one of a pair*
Porcelain with a blue underglaze decoration of waves, dragons and clouds on a white ground
China, Qianlong Period (1736–95)
Chased and gilt bronze mount
H. 80 cm
Inv. CAM 14

Moïse de Camondo kept little from his family's collections. This vase and its pendant, like most of the vases in the mansion's galleries, are an exception. They were formerly in the collection of his uncle, Count Abraham Behor de Camondo, and were bought by his nephew at auction after his death.

p. 241 *Lidded vase, one of a pair*
White marble
c. 1760–70
H. 62 cm
Inv. CAM 17

p. 242 *Gallery on the lower ground floor*
Beyond the open door at the end, a small hallway leads up to a door to the garden. In the niches, Moïse de Camondo placed a set of four wooden tripods painted grey with early 17th-century Chinese *gu* stoneware vases with a green glaze.

p. 243 *Fountain*
Red royal marble, lead
c. 1750–60
H. 180, W. 190, D. 69 cm
Inv. CAM 30

Since its purchase in 1927, this fountain has welcomed visitors entering the mansion from the covered motor car entrance. It was formerly in the dining room of the Château de Saint-Prix in Montmorency Forest, property of Baron Double.

Notes

From Istanbul to Paris pp. 22–55

1 Although they were foreign nationals – until 1865 the family was under Austrian protection, then Italian – the Camondos had been granted an exclusive right to own buildings and land on Ottoman territory. Cf. Nora Şeni, 'The Imprint of the Camondos in 19th Century Istanbul', *International Journal of Middle East Studies*, 26, 1994.

2 The Edicts of the Sublime Porte were written in a rigid form of rhetoric. Laws and regulations derived their legitimacy from the preservation of the established order. In 1839 the raft of new measures voted in violently threatened the hegemony of this rule. This was the beginning of a lengthy confrontation between modern-minded reformers, influenced by the Europe of the Enlightenment, and conservatives.

3 In 1839, the government issued paper money for the first time. As these bills were made out by hand they were easily forged and a few months later, to prevent jeopardizing the Empire's commerce, a considerable number of fake banknotes had to be removed from circulation.

4 See Steven Rosenthal, 'Foreigners and Municipal Reforms in Istanbul', *International Journal of Middle East Studies*, II, 1980.

5 In Paris and London, the seal of the Haute Banque – which sought to take the place of the aristocracy – became increasingly prominent as the volume of business grew.

6 Abraham Behor de Camondo's will, 1889 (AMNC).

7 Cf. *Les Statuts de la Société des tramways de Constantinople,* 1870, p. 3, quoted by Nora Şeni and Sophie Le Tarnec, *Les Camondo ou l'éclipse d'une* fortune (Arles, Actes Sud, 1997) p. 285, note 9. Abraham Behor believed in the future of this form of transport. In a letter to Nissim dated 4 June 1874, he mentions setting up 'a repair workshop in Constantinople which could even become a tram construction workshop' (AMNC).

8 Abraham Behor recruited a head for his school in France himself and took a close interest in the progress of educational methods. He issued teaching guidelines, supervised the award of annual scholarships, and praised good pupils personally.

9 Abraham Behor was shocked by the plight of his fellow Jews. Throughout the 18th century, the Jews of the Ottoman Empire had grown gradually poorer. Cf. Şeni and Le Tarnec, *op. cit.*, pp. 14–16.

10 Over the years to come, the Universal Israelite Alliance set up schools throughout the Ottoman Empire, from Salonica to Alexandria. Teaching in French brought lasting changes to the linguistic, professional and mental attitudes of the Jewish communities in the Near East.

11 In a stirring speech, Nissim, Moïse's father, presented the Alliance to the Istanbul community: 'Ultimately, the Alliance's sole aim is to protect Israelites who are suffering simply because they are descendants of Abraham, to uproot the preconceived ideas which still exist among us … and to lead our brothers through education and work to become the equals of the peoples into whose midst they have been thrown by the terrible and mysterious hand of fate. It is in Paris, a centre of civilization, that several generous men have come together to conceive the grand design of a Universal Israelite Alliance' (UIA Archives, Turkey, I, B, 3).

12 The Jewish and Christian secular elites in the Ottoman empire increased their power in their respective communities to the detriment of religious institutions; from the mid-19th century they consolidated their positions by practising a particular type of charity (considered an expression of 'the love of mankind', therefore *a priori* irrespective of race or religion). Yet their generosity was expressed towards their coreligionists. It was not charity as such, that is, it was dispensed not in the name of the love of God but that of Reason and Progress. The sort of education it promoted enabled minority groups in the Empire to integrate on an equal basis. The pursuit of equal rights became a plausible project. They promoted education, health and hygiene and initiated new forms of social control. But whereas Jewish philanthropists such as Abraham Behor promoted the teaching of Turkish and French, the Greeks founded Hellenic linguistic and literary societies. They built museums in which they set out a national identity and memory, an official history, and the teaching of the Greek language was promoted in the schools they founded. Cf. Nora Şeni, *Les Inventeurs de la philanthropie juive* (Paris, La Martinière, 2005).

13 Letter from Nissim de Camondo to Abraham Behor, 17 February 1869 (AMNC). Their letters were kept in correspondence books: for all their administrative and business correspondence, the Camondos complied with French commercial law, whereby anyone in business had to keep copies of letters sent. To obtain copies, these letters, handwritten in copy ink, were placed under the register's very thin, numbered pages, dampened beforehand, and pressure was applied. Several machines for copying letters were invented. *Larousse commercial illustré*, 1930.

14 'I ordered the three-quarter coupé for grand papa. Please sell everything before you leave, carriages and horses,' Abraham Behor wrote to Nissim, who was still in Istanbul, on 11 August 1869. As for his coachman, he added that he was 'knowledgeable and capable, one can trust him. He is an Englishman recommended to me here …. He was with the Murats for a long time.' See Şeni and Le Tarnec, *op. cit.*, p. 90.

15 Financing his policies and the needs of an infant state put Victor Emmanuel II in great need of philanthropy. He ennobled several Levantine Jewish families. We know that Abraham Salomon, amongst other generous gifts, gave considerable sums to the orphanage in Turin and to the Italian school and hospital in Constantinople. See Şeni and Le Tarnec, *op. cit.*, p. 57.

16 Arthur Meyer, *Ce que mes yeux ont vu* (Paris, Plon Nourrit, 1911), p. 305.

17 Émile Zola, *La Curée* (1871). Several other mansions built around the Parc Monceau at that time, of which Zola made notes and sketches, also served as the models for fictive residences. See Zola's preparatory notes for *La Curée*, Bibliothèque Nationale de France, Paris, Département des Manuscrits, N.a.fr., 10282, F° 270.

18 Panels, probably from this boudoir, are now in the Musée des Arts Décoratifs.

19 At the auction of the Pereire collections on 6 and 7 March 1872, Abraham Behor bought Lancret's *Mademoiselle Salé*, Van Loo's *Portrait of a Man*, Teniers' *Game of Backgammon* and Bida's *Pilgrims Returning from Mecca*. These pictures were sold at auction at Galerie Georges Petit after his death, on February 1893 (nos. 10, 11, 23 and 88). He also attended the Baron Double auction, where he acquired a chandelier and wall lamps (nos. 286 and 300), which were resold on 1, 2 and 3 February 1893 (nos. 260 and 261). On 7 June 1873, Nissim bought Courbet's *Hunters in a Forest* and Dupré's *Farm Interior in the Berry* at the auction of the Faure collection. These pictures were resold at the Hôtel Drouot, Paris, on 18 November 1910 (nos. 18 and 21).

20 Edmond and Jules de Goncourt, *Journal, mémoires de la vie littéraire 1851–1896* (1887–96) (Paris, Robert Laffont, 2004) vol. II, p. 651.

21 *L'Art et la Mode*, 1881, p. 26.

22 Their numerous decorations are listed in the chronology.

23 *L'Art et la Mode*, 1884, p. 344.

24 Édouard Drumont, *La France juive, essai d'histoire contemporaine* (Paris, Marpon & Flammarion, 1886) vol. II, p. 154. The book was an extraordinary success. It was reprinted almost two hundred times and established the lexicon for decades of virulent anti-Semitism. The Camondos appear throughout.

25 Oil on canvas, signed and dated 1882 (inv. CAM 785).

26 Léon Alfassa married Clarisse de Camondo in 1867. As a senior executive of Isaac Camondo & Co., he caused a bankruptcy amounting to several million francs in April 1885. See Şeni and Le Tarnec, *op. cit.*, pp. 119–23.

27 Concerning his collections, see Şeni and Le Tarnec, *op. cit.*, pp. 185–90.

28 In 1893, Isaac bought eight pictures by Degas, two pictures by Monet (*The Seine at Port-Villez* and *Sailing Boats, Regatta at Argenteuil*) and Manet's *Lola de Valence*.

29 Gabriel Astruc, *Le Pavillon des fantômes* (1927) (Paris, Belfond, 1987), p. 139.

30 *Ibid.*, p. 139.

31 *Le Théâtre*, June 1906. Regarding Isaac the composer, see Şeni and Le Tarnec, *op. cit.*, pp. 165–74.

32 Regarding the aid Astruc gave Isaac, see *ibid.*, pp. 178–85.

33 Guillaume Apollinaire, *Chroniques d'art. 1902–1918* (Paris, Gallimard, 2002) p. 488.

34 *Le Gaulois*, 16 October 1891.

35 The Russian-born banker Charles Ephrussi was also a collector and owner of *La Gazette des Beaux-Arts*. His social life partly inspired Proust's character Charles Swann. He met Renoir in 1875 at Henri Cernuschi's mansion.

36 Oil on canvas, signed and dated 1880, Fondation Bührle, Zurich.

37 Isaac Camondo & Co. ceased to exist on 31 December 1917, following the deed of dissolution granted by the notary Charpentier on 7 November 1917, and the annulment of its licence on 1 January 1918 (see Moïse de Camondo's correspondence, 1 August 1921, AMNC). The bank's archives were partially deposited in the Archives nationales by Léon Reinach in 1939 (fonds 1AQ), and the remainder is now in the Musée Nissim de Camondo.

38 A year after their divorce, Irène married Count Sampiéri and renounced her Jewish faith to become a Catholic. Moïse seized upon this pretext to distance his children from their mother. Count Sampiéri ran the stables of Count Boni de Castellane. See Boni de Castellane, *Comment j'ai découvert l'Amérique* (1924), in *Mémoires de Boni de Castellane* (Paris, Perrin, 1986) p. 156 and Şeni and Le Tarnec, *op. cit.*, pp. 205–7.

39 Seven photo albums were donated to the museum by Mme Gaisenband, Béatrice de Camondo's niece, in 1989 (inv. CAM 1989.1.1–7).

40 Moïse de Camondo's correspondence, 10 November 1924 (AMNC).

41 *Ibid.*, 19 February 1930.

42 A precise list of these vehicles from 1895 to 1935 (make, type and number plate) was established from correspondence, insurance and administrative documents (AMNC).

43 Jacques Kelp, *Cinquante ans par Monts et Vallons* (Paris, Georges Lang, 1935) p. 14.

44 Nissim de Camondo's war correspondence comprises 286 letters written between 1914 and 1917 and their typewritten transcriptions (AMNC).

45 Nissim de Camondo's correspondence, 2 December 1915 (AMNC).

46 *Ibid.*, 25 January 1916 (AMNC).

47 Joseph Kessel, *Les Temps sauvages*, 1975 (Paris, Gallimard, 2001). Joseph Kessel was in Squadron 39.

48 Nissim de Camondo's correspondence, 16 April 1916. Numerous photographs taken by Nissim are in the museum's archives (AMNC).

49 *Ibid.*, 19 September 1917 (AMNC).

50 *Ibid.*, 4 April 1919 (AMNC).

51 Following a declaration by Maurice Barrès concerning the need to preserve artworks, whether state or privately owned, a commission was created in June 1918 to facilitate their evacuation. Moïse de Camondo's collections were sent to Tours for safekeeping. See Şeni and Le Tarnec, *op. cit.*, p. 251–52. To protect the mansion, the windows were filled in with sandbags (see p. 314).

52 Letter dated 27 November 1927 (AMNC).

53 *Ibid.*, 4 April 1919 (AMNC).

54 Cf. Régis Vian des Rives (ed.), *La Villa Kérylos* (Paris, Les Éditions de l'Amateur, 1997).

55 Moïse de Camondo's correspondence, 4 April (AMNC).

56 Concerning Léon Reinach, see Filippo Tuena's fictionalized biography, *Le Variazioni Reinach* (Milan, Rizzoli, 2005).

57 Account by Mme Appel, a survivor of Drancy, where she was a prisoner with the Camondos and became friends with Fanny. Account recorded by Sophie Le Tarnec in 1998.

A Mansion in the 18th-Century Style pp. 57–79

1 For more about mansions in the west of Paris, see Yvan Christ, Jean-François Barrielle, Thérèse Castieau, Antoinette Le Normand-Romain, *Champs-Élysées, Faubourg Saint-Honoré, Plaine Monceau* (Paris, Veyrier, 1982), and Gérard Rousset-Charny, *Les Palais parisiens de la Belle Époque* (Paris, Délégation à l'Action artistique de la Ville de Paris, 1990). The shift to the west took place from the Faubourg Saint-Honoré to Étoile or Monceau, then in the late 19th century moved down towards Iéna and Trocadéro, and the Champ-de-Mars on the other side of the Seine.

2 It was now the home of senator Gaston Menier, son of the well known chocolate manufacturer Émile Menier. Émile, whose head office was in a mansion in rue de Châteaudun (1882–83, by Eugène Ricard), lived in the prestigious residence at 5 avenue Van-Dyck, designed by Henri Parent in 1870. His son Henri had a more modest mansion built at 8 rue Alfred-de-Vigny (1880, again by Henri Parent), and in 1878 his brother Gaston bought the Lecomte mansion at 4 avenue de Ruysdaël (1875, by Henri Pellechet, the Pereire brothers' regular architect), before acquiring Abraham Behor de Camondo's mansion at 61 rue de Monceau in 1893.

3 Nora Şeni and Sophie Le Tarnec, *Les Camondo ou l'éclipse d'une fortune* (Arles, Actes Sud, 1997). Adopted by the most powerful industrialists and bankers of the time, the Parc Monceau district epitomized the triumph of the power of money under the Third Republic. In the turbulent context of the two last decades of the century (from the so-called Decorations Scandal to the Dreyfus Affair), bankers around the Parc Monceau all suffered the same 'opportunist's' fate: they were gradually distanced from power by the radical left and subjected to public condemnation fuelled by the upsurge of increasingly anti-Semitic and xenophobic populism.

4 Inaugurated in 1896. Henri Cernuschi was a leading figure of Italian patriotism but also the founder of the Banque de Paris et des Pays-Bas. He was close to the Pereire family, and it was their architect, William Bouwens van der Boijen, Léon Vaudoyer's adoptive son, who designed his mansion. In 1865, Bouwens, Crédit Lyonnais' architect, had built Eugène Pereire's mansion at 47 rue de Monceau (bought in 1868 by Adolphe de Rothschild after the liquidation of Crédit Mobilier and now demolished). He designed a dozen prestigious mansions in Paris. Most of those he built for the great Jewish bankers were located around the Parc Monceau and built in the first decade of the Third Republic.

5 It was opened to the public in 1913, after the death of its donor, Nélie Jacquemart-André. Her husband, Édouard André, a member of one of the major protestant banking families in the south of France, moved in Bonapartist circles, and it was an architect specializing in châteaux, Henri Parent (Joseph-Antoine Froelicher's son-in-law), who was commissioned to design his mansion in boulevard Haussmann in 1868. He was the first to adopt the Louis XVI style which Empress Eugénie had brought back into fashion and which became the international trademark of French style for almost a century.

6 Built between 1878 and 1888, the Palais Galliera (whose design and building the Duchess de Galliera had entrusted to Léon Ginain, Charles Garnier's great rival) is one of the finest examples of this skilful mannerism. It was inspired by the second French Renaissance but infused with great rationalism, which offset the rhetorical excesses of Garnier's Paris Opéra. In 1886, political circumstances, linked to the duchess's support for the re-establishment of the Orléanist monarchy, put paid to her project of installing her collections in Paris. But in particular, the creation of the Musée Guimet in place d'Iéna, designed by the Lyon-based architect Jules Chatron in 1885, overlapped with the site's new cultural orientation, shared by the Palais du Trocadéro and its extraordinary museum of comparative sculpture (conceived by Viollet-le-Duc and opened in 1882).

7 From the beginning the park was located just inside the Farmers General Enclosure, whose boundary was marked by the Chartres rotunda on boulevard de Courcelles. Boulevard Malesherbes' crow's foot trajectory from place de la Madeleine bends at place Saint-Augustin to run alongside the park, then traverses the Plaine Monceau obliquely. The decision to turn the entire area into a residential district contrasted starkly with the first town planning projects, which included a major railway station.

8 Jean Autin, *Les Frères Pereire, le bonheur d'entreprendre* (Paris, Perrin, 1984).

9 The Parc Monceau took over from the Champs-Élysées, where almost all of the mansions built in the mid-19th century have disappeared. The most luxurious was the exuberantly rococo residence of Countess Lehon (wife of the Belgian ambassador), built in 1846 by Louis Moreau on the Rond-Point des Champs-Élysées. Around the Parc Monceau, Abraham Behor de Camondo's mansion (61 rue de Monceau) was built in 1870–74 by Denis-Louis Destors; Émile-Justin Menier's residence (5 avenue Van-Dyck) by Henri Parent in 1872–74, Henri Cernuschi's (7 avenue Vélasquez) in 1874 by William Bouwens van der Boijen, the same year as Auguste Dreyfus's (3 avenue Ruysdaël, demolished). They were followed by the mansions of Émile Pereire (10 rue Alfred-de-Vigny, 1879–81, by William Bouwens van der Boijen) and Joseph Reinach (6 avenue Van-Dyck, 1887, by Alfred-Nicolas Normand).

10 The same is true of its exact contemporary, the Paris Opéra.

11 Act of sale signed 5 and 6 March 1863 before the notaries Adeline and Fould (Archives nationales, Minutier central, CIII, 851). The house built by Adolphe Violet is registered as having been finished in October 1864 (Archives de Paris, D¹P⁴740, 1862). See Michel Borjon (ed.), *Musée Nissim de Camondo. Recherches historiques et archéologiques* (Paris, Grahal, 2002), a study carried out for the Service national des travaux.

12 Alfred Armand and Jules Pellechet were the Pereires' usual architects and, as shown by the list compiled by Tiphaine Zirmi in 'Alfred Armand (1805–1888): un architecte collectionneur' (thesis, École Nationale des Chartes, 2003), their characteristic response to the demands of urban layout (in the tradition of Ignace Hittorff and Charles Rohault de Fleury) led them to design more ordinary-looking edifices. Built in alignment and rendered commonplace by the standardized design of their façades, they sit comfortably with the type of bourgeois buildings built in the neighbouring streets by Auguste Tronquois and Joseph Lesoufaché. Although luxurious, they are in fact more akin to the 'petits hôtels' which sprang up during the Third Republic than the palatial detached villas set deep in the greenery of their own grounds, whose prototypes were the Hôtel Pereire, and, on a less grand scale, the Hôtel Violet.

13 The family's origins were modest. His father was unrelated to the illustrious Parisian architect and property developer of the same name (Jean-Léonard Violet, who developed the Plaine de Grenelle, during the 1820s). I would like to thank Élisabeth Pillet for the additional research she carried out at the Archives Nationales, based on the study by Michel Borjon.

14 Laurent Poupard, *Marbres et marbreries. Jura*, Inventaire général des monuments et des richesses artistiques de la France, 'Images du patrimoine' collection (Paris, Erti, 1997). The crisis in 1884 caused the quarry at Damparis to be declared bankrupt, despite its prestigious commissions (the Fontaine Saint-Michel, the monolithic columns of the Église de la Trinité and the balustrades of the Palais Garnier in Paris).

15 Pereire still owned the neighbouring vacant plots. Following a complementary sale dated 23 June and 29 July 1863, arranged by the notaries Adeline and Fould (Archives nationales, Minutier central, CIII, 865), there was an exchange of land on 12 December 1866 (CIII, 988).

16 A plan now in the Musée Nissim de Camondo (inv. CAM 1996.1.1.) shows the initial layout, with storerooms opening onto the semicircular courtyard and stables on the right-hand side connecting with the service entrance in the mews. The covered entrance was redesigned by Sergent during the rebuilding of the semicircular courtyard façade of the outbuildings. The high-vaulted gateway itself (in a style fairly faithful to that of the reign of Louis XV and in complete contradiction to the Gabrielian design of the new mansion) is part of the original building – as suggested by the regularity of the dressing.

17 Plain entablatures, profiled cornices and a large broken roof with undecorated stone dormer windows evoke the 17th-century tradition.

18 It is reminiscent of the Hôtel Pontalba, built in 1839 by Louis Visconti in rue du Faubourg Saint-Honoré.

19 The most prestigious formula in the 19th century was the hôtel-château, set well back from the street with a decorative gateway between two entrance pavilions. A less ambitious version did away with the main building's wings, pavilions and porch, reducing it to a large detached pavilion in a garden. Much rarer was the semi-detached building set between courtyard and garden that was popular in the 18th century. The terraced main building reappeared only in 'petits hôtels' (small mansions), a formula closer to the traditional middle-class residence on the street itself or set slightly back behind a shallow garden, and which usually entailed doing away with those aristocratic emblems, the outbuildings and stables. But they were no longer needed since the owner now travelled by rental cars or public transport.

20 The deed of sale signed on 27 June 1870 (Archives nationales, Minutier central, XCIX, 1080) describes a residence comprising 'a ground floor consisting of a hall, a main staircase, a service staircase, large and small drawing rooms, a dining room and staff quarters; a first floor consisting of a drawing room, a boudoir, two bedrooms with toilets, two bathrooms and showers; a second floor consisting of a small drawing room, a library, five bedrooms with a toilet and a linen room ; and a third floor in the attic, consisting of six servant's rooms and a water cistern'. The estimate for the demolition in 1911 indicates the existence of a water cistern on the attic floor.

21 'Compact' here is a relative term. The mansion itself had 1,700 square metres of living space: 250 square metres on each of the two floors in the outhouses, and 300 square metres on each of the four floors of the main house (ground floor, two floors upstairs and an attic floor). The whole space was ten times larger than a typical middle-class apartment.

22 Bill of sale dated 26 August 1872 (Archives nationales, Minutier central, XCIX, 1091).

23 It foreshadows the pavilion Pierre Patout built in the middle of the Exposition Internationale des Arts Décoratifs in Paris in 1925, except that it is to the art of their own time and not that of the 18th century that the modernist interwar generation directed their attention. It is also revealingly different to Jean-Louis Pascal's imposing design for a 'mansion for a rich banker', with which he won the Prix de Rome in 1866.

24 Edmond and Jules de Goncourt's *L'Art du XVIIIᵉ siècle*, was published by Rapilly in 1873 and 1874 in two volumes (its publication in instalments had begun in 1859). At the same time, Empress Eugénie's passion for the Marie-Antoinette style had prompted an important publication by the engraver Rudolf Pfnor, *Architecture, décoration et ameublement, époque Louis XVI, dessinés, gravés d'après les motifs choisis dans les palais impériaux...*(Paris, Morel, 1867). It followed a collective work initiated by Hippolyte Destailleur on French classical art (H. Destailleur, R. Pfnor, Carresse, Riester, *Recueil d'estampes relatives à l'ornementation des appartements aux XVIᵉ, XVIIᵉ et XVIIIᵉ siècles*, Paris, Rapilly, 1863).

25 Interior decoration interested him less, probably because none of the great 18th-century interiors had been out of the market for a long time. An active protection policy, supported particularly by the Commission du vieux Paris (founded in 1897), now imposed their protection in their original setting. This led to the revision of the law on historic monuments in 1913, reflecting the public interest in cultural heritage (even privately owned) and favouring far more extensive protection of buildings, including their interior decoration. The chronology is significant: Alphonse de Rothschild was the first, in 1863–68, to have Léon Ohnet, with the interior decorator Émile Petit, install Ledoux's decorations from the Château de Louveciennes in the extension to the Hôtel Saint-Florentin in rue de Mondovi. In 1866, Hippolyte Destailleur utilized those from the Arsenal for the Countess de Behague. In 1876, Henri Parent acquired the panelling from Bercy for the Doudeauville; in 1881, Destailleur the panelling from Mayenne for the Cahen d'Anvers; in 1887, Félix Langlais, the panelling from Samuel Bernard for Edmond de Rothschild. The series ends in 1892 with Ernest Sanson's reuse of the panelling from the Hôtel Dodun for Baron de Breteuil. Moïse de Camondo could only manage to acquire panelling from the apartment of Count de Menou (built in rue Royale in 1782–85 by the architect Pierre-Louis Le Tellier), at auction in 1910–11, one of the last of its kind. His other panelling is less prestigious and more provincial in origin. But he may also have wished to place his exceptionally fine furniture in a setting that would not compete with it. Although it meant upsetting their original order, Sergent adapted the panelling to his architectural composition.

26 In 1908, Isaac de Camondo donated his collections to the Louvre, where, after his death in 1911, they were transferred from 1914 onwards.

27 In 1917 Ernest Cognacq and his wife Marie-Louise Jay showed the works they had acquired in the 'Samaritaine de luxe' store in boulevard des Capucines, before donating them to the City of Paris in 1928.

28 In 1921, Edward and Julia Tuck, who lived on the Champs-Élysées, then later near the Château de Malmaison at Rueil, donated their collection of Louis XV objects and furniture to the Musée du Petit Palais, where it was on display from 1930 before Mrs Tuck died.

29 Among the publications demonstrating this are *Le Baron Sinaï* (1897) and *Israel* (1898) by Gyp (Sibylle-Gabrielle de Mirabeau, Countess de Martel de Janville).

30 Moïse de Camondo's will, drawn up in 1924, is absolutely explicit on this point: 'this decorative art which has been one of France's glories, during the period I have loved above all others'.

31 Great though social prejudices were at the beginning of the 20th century, they were no longer based on the historical privileges of the aristocracy. One could no longer be surprised, like Countess de Damas (*Lettres de la comtesse Charles de Damas à Adélaïde de la Briche. 1791-1792*, Paris, Paris-Musées, 2006, p. 15), at the disappearance of all hierarchy within the aristocracy in exile: 'As you should know that the principles of equality are just as widespread on the banks of the Rhine as the Seine; those ennobled fifty years ago want to march side by side with M. de Rieux; officers want to name their chiefs; one speaks only of being free, equal, of abolishing every distinction and privilege between nobles.'

32 Commissioned by James de Rothschild. See Pauline Prévost-Marcilhacy, *Les Rothschild, bâtisseurs et mécènes* (Paris, Flammarion, 1995).

33 Between 1870 and 1875, Charles Questel built an exact replica of the famous gilt gallery in the Hôtel de Toulouse (1870–75) for the Banque de France. Honoré Daumet enlarged the Château de Chantilly (1875–82) for the Duke of Aumale. Félix Langlais rebuilt the Hôtel de Pontalba (1878–79) for Edmond de Rothschild. Alfred Aldrophe designed the Hôtel Gustave de Rothschild in avenue de Marigny (1873–83), and the Hôtel Thiers in place Saint-Georges (1873), in a conventional Louis XVI style. Jules Reboul, Henri Parent's nephew, adopted an extremely monumental and luxurious Louis XIV style for the Hôtel Potocki (1879–81). Between 1896 and 1904, Charles Mewès, better known for his ocean liners and hotels, built an outlandish copy twice the size of the illustrious Hôtel de Salm at Rochefort-en-Yvelines, for the banker Jules Porgès.

34 Albert de Rothschild's palace in Vienna (1876, demolished) and Waddesdon Manor, Buckinghamshire (1877). He also restored the Château de Courances (1873) for the De Ganay family and Vaux-le-Vicomte (1877) for the Sommiers. In Paris, he built the hôtels de Béhague (1866), de Luynes (1879) and Cahen d'Anvers (1881).

35 Built for the Duke de Massa. In the same spirit, one should note the Château de Laversine, built in 1882–92 by Alfred Aldrophe for Gustave de Rothschild.

36 Hôtels Porgès and de Breteuil (1892), de Ganay (1894), Bischoffsheim (1895), Lebaudy (1900), Kessler (1905), de la Trémoïlle (1912), etc.; see G. Rousset-Charny, *op. cit.*, pp. 62–139. It was with the Hôtel de Castellane, the illustrious Palais Rose on avenue Foch (1895, demolished), that he properly acquired his reputation as an imitator of classical French art.

37 He is particularly known for the Hôtels de Sourdeval, avenue de New-York (1892), de Moustiers, avenue Georges-V (1899) and Jacques Doucet, rue Spontini (1904).

38 Hôtels de Béhague (reconstructed, 1895), and the Baron Roger (1898), Errazu (1903) and Louis Renault (1912) mansions. He also restored the Château de Champs (1896–99) for the Cahen d'Anvers.

39 The Art Nouveau architects Hector Guimard and Jules Lavirotte may be considered as exceptions, as were the modern rationalists Anatole de Baudot, Paul Guadet and Auguste Perret, but without including references to the great examples of the past. It never occurred to their colleagues in the modern decorative art movement (Auguste Bluysen, Adolphe Bocage, Georges Chedanne, Frantz Jourdain, Charles Plumet, Henri Sauvage, Tony Selmersheim, Xavier Schoellkopf) to comply with the period-style architecture of architects and property developers such as Sélonier and Ragache. Only Richard Bouwens van der Boijen practised both styles, whilst endeavouring to modernize the classical references to which he alluded.

40 The term 'hôtels d'exposition' is borrowed from Michel Steve, *René Sergent et le néo-classicisme 1900* (doctoral thesis, Université Paris IV, 1993), pp. 532 and 543. This metamorphosis of the mansion into exhibition gallery is especially noteworthy in that it occurred at the same time that confusion arose between the terms for a prestigious private mansion – 'hôtel particulier' – and a grand hotel for travellers.

41 The layout of the new mansion was strikingly similar to the one in rue Hamelin, many of whose features were reused almost unchanged. Moïse de Camondo knew exactly what he wanted from his architect, but did not impose limits on his design and composition.

42 This occurred after an abortive reform, in which the modernization of the teaching of architecture advocated by Viollet-le-Duc came up against the resistance of the 'bosses'. See Frédéric Seitz, *Une entreprise d'idée, l'École spéciale d'architecture, 1865-1930* (Paris, Picard, 1995).

43 René Bétourné, *René Sergent architecte. 1865-1927* (Paris, Horizons de France, 1931) p. 6.

44 'To imitate in the fine arts is to produce the resemblance of something, but in something else which becomes its image', Antoine Chrysostome Quatremère de Quincy, *Essai sur la nature, le but et les moyens de l'imitation dans les beaux-arts* (Paris, Treuttel et Würtz, 1823) p. 3.

45 Before publishing *Pastiches et Mélanges* in 1919, Marcel Proust wrote eight articles on the Lemoine Affair in *Le Figaro* between February 1908 and March 1909, all of which are pastiches of the masters of literature. More caricatured is the approach of Paul Reboux and Charles Muller, the first edition of whose *À la manière de...* was published by Grasset in 1907.

46 This was true as long as one knew them. The first serious reference work was the exceptional series of photograph albums compiled by Jules-Félix Vacquier and published by F. Contet. The first volume, on the Hôtel Biron, was published in 1909. It was followed by three volumes on the Faubourg Saint-Germain in 1910–12, then a combined edition, *Les Vieux Hôtels de Paris* (1912, often reprinted). The series continued until the 1930s. While he

was designing the Hôtel de Camondo, René Sergent could therefore draw on this precise documentation without recourse to the great engraved publications of the previous century.

47 Reading the accounts may explain this level of aesthetic concern, in the form of expense. The mansion cost nearly 2 million gold francs (1,945,746 francs according to the architect's accounts, dated 20 October 1914), roughly equivalent to 6 million euros today. The construction itself accounted for 40 per cent of this sum, the finishing less than 20 per cent, heating and comfort 16.4 per cent and decoration 23 per cent (the considerable sum of 449,105 francs). One can understand the protests of the building contractor, Michau & Douane (letter to R. Sergent dated 3 October 1914): he had undertaken the work for a fixed sum, not anticipating that this level of quality was expected nor that the decorators would be constantly on site. Two of them monopolized the largest share of the expenses: the firm of Housse & Guillemin received 255,600 francs and the Decour company 74,305 francs. The rest went to the contractors who carried out the gilding and wrought iron (Baguès did the staircase), and the house painters.

48 Jules Lavirotte and Adolph Bocage in particular come to mind, but also Gustave Rives and Charles Lefebvre, whose work was in the Louis XVI style only in its accumulation of authentic details on an entirely unrelated structure.

49 Its rigour was such that the purely sculptural use of mass and volume was forbidden, restricting itself to elaborating surfaces by their geometry (plan/cross-section/elevation). This linear approach played on the transposition of space in the plan: the revelation or non-revelation (or, possibly, discordance) of the exterior vis-à-vis the interior – an exercise in which Sergent became a master.

50 Count de Fels largely contributed to the rediscovery of Gabriel with his 1912 publication of a standard reference work (Edmond Frisch, Comte de Fels, *Ange-Jacques Gabriel, premier architecte du roi, d'après des documents inédits,* Paris, Émile Paul, 1912). As René Sergent's client at the Château de Voisins (1903–6), he was his first real mentor, urging him to adopt the language of the 18th-century architect. Concerning the importance of the 'modern Louis XVI' style in the second decade of the 20th century in Paris, see Hélène Guéné, *Décoration et haute couture. Armand Albert Rateau pour Jeanne Lanvin, un autre Art déco* (Paris, Les Arts Décoratifs, 2006) pp. 13–15.

51 On Sergent's plans, the courtyard level is 45.23 metres, and the garden level 47.92 metres, to the right of the façade – a difference of 2.69 metres (transforming the rear part of the ground floor into a sunken service floor lit by large basement windows).

52 One should also praise the extreme modernism of his work, which discards the academic conventions of the classical repertoire to exploit the site to the full. Everything about the mansion's composition depends on the interplay of site and form, its mirror effects, its correspondences and conflicts.

53 A mannerist variation on the theme of the central plan of the villa Rotunda, it enhances the longitudinal axis with two façades, one of which is a perfect example of canonic style while the other alludes to the Venetian vernacular tradition. This stylistic exercise has become a standard reference which even the modernists retained, notably Le Corbusier.

54 The hall and staircase fit so tightly together that the regularity of their volumes is broken, as though compressed by the unitary dynamics of the spaces. Even the decoration is subjected to this constriction, which destroys its autonomy, particularly the very unconventional cornice. Sergent borrowed his references from Gabriel (the École Militaire), but is not afraid to adapt them to the spatial rhythm of his own handling of volumes.

55 This aspect of the Hôtel Camondo has been explored in two standard reference works: Marie-Noël de Gary and Gilles Plum, *Les Cuisines de l'hôtel Camondo* (Paris, Union centrale des arts décoratifs, 1999) and Marie-Noël de Gary, 'L'hôtel de Moïse de Camondo', Jean-François Belhoste (ed.), *Le Paris des centraliens, bâtisseurs et entrepreneurs* (Paris, Action artistique de la Ville de Paris, 2004) pp. 212–15.

56 The wall and vaults were built in stone from Tercé, a commune in the Poitou known for its fine-grained limestone. The architect often made do with stucco stone, that was far less expensive and less difficult to use. This concern for authenticity is revealed in the very low cost of the stucco work: 4,220.20 francs. Sergent, who was fond of 'dry' construction, only used plaster for the floors and partitions. The only use he made of reinforced concrete was in the foundations, unlike major Art Nouveau architects such as Anatole de Baudot and Paul Auscher.

57 From here, vehicles can leave via the mews leading to boulevard Malesherbes, using a one-way system facilitating traffic.

58 There was originally a jardinière. The year before he died, Moïse de Camondo had it replaced by this imposing fountain in the style of the antique nymphaeum.

59 On the house near Primrose Hill, see Françoise Boudon, Paul Dufournet, François Loyer, *Hector Horeau 1801–1872* (Paris, CERA, 1979), pp. 61–62. Echoing it is the project for a mansion presented by Viollet-le-Duc in the *Entretiens sur l'architecture* (no. 17, vol. II, Paris, Vve. A. Morel, 1872), pp. 281–90. Reused by Anatole de Baudot, it also inspired Charles Mewès for Sacha Guitry's mansion on the Champ-de-Mars, Hector Guimard for the Hôtel Nozal and Auguste Perret for the La Saulot hunting lodge – and René Sergent himself, in 1908, for the mansion of the couturier Jean-Philippe Worth on the Champ-de-Mars.

60 Their coldness evokes the atmosphere of the great hotels. There is a reason for this. Not only were the requirements of the mansion and tourist hotel similar in some ways – in the importance given to service and food, for instance – but from the beginning of the 20th century the architects who specialized in the 'grand goût français' worked both for a luxury international clientele and for the Paris elite. The first to do so was Charles Mewès, who designed the Ritz (1896–98) in Paris then the Carlton (1900) in London. Paul Nénot followed with the Hôtel Meurice in 1908, then Walter-André Destailleur with the Crillon (1909) and finally René Sergent, the most prolific of them all, with the Grand Hotel in Rome (1906), the Savoy (1907–10) and Claridge's (1909) in London, the Stéphanie in Baden-Baden (1909) and the Trianon-Palace at Versailles (1910).

61 In the same way, the staircase up to the private apartments is detached from the walls and on a smaller scale, like the staircase of a shop, whilst retaining the pomp of the imperial format: what better way to express the passage from the reception floor to the private apartments? These remarks owe much to Hélène Guéné's acutely observant analysis of the building, and this text naturally echoes her comments.

Building a collection pp. 81–117

1 *Alla certosina* marquetry was perfected in Italy in the late 15th century and used for the stalls and panelling of the Carthusian monastery at Pavia, after which it was eventually named. It is often characterized by the use of ivory, bone or mother-of-pearl and was reused by revivalist furniture makers in the 19th century.

2 Inventory of the mansion compiled in 1910, p. 16 (AMNC).

3 On Charles Ephrussi, see Auguste Marguillier, 'Charles Ephrussi', *Gazette des Beaux-Arts,* 1905, vol. II, pp. 353–60, and Philippe Kolb and Jean Adhémar, 'Charles Ephrussi (1849–1905). Ses secrétaires: Laforgue, A. Renan, Proust. "Sa" Gazette des Beaux-Arts', *Gazette des Beaux-Arts,* 1984, vol. I, pp. 29–41.

4 The pavilion was bought on 24 August 1878. It had been partially stripped of its interior decoration, which was installed in the former Hôtel de Saint-Florentin by Alphonse de Rothschild in 1863. Mme de Lancey's collection was sold at two auctions: her magnificent jewellery at the Hôtel Drouot on 8–12 April 1889 and her furniture and objets d'art at Galerie Sedelmeyer on 10–13 December 1890.

5 Saturday 3 June 1882, Edmond and Jules de Goncourt, *Journal, mémoires de la vie littéraire 1851–1896* (1887–1896), unabridged text compiled and annotated by Robert Ricatte (Paris, Robert Laffont, 1989) vol. II, p. 943 (Ricatte quotes Isaac de Camondo by mistake in the reference).

6 On the mansion in rue de Bassano, see *La Semaine des constructeurs,* eighth year, no. 16, 20 October 1883, p. 186–88, ill. 148.

7 This residence, built for the financier Paul Poisson de Bourvalais in 1706 by the architect Bullet de Chamblain, had belonged to Princess de Conti and her heir, the Duke de La Vallière, and was subsequently occupied by Madame de Pompadour. The house, restored by Walter-André Destailleur, and its park, redesigned by Achille Duchêne, were

described by Charles Cahen d'Anvers in *Le Château de Champs* (Paris, Imprimerie nationale, 1928; Moïse de Camondo owned a copy), then in the luxurious *Gazette illustrée des amateurs de jardins,* in the 1933–34 edition: Ernest de Ganay, 'Le Château de Champs' (Paris, Société des amateurs de jardins, 1933).

8 *Louis Cahen d'Anvers* by Léon Bonnat, 1901, and *Louise Cahen d'Anvers* by Carolus-Duran, both still in the Château de Champs.

9 Through the Cahen d'Anvers (Yvonne Cahen d'Anvers [1899–1977] married Anthony de Rothschild [1887–1961]), the Alfassas and the Reinachs. Béatrice Ephrussi de Rothschild (1864–1934), who built an extravagant villa at Cap-Ferrat from 1905 to 1912, was related by marriage to Léon Reinach, Moïse de Camondo's future son-in-law; see Régis Vian des Rives (ed.), *La Villa Ephrussi de Rothschild* (Paris, Les Éditions de l'Amateur, 2002).

10 45–49, rue de Monceau. The mansion was built in 1865 by William Bouwens van der Boijen for Eugène Pereire and was bought by Adolphe de Rothschild in 1868, then inherited by Maurice de Rothschild in 1907. In 1914, Maurice de Rothschild commissioned René Sergent to produce plans for the house's modification, but they were rejected. On the Rothschild residences, see Pauline Prévost-Marcilhacy, *Les Rothschild, bâtisseurs et mécènes* (Paris, Flammarion, 1995).

11 Although knowledgeable and eclectic in his tastes, Henri de Rothschild had the Château de La Muette rebuilt by Lucien Hesse in 1914 in a rather aridly classical style. He donated his large collection of 15th- to 19th-century political and literary correspondence to the Bibliothèque Nationale in 1933.

12 Baron Ferdinand de Rothschild, 'Bric-à-Brac' published by Michael Hall, 'Bric-A-Brac. A Rothschild's Memoir of Collecting', *Apollo*, July & August 2007, p. 50-77, quoted p. 55.

13 He began as a curatorial assistant in 1901 and was appointed Head Curator in 1933.

14 The Dreyfus lived at 101 boulevard Malesherbes, where Gustave Dreyfus had installed his prestigious collection of Renaissance artworks, notably small bronzes, eventually bought by Duveen when the collector died in 1914 (except for a bust by Mino da Fiesole, which was donated to the Louvre). On Carle Dreyfus, see *Collection Carle Dreyfus léguée aux musées nationaux et au musée des Arts décoratifs* (Paris, Réunion des Musées Nationaux, 1953), exhibition catalogue with prefaces by Albert S. Henraux, Georges Salles and Pierre Verlet.

15 CAM 108. 'A life-size bronze bust with a red marble plinth and chased and gilt bronzes. Bought in Berlin via the intermediary of M. Paul Vitry', on 5 January 1929 (purchase book, volume 2, AMNC).

16 He bought a red Morocco leather portfolio (CAM 81), a desk chair stamped by Jean-René Nadal (CAM 136), a writing table stamped by Jean-François Dubut (CAM 193), a pair of Sarrancolin marble columns (CAM 329), a white marble lidded vase (CAM 432), a pair of 'Chantilly porcelain' vases (CAM 612), and the desk armchair by the chair-maker Étienne Michard (CAM 199) in the Salon des Huet, and which the account of the Doucet auction, published in the *Gazette de l'Hôtel Drouot* (June 1912 supplement, p. 2), states was 'fiercely bid for by Count Louis-René de Grammont, M. Fournès and M. Carle Dreyfus, and went to the latter for 33,500 francs'.

17 In 1932 he was finally appointed a member of the Commission des arts plastiques rattachée au Comité consultatif d'action artistique, 'with a view to studying all questions pertaining to the growth of French art and thought abroad' (AMNC).

18 On the antique dealers, see Jean-Louis Gaillemin, *Antiquaires* (Paris, Éditions Assouline, 2000).

19 Bing dealt in antique furniture, Japanese art and contemporary artists in his gallery 'L'Art Nouveau'. A Louis XV wall clock was bought from Bing on 18 January 1912, and later resold (AMNC). On Bing, see Gabriel P. Weisberg, Edwin Becker and Évelyne Possémé (ed.), *Les Origines de l'Art nouveau. La Maison Bing,* exhibition catalogue (Amsterdam and Paris, Van Gogh Museum-Fonds Mercator, Les Arts décoratifs, 2004).

20 The list of some sixty names on invoices also includes Bensimon, Cailleux, Guiraud, Helft, Lévy, Lion, Mayer, Stettiner, and for only two purchases Édouard Jonas, Ernest Cognacq's principal antique dealer and advisor.

21 A few works from the Rodolphe Kann collection were acquired via the intermediary of Duveen: a pair of soft-paste Chantilly porcelain glass coolers (CAM 391) and a pair of gilt bronze wall-lights (CAM 665). Duveen Brothers invoice, 10 January 1908, AMNC). On Duveen, see Meryle Secrest, *Duveen: a life in art* (New York, Alfred A. Knopf, 2004).

22 Such as the 'casket decorated with bronzes guaranteed early Louis XV period', listed in an invoice dated 4 July 1891, which Moïse later parted with (AMNC).

23 Like the two *bergères* 'Louis XV style modern wood mended upholstery', acquired in 1893 (invoice, 4 October) and two years later 'three small Louis XVI style tables' (invoice, 14 January 1895), all subsequently resold (AMNC).

24 Antique dealers pointed out to him that the bronzes on a small Louis XV table were modern (invoice, 6 September 1892), that those on another table were of doubtful authenticity (invoice, 19 October 1893), and that the Meissen porcelain figures on a clock signed by the bronze founder Saint-Germain were not the original ones: 'As I pointed out to you, I fear that the two Saxony figures do not belong to the clock' (invoice dated 20 October 1894, AMNC).

25 CAM 636; 'a Louis XVI marquetried chest of drawers decorated with bronzes signed Graner [*sic*] guaranteed period', purchased for 9,000 francs from Seligmann (AMNC).

26 Two Louis XV wing chairs, bought in October 1893, were exchanged in October 1894 for a Louis XVI marble and gilt bronze clock, which was in turn sold; cf. invoice dated 13 October 1894: '1 white marble and gilt bronze clock from the time of Louis XVI for two large Louis XV marquises white ground plus 3,500 F' (AMNC).

27 Folios 88–90 of the first book (AMNC).

28 Count Bozon de Talleyrand-Périgord, Prince de Sagan, had just had this building built by the architect Louis Joliet at the end of the plot next to his own mansion, formerly the Hôtel de Monaco. He went on to build 17, 19, 19 b (in 1884), 21 (in 1889), 23 (in 1876), 23b (in 1885), 25 (in 1877) and 27 (in 1879). The mansion at number 21 is a prestigious residence with reception rooms on the first floor, including a smoking room (with a conservatory on the courtyard side), small drawing room, large drawing room, large dining room and pantry. It was organized around the central landing of the staircase, forming a gallery. A second staircase led up to the private apartments. Cross sections show Louis XVI decoration with panelling (building permit, Archives de Paris, Vo 11 776). My thanks to François Loyer and Alexis Markovics for their archive research concerning the mansions in rue de Constantine and rue Hamelin.

29 In 1880, like the young Irène Cahen d'Anvers, Adèle Heimendahl, née Ocampo, had posed for Renoir; see *Auguste Renoir. Catalogue raisonné de l'œuvre peint, I. Figures* (Lausanne, Éditions Durand-Ruel, 1971), fig. 345; and Anne Distel, 'Charles Deudon (1832–1914) collectionneur', *Revue de l'Art,* 1989, no. 86, p. 61, notes 19 and 20.

30 'Sublet by M. Heimendahl to M. Count Moïse de Camondo', private agreement drawn up on 10 October 1891 (AMNC).

31 'Description and state of the furniture and furnishings in the mansion at 21 rue de Constantine, sublet by M. R. Heimendahl to M. Count Moïse de Camondo', dated 10 October 1891 (AMNC).

32 The furniture was valued at 400,000 francs (AMNC).

33 The 'two long Louis XVI-style mirrors in three pieces with giltwood console tables with marble tops' in the small drawing room in rue de Constantine were bought and placed in a strategic position in the mansion in rue de Monceau, at the entrance to the Salon des Huet (CAM 307). Moïse de Camondo also bought the Aubusson carpet now in the Large Study (CAM 117).

34 Their friendship with the Ephrussi brothers is confirmed by a number of details: thus Moïse de Camondo offered Mme Jules Ephrussi a Meissen porcelain figure, bought at the Henri Chasles auction in December 1907 (invoices, AMNC).

35 Unfortunately we know nothing of the furnishing of the apartment in avenue d'Iéna.

36 Building permit, December 1897 (Arch. Paris, Vo 11 1682). The architect Paul Rouyrre worked with Léon Chatenay, Princess de Sagan's architect in rue de Constantine. The plot in rue Hamelin had been bought by the Banque de France in 1897 (cadastre de 1876, D1 P4 531). The mansion had a surface area of 500 m² per floor. Due the plot's

narrowness (only three windows per floor on the street), the ground plan was compact and the main staircase was lit by a skylight (information provided by François Loyer and Alexis Markovics).

37 Letter from Moïse de Camondo to Rouyrre: 'My friend Charles Ephrussi strongly advises me to visit the mansion that Madame Bernstein is having built in rue Hamelin' (6 June 1898, AMNC).

38 The mansion consisted of 'cellars, ground floor, a first floor, a second floor and an attic floor' ('Lease by Madame Veuve Bernstein to M. Count de Camondo', signed before Jules Plocque and Robert Olagnier, notaries, 1 rue d'Hauteville, Paris, dated 7 June 1898. The lease began on 1 April 1899 and was renewable every three years. It was renewed for the last time for the period 1911–14. The annual rent was 30,000 francs). The mansion belonged to Mme Ida Seligman, M. Marcel Bernstein's widow, who lived at 16 rue Murillo (AMNC).

39 The second-floor dining room was probably for the children. It seems that Moïse de Camondo furnished an apartment for himself on the ground floor.

40 Letter to Rouyrre, 6 February 1899: 'I was at rue Hamelin yesterday with one of my friends and an upholsterer and furnisher. Both told me the mansion would never be ready for 1 March. I think so too. You told me several times that the mansion would be finished on 1 March: this seems to me impossible, I repeat, as I have already told you, I am not in a hurry and grant you, if necessary, a delay of a month' (AMNC). The elevations attached to the building permit show Louis XV-style decoration, and one can presume that Moïse de Camondo's final decorations were more Neoclassical in taste. An inventory dated 20 July 1909 lists the first floor as follows: large drawing room, small drawing room, large gallery, small galleries and staircase, dining room.

41 Such as the 'white marble and gilt bronze chimney-piece with console supports and satyr's head', bought from Seligmann (invoice, 27 April 1897) and which he installed in the large drawing room of his mansion in rue de Monceau (invoice, 27 April 1897). The chimney-pieces in the Salon des Huet, Small Study and his bedroom in rue de Monceau also came from this residence.

42 CAM 191; invoice, 6 May 1899, paid 36,500 francs.

43 CAM 126; invoice, 8 June 1899, for the considerable sum of 280,000 francs.

44 CAM 120; invoice, 3 April 1909, paid 170,000 francs.

45 The lease of the mansion in rue Hamelin was terminated and Moïse de Camondo had to leave on 15 July 1913; the residence was subsequently let to Countess Tolstoy (14 February 1913, AMNC). Moïse de Camondo took with him most of the decorations he had installed but agreed to leave others, such as the antique pier glass in the small drawing room and the overdoor in the library (bought in 1899). The marble dresser in the dining room was offered to Countess Tolstoy, but was eventually taken away (letter from Moïse de Camondo to Carl Imandt, architect, dated 21 February 1913).

46 The epithet was coined in Istanbul.

47 Auctions at the Hôtel Drouot, 14–15 November (Countess de Camondo's jewellery), 18 November (pictures, ancient and modern) and 21–23 November 1910 (objets d'art, furnishings, tapestries).

48 A few Turkish carpets would add colour to the floors of the secondary galleries in rue de Monceau.

49 José Laguna y Perez (?–1881), Alberto Pasini (1826–99), Henri Léopold Lévy (1840–1904).

50 Letter dated 21 July 1910. The furniture not sold at auction was sold privately: for instance the asking price for a 'smoking-room cabinet (inlaid with mother-of-pearl)' was 1,000 francs.

51 The use of models and not solely drawn elevations was a new feature of architectural practice. The A. Cruchet company received an order for a model of the main staircase in April 1911 (note of memos, October 1914, AMNC). For the monumental consoles supporting the lintel across the bay in the Large Study, 'instead of the execution stipulated in the estimate, four studies in clay, moulded in plaster with three presentations' were necessary for Moïse to make a final decision ('Mémoire des Travaux exécutés … par A. Decour, Tapissier, 41, Rue Joubert à Paris – year 1913', p. 12, AMNC).

52 Moïse de Camondo's approach was the opposite to that of Boni de Castellane, a member of one of France's oldest families, who denounced the removal of panelling and started another trend: re-creating historic interiors using new materials. The Palais Rose, built by Ernest Sanson in 1895, was the finest expression of this movement.

53 CAM 118; invoice, 30 September 1911 (AMNC).

54 On the history of this panelling, see Bruno Pons, *Grands Décors français: 1650–1800, reconstitués en Angleterre, aux États-Unis, en Amérique du Sud et en France* (Dijon, Éditions Faton, 1995) pp. 380–93.

55 CAM 235 and CAM 304; invoices, 14 January 1911. The panelling in the Dining Room consisted of two overdoors and door casings, and five window casings (and a sixth incomplete one). It was complemented with moulded panelling.

56 Invoice dated 30 December 1911 (AMNC).

57 CAM 634; invoice dated 12 September 1912 (AMNC).

58 The chimney-pieces in the Large Study (CAM 48) came from the same house. Between the wars, there were fewer and fewer Parisian interior decorations on the market, due to ever stricter protective measures, so provincial panelling was increasingly bought, especially by the American museums.

59 The interior decorators A. Decour, founded in 1834, had premises at 41 rue Joubert; then, from June 1914, at 26b rue François-I. Moïse de Camondo enlisted the services of this reputable company which had decorated several Rothschild residences including Waddesdon Manor in the 1880s (information kindly provided by Selma Schwartz). Decour had also business in the United States, where he worked on Henry Clay Frick's house in New York in 1915.

60 Letter to René Sergent, 25 January 1913: 'Since the two galleries are in wood, it would be absolutely illogical to do the private staircase that joins the two galleries in different materials'. Eventually, contrary to the first estimate, this stairwell was also panelled.

61 Gabriel's design in the Petit Trianon was not copied, although the wrought iron balustrade had been published in detail by Rodolphe Pfnor in his *Architecture, décoration et ameublement, époque Louis XVI, dessinés, gravés d'après les motifs choisis dans les palais impériaux…* (Paris, A. Morel, 1865) pl. V, VI, X and XI. The gilding of the wrought ironwork was an opportunity for Moïse de Camondo to reveal his sense of detail. On 28 October 1913, he wrote to the architect René Sergent: 'Dear M. Sergent, after the meeting today, I spoke at length with Bourdier on the subject of the gilding of the staircase balustrade. Bourdier believes that we will never achieve a satisfactory result with the gold that has been used; in his view LEMON GOLD should be used, and then patinated by a man absolutely specialized in this. It seems to me that if this is so, and having expressed my displeasure to the Baguès company, you could persuade them to address themselves to Bourdier for this work, obviously at their expense, since they owe me a job well done and which gives you and myself entire satisfaction. Bourdier is also surprised that the bronze ornaments were not gilded by electrolysis, which, according to him, would have yielded a better result.' (AMNC).

62 In the Large Drawing Room, four window catches and two locks came from the Mme Lelong collection (CAM 118), as did the locks and window catches in the Salon des Huet (CAM 185), which served as models for the copies made by the Bricard company, who supplied all the mansion's door and window fittings and locks.

63 The varnished oak panelling *à la capucine*, fashionable around 1700 (châteaux de Bercy, *c.* 1710 and Meudon), was later used solely in libraries and religious buildings (for choir stalls, sacristies, rectories, etc.). In the 19th century, it took on a more masculine appearance, won over by the very austerity that had led to its rejection in the 18th century.

64 These colour schemes were already used in the 18th century, for instance in the new dining room in the Hôtel Crozat in place Vendôme in 1744. It was a new colour scheme at the time, the water-green ground set off with dark green relief effects (described in Pons, *Grands Décors français, op. cit.*, p. 18).

65 As Baron Edmond de Rothschild did at 41 rue du Faubourg-Saint-Honoré, built by Félix Langlais in 1878, whose drawing rooms are all decorated with gilt panelling. See Pauline Prévost-Marcilhacy, 'L'hôtel d'Edmond de Rothschild', in *La Rue du Faubourg-Saint-Honoré*, exhibition catalogue (Paris, Délégation à l'action artistique de la Ville de Paris, 1994) pp. 149–58.

66 The dresser, comprising a 'solid moulded top…with inlaid pilasters, backboard and four sculpted consoles, moulded back panel and base',

was made by Gilis from a model supplied by Decour (invoice from Ch. Gilis, 8 September 1913, AMNC).

67 In the Potocki mansion, designed by Jules Reboul (finished in 1884), the Béhague mansion, by Walter-André Destailleurs (1895–1904), the Polignac mansion by Grandpierre (from 1904). In the dining room in rue Hamelin there was a Sarrancolin marble dresser, which was removed. In the end, a new, more spectacular console was made for rue de Monceau.

68 CAM 45; probably acquired before 1907.

69 The decorator Decour was given the task of cleaning the tapestries, lining them if necessary and mounting them on stretchers.

70 Pons, *Grand Décors français, op. cit.*, pp. 142–43.

71 CAM 114 (bought before 1907). Moïse de Camondo did not buy the two other tapestries in the set, sold with the Jules Ephrussi collection on 29 May 1929 (nos. 12 and 13), because there was no place for them in the panelling then.

72 Small carpets decorated with lambrequins and bouquets of flowers dating from the mid-century (CAM 177 and CAM 179), large compositions inspired by Charles Le Brun for the famous commission for the Grande Galerie in the Louvre (CAM 176), and early 18th-century arabesque decorations (CAM 178; bench cover). On the Savonnerie carpets, see Pierre Verlet, *The James A. de Rothschild Collection at Waddesdon Manor, The Savonnerie* (London and Fribourg, The National Trust–Office du Livre, 1982).

73 'Memo of work done…by A. Decour, Upholsterer… – 1913–1914', p. 6 (AMNC); the two *voyeuses* were then put in Moïse de Camondo's bedroom.

74 CAM 70. See Pierre Verlet, 'Les meubles sculptés du XVIIIe siècle, quelques identifications', *Bulletin de la Société de l'histoire de l'art français*, 1937, pp. 268–69, and *Le Mobilier royal français, II : Meubles de la Couronne conservés en France* (Paris, Plon, 1955) note 39.

75 CAM 232; invoice for 550,000 francs from Fabre et fils, 5 June 1923 (AMNC). The door tapestries were woven for the Marquis of Marigny in 1775.

76 For which they had very probably been woven a few years earlier and which the frugal Moïse de Camondo had decided not to replace. The curtains in the library were made from those formerly in the bedroom, the lampas in the small drawing room was reused in Béatrice's bedroom, and the lampas originally in the drawing room was used in Nissim's drawing room. Decour was given the task of adapting the curtains for the windows in rue de Monceau.

77 Venetian blinds were also fitted in the windows of the Large Study.

78 In this mansion designed by Louis Parent in the Louis XVI style, the 18th-century collections were displayed more as they would be in a museum: the windowless hall and drawing room were lit by skylights, and the drawing room is in a Louis XIV-Régence style, in contradiction to the exterior architecture.

79 The Hôtel Cernuschi, finished in 1874, was designed by William Bouwens van der Boijen. Writing about this mansion in 1875, when the residence had not yet become a museum, the Goncourt brothers described it as a 'hôtel-musée' that was 'a milieu as imposing and cold as the Louvre…not the hospitable and pleasant surroundings of a dwelling' (1 July 1875, Goncourt, *Journal, op. cit.*, p. 651).

80 Letter, 9 February 1914 (AMNC).

81 For the first purchase attempt, Moïse de Camondo had advanced the sum, and finally, in 1920, he participated in the definitive acquisition (receipt for a cheque for 10 000 francs, signed by Louis Metman, dated 14 January 1920 and letter from the minister of Public Instruction and Fine Arts, dated 13 February 1920 [AMNC]). See 'La Société des Amis du Louvre', in *Les Donateurs du Louvre*, exhibition catalogue (Paris, Réunion des musées nationaux, 1989) pp. 98–100. In March 1928 he also contributed to the subscription for the purchase at auction of the Degas drawings and monotypes for Ludovic Halévy's *Petites Cardinales*, in order to ensure its publication (letter from Léon Comar, 20 March 1928). But when the edition was finished, 'given his small participation', he declined the offer of a monotype, preferring to be reimbursed instead (letters to Léon Comar, 26 March and 6 June 1928, AMNC).

82 Following the observation made in the rules: 'Most paintings, drawings and prints by modern artists are still usually presented in frames slavishly imitating antique frames. There are at present no frames which match not only these works but also the modern furniture they have to accompany. ...M. Count de Camondo, member of the board of the Union Centrale des Arts Décoratifs, has had the idea, with a view to remedying this situation, of instating a Competition and endowing it with a prize.'

83 Letter to Mme Marin-Berryer, antique dealer at Nonancourt, 10 December 1917 (AMNC).

84 Letter to Henri Petitpas, 3 May 1929 (AMNC).

85 He sold him the second commode by Garnier in 1929.

86 Linke, for instance, and Zwiener, who in 1895 delivered a complete bedroom suite to Emperor Wilhelm II at the royal castle in Berlin, an unbridled Louis-XV style creation showing the influences of Bernard Van Risenburgh, Joseph Baumhauer and Jean-François Œben. See Wilfried Baer, *Eine Schlafzimmer-Austattung von Julius Zwiener. Ein Auftrag Kaiser Wilhelms II. für das Berliner Schloss. 1895–1900,* Berlin, Verwaltung der Staatlichen Schlösser und Gärten Berlin, 1989.

87 Anecdote recounted by Marcelle Goldschmidt, née Dreyfus, Gustave Dreyfus' daughter and Carle's sister (verbal account given by Hubert Goldschmidt, March 2007).

88 In 1960, Adrien Fauchier-Magnan recalled the great collectors of the interwar period whom he had frequented: 'various members of the Rothschild family, Countess de Béhague, Mme Burat, Princess de Poix, the Marquis de Biron, ..., Count de Camondo, M. Martin le Roy, M. Veil Picard, M. David Weill, M. Gulbenkian, etc.' *C'était hier... [souvenirs d'un demi-siècle]* (Paris, Éditions du Scorpion, 1960) p. 49.

89 The collection was catalogued by Jean Messelet as soon as the museum opened under the following categories: panelling, chimney-pieces, furniture, chairs, screens, miscellaneous objects, bronzes, precious metalwork, ceramics and glass, sculptures, paintings and pastels, drawings, prints, tapestries, carpets. Nadine Gasc and Gérard Mabille adopted a slightly different order in *Le Musée Nissim de Camondo* (Paris, Musées et monuments de France, 1991).

90 Pieces from three services were reunited: the 1784 'Lefèvre' service (CAM 293), bought from Seligmann before 1907 and formerly in the Double collection, the 1786 'Eden' service (CAM 292), bought in 1911 from Stettiner and the 1792 'Lefébure' service (CAM 258); additional pieces from these service were later bought.

91 'It was by mistake that you were given my name as an owner of 18th-century drawings. It was probably the collection of my cousin, Count Isaac de Camondo, which is now the property of the Louvre. I have no drawing from that period or from any other', letter to M. Hermann Loeb, president of the Prestel company, 1 May 1934 (AMNC).

92 Letter, 9 February 1931 (AMNC).

93 He did not collect miniatures despite these works being highly sought after at the time: 'I hasten to inform you that I do not collect miniatures,' he replied courteously in a letter to Mlle Jumel on 6 May 1927. And indeed there were none in his collection except for the large miniature he inherited from his father, *The Children of King Murat*, and two gouaches by Jean-Baptiste Berthier, but they were closer in size to paintings than the small objects usually denoted by the term miniature.

94 On the life of Henry Clay Frick, see Martha Frick Symington Sanger, *Henry Clay Frick: an Intimate Portrait* (New York, Abbeville Press Publishers, 1998), and on the mansion on Fifth Avenue, see Charles Ryskamp *et al.*, *Art in the Frick Collection: Paintings, Sculptures, Decorative Arts* (New York, Harry N. Abrams, 1996).

95 Only one picture is now attributed to him (by Alastair Laing), *Meal During the Hunt* (CAM 441), an early work, first attributed to Jean-François de Troy when it was acquired in 1923 due to its very specific subject matter. However, Boucher is triumphantly present in the tapestries.

96 Thérèse Burollet, *Le Musée Cognacq-Jay* (Paris, Les Presses artistiques, undated).

97 Sophie Le Tarnec, Bertrand Rondot, 'Les Camondo et la vénerie', *Vénerie*, no.164, December 2006, pp. 66–69.

98 Collectors had grown wary of these objects due to the many fakes then in circulation, which experts were not yet able to systematically identify (as Christian Baulez and Vincent Bastien have kindly suggested). See Frederick Litchfield, 'Imitations and Reproductions, I, Sèvres

Porcelain', *The Connoisseur*, XLIX, 1917, pp 3–14, and Pierre Verlet, *Les Grands Services de Sèvres* (Paris, Éditions des musées nationaux, 1951).

99 CAM 100. The set was bought in 1897 from Seligmann (invoice dated 17 May). In 1899, Moïse de Camondo also acquired from Seligmann 'a vase in early Sèvres soft-paste porcelain' (invoice, 1 February), for the considerable sum of 31,000 francs, but the mention of a hard-paste base leaves its integrity open to doubt and he parted with it when he bought the paintings by Huet the following year. He finally declared: 'I am not a collector of porcelain' in a letter to Count R. de Lavigerie on 23 November 1929, referring to the porcelain bust of Louis XV by Menrecy at the Yanville auction.

100 CAM 194; bought for 230,000 francs from Bensimon (invoice, 30 September 1934).

101 He asked antique dealers to provide the provenance of the most important pieces. Lion wrote to him on 14 January 1913: 'Here is the information you asked for concerning the guéridon table decorated with Sèvres'. Research was carried out for certain works. Regarding the paintings by Hubert Robert, the notary Louis Bossy wrote to him on 8 March 1927: 'Mme Hubert Robert née Loos's will, authentic, 13 July 1821, makes no mention at all of the works of art which interest you. I have found in the notarized papers drawn up after her death on 6 September 1821 that the inventory was compiled after her death by Maître Delacour, notary in Paris (whose successor is Maître Salle...), on 18 August 1821. You might address yourself to Maître Salle with some chance of success'. Moïse de Camondo replied on 10 March 1927: 'then I will consult your colleague, Maître Salle'.

102 Bertrand Rondot, 'Moïse de Camondo and the Price of "Association"', *Furniture History*, vol XLIII, 2007, p. 303-314.

103 CAM 133; invoice, 6 March 1913.

104 On 14 January 1913, Lion wrote: 'This information was given to me by the last owner, Monsieur de Champeaux, navy commander, at Autun'.

105 The standard reference work, giving the biographies of the cabinetmakers, was published ten years after this purchase, in 1923: Comte François de Salverte, *Les Ébénistes du XVIIIe siècle. Leurs œuvres et leurs marques* (Paris and Brussels, G. van Oest, 1923).

106 Probably Croisilles and not Croissilles. The exchange also included a marquetried oval table and 125,000 francs in cash (the table by Carlin was bought for 220,000 francs from Seligmann in December 1908 [invoice, 8 December]).

107 CAM 126; invoice, 8 June 1899. Seligmann bought it from General de Charrette, according to whom 'it came from Ménage de Pressigny..., to whom it had apparently been given by Queen Marie-Antoinette'. The table may well have belonged to Farmer-General François-Marie Ménage de Pressigny, who lived at 25 rue des Jeûneurs in Paris and was sentenced to death by the Revolutionary Tribunal on 19 Floréal An II, 'for being an accomplice to the plot against the people by adding water and ingredients harmful to citizens in tobacco'. His possessions, which included several pictures by Fragonard, were confiscated. In the 19th century, the writing table belonged to Baron d'Aubigny et de Charette but not to 'General de Charette, head of the royalists', as claimed in the invoice.

108 On *bonheur du jour* (stepped back) writing tables decorated with porcelain plaques, Geoffrey de Bellaigue includes a table of known pieces in *The James A. de Rothschild Collection at Waddesdon Manor, Furniture, Clocks and Gilt Bronze*, vol. II (London and Fribourg, The National Trust-Office du Livre, 1974) note 100, p. 480; see also *European Furniture in The Metropolitan Museum of Art. Highlights of the Collection* (New York, The Metropolitan Museum of Art, New Haven, Yale University Press, 2006), note 63, pp. 156–58, by Daniëlle O. Kisluk-Grosheide.

109 CAM 153; bought on 30 March 1935 from Jean Seligmann (purchase book, volume 2, AMNC).

110 Christian Baulez, 'Le grand cabinet intérieur de Marie-Antoinette. Décor, mobilier et collections', in *Les Laques du Japon. Collections de Marie-Antoinette*, exhibition catalogue (Paris, Réunion des Musées Nationaux, Münster, Museum für Lackkunst, 2002) p. 39.

111 CAM 202; its provenance is unknown but it was already in the mansion in rue Hamelin.

112 Christian Baulez, 'Identification de quelques meubles des collections de Versailles, Compiègne et Chantilly', *Bulletin de la Société de l'histoire de l'art français*, 1977, pp. 161–69; Pierre Verlet, *Le Mobilier royal français, IV:*

Meubles de la Couronne conservés en Europe et aux États-Unis (Paris, Picard, 1990) pp. 150–55, note 40.

113 CAM 192; invoice dated 31 May 1933.

114 Confirmed by the account by the Marquis de Saint-Seine published in *Connaissance des Arts* in March 1958 (no. 73, p. 5).

115 See E. Williamson, *Les Meubles d'art du Mobilier national* (Paris, Baudry et Cie, 1883) pl. 49.

116 Théodore Vacquer, *Maisons les plus remarquables de Paris construites pendant les trois dernières années [...] relevées et dessinées par Th. Vacquer...* (Paris, A. Coudrillier, undated).

117 CAM 36; invoice from S. Guiraud, 3 October 1911: 'Two Oriental lacquer corner-cupboards decorated with Louis XV period gilt bronzes', bought for 32,000 francs.

118 CAM 121; acquired from Arnold Seligmann, invoice dated 7 March 1921, bought for 220,000 francs, 200,000 francs of which were paid in National Defence coupons...

119 CAM 123. These two pieces, formerly in the Édouard Kann collection, were bought from his daughter, Mme Delaunay, via Wildenstein as intermediary, for the colossal sum of 800,000 francs in November 1930.

120 CAM 49. The purchase book notes the acquisition of these two pieces separately, on 29 November 1922, without mentioning the antique dealer: 'A large Louis XVI-period cabinet...stamped by Leleu. 80,000 / A second, identical piece... 25,000. To this price must be added the two magnificent gouaches given in exchange.' The museum has the invoice, dated 29 November 1922, for the latter, made out by Chastel: 'A Louis XVI-period rosewood cabinet with bronzes, two doors and two drawers, stamped by Leleu, 30,000 francs' (why such a considerable difference in price?). In 1912, Moïse de Camondo had bought from Seligmann the two cabinets stamped by Leleu in the dining room 'both guaranteed 18th century', but a quick examination reveals that they had been entirely reveneered. (invoice, 8 January).

121 CAM 189. The first, invoiced on 28 May 1898, the second, invoiced on 4 July 1928. Already in 1922, Davis had offered him a pair of 'commodes that are so close one could treat them as a pair. They are from the Régence period, very rare in form, and with very beautiful fittings. Mr May asked me to write to you about these pieces, which he thought would interest you' (letter, 15 May 1922). Davis included precise dimensions, but Moïse de Camondo replied that he bought 'only Louis XVI furniture' (letter, 17 May 1922).

122 CAM 188; bought from Larcade (invoice date 9 March 1907).

123 'I assert, Monsieur le Comte, that I am absolutely stupefied that someone should have said to you that the bronzes on these two pieces are modern, given that these pieces are marvels and that they have been examined and admired by two people who, in my view, are the most competent in Paris. These pieces of furniture are indisputably genuine!' Letter, 28 October 1907. Unfortunately, the identity of the two people cited is unknown.

124 The marble bust (CAM 412) was bought from Sarrazin; for the bronze bust, see note 16.

125 CAM 165 (invoiced by Kraemer on 23 January 1912) and CAM 616 (invoiced by Larcade on 15 March 1918). Moïse de Camondo had the presence of mind to describe the plaster bust in flattering terms to a potential borrower of the marble, maintaining that the plaster 'is unanimously considered...to be perhaps superior in interest to the marble and is even preferred by certain collectors' (Louis Réau mentions it again in his monograph. Cf. *Houdon, sa vie et son œuvre* (Paris, F. de Nobèle, 1964) III–IV, p. 14, fig. 9 c). Another example of marble and plaster pairs in the collection is Jean-Jacques Caffieri's *Fidelity*, whose marble (CAM 163) was joined by a plaster version (CAM 784) in 1902 (bought via Seligmann as intermediary at the Miallet auction, 9–10 June).

126 CAM 325 (Wildenstein's invoice, 8 January 1918) and CAM 230 (Seligmann's invoice, 5 February 1898). The two bronzes by Thomire were believed to be by Pigalle when they were acquired, as attested by the inscription engraved on the plinth. See Jean Messelet, *Musée Nissim de Camondo : catalogue des collections*, revised and enlarged by Bertrand Rondot, with the participation of Xavier Salmon and Béatrice Quette (Paris, Réunion des Musées Nationaux / Union Centrale des Arts Décoratifs, 1998).

127 The screen was bought from Seligmann in 1911 (invoice, 29 September, CAM 203), the panel from Bensimon in 1934 (invoice, 30 April), and the frame from Rotil (invoice, also 30 April, CAM 204).

128 Two pairs of fruit dishes with domed lids, one rectangular and one square (the latter exchanged for two of the same type but round; CAM 257), belonging to another court service, known as the 'Moscow' service, and a terrine, two *pots à oille* and four buckets from the Orloff service (CAM 252, 253 and 255). The earliest major purchase was a *pot à oille* by Auguste (CAM 254), bought on 31 October 1928.

129 Philippe Bordes, 'Portraiture in the mode of genre: a social interpretation', *French Genre Painting in the Eighteenth Century*, Philip Conisbee (ed.), *Center for Advanced Study in the Visual Arts Symposium Papers*, XLI, *Studies in the History of Art*, 72, Washington, National Gallery of Art, 2007, p. 257–73.

130 Acquired on 1 June 1935 from Bauer (CAM 146); his last purchase, in August 1935, would be eight gilt bronze curtain hooks (CAM 674, invoiced by Édouard Jonas on 2 August). They were the same model as a pair of wall-lights acquired at the Rodolphe Kahn auction, and were intended for Moïse de Camondo's bedroom.

Behind the scenes pp. 244–81

1 In private households, these spaces gradually became smaller as technology advanced.

2 Marie-Noël de Gary, 'L'hôtel de Moïse de Camondo', *Le Paris des centraliens, bâtisseurs et entrepreneurs*, Jean François Belhoste (ed.) (Paris, Action artistique de la Ville de Paris, 2004), pp. 212–15.

3 After the bank closed, in 1917 the archives and secretariat were installed on the first floor of the outbuildings, above the stables, as shown by a plan of the premises (AMNC).

4 Ripolin was named after the Dutch inventor Riep and *olin* (oil). This washable paint was used in all the service rooms and outbuildings. Records of payments to the interior decorator Feist (AMNC).

5 Marie-Noël de Gary and Gilles Plum, *Les Cuisines de l'hôtel Camondo* (Paris, Ucad, 1999).

6 In the 1890s, Jules Cubain, who graduated from the ECP in 1871, and his brother Maurice, who graduated from the ECP in 1883, took over the former Baudon et Coquelle company, founded in 1839. The firm became Cubain Frères, then, after Maurice's death in 1900, J. Cubain et Cie, ingénieur-constructeur ECP, and later J. Cubain et ses fils. The company's Paris offices were in rue de Bondy and its factory at Saint-Ouen, in the Paris suburbs.

7 The law passed on 31 July 1917 obliged all employers to declare all staff in their employ whose salary exceeded 3,000 francs a year. Moïse de Camondo complied, but did not declare his low-paid staff. Nonetheless, from 1917 to 1934 Tédeschi compiled tables listing the names of all employees, their posts and wages. In September 1921 those with board and lodging at rue Monceau were Pierre Godefin, butler, Paul Méchain, manservant, Charles Courtain, underbutler, Louis Charnet, manservant, Édouard Durand, manservant, Anna Davezac, laundry maid, Arthur Colliard, Pierre Pêcheux, Martin Fuertès, Paul Duron, footmen. With lodging only: Camille Clermont, mechanic, Aloze, washer, M. and Mme Blond, concierges, and Joseph Richer, concierge.

8 The description of the work carried out in 1912 indicates the layout of this floor. 'In 1928, I lodged in a room above the porch. It was very comfortable – there was even carpeting in the bedrooms' (oral account by Maurice Mirliry, kitchen boy, born 1900).

9 An oral account by Gérard Boucheron, recounted by his father Louis, a guest at the 'Marsan lunches' which Moïse de Camondo gave for those involved in the decorative arts. The table services used were not included in the bequest.

10 He entered Moïse's service in 1905, after the death of Countess Abraham Behor de Camondo.

11 Moïse de Camondo's pelisse came from Revillon.

12 A kind of caviar made from pressed and dried grey mullet or mullet roe.

13 Ch. Mildé Fils et Cie built the Drouot generator station in 1886 and the Compagnie de l'Ouest Parisien 'Ouest-lumière' in 1899. The firm's premises were initially at 3 rue de Monceau and 26 rue Laugier, then at 51 and 56–60 rue Desrenaudes in the 17th arrondissement. Charles Mildé began manufacturing electrical equipment in 1873. His son Charles Jean Alexandre Ernest (born 1886) graduated from the École Centrale in 1910. Just before the war, the firm published commercial catalogues, including *L'Electricité à la campagne*, with plates and texts by Frantz Jourdain, mentioning the firms main installations all over France, and listing 1914 prices.

14 Marcel Proust, *In Search of Lost Time, Within a Budding Grove* (1919).

15 The light bulb was developed for domestic lighting in 1878 by Joseph Wilson Swan in Britain and Thomas Edison in the United States.

16 Boni de Castellane, 'Comment j'ai découvert l'Amérique' (1924), *Mémoires de Boni de Castellane 1867–1932* (Paris, Perrin, 1986) pp. 143–44.

17 Light bulb deliveries list Mildé bulbs, then from 1929, Philips and Mazda bulbs.

18 '...carpet of sockets beneath an insulating sheath and fabric covering'. The same system was also mentioned in the chauffeur-mechanics' lodgings apartments in the outbuildings.

19 Compagnie Parisienne du Nettoyage par le Vide, a central vacuum cleaning system, Rulf frères.

20 In 1880, Charles Kula took over Seyffert, a cabinetmaker that specialized in bathroom furniture, diversified into taps and created a plumbing and roofing company. In 1897, he moved his workshop to 21 rue de Viète and opened a showroom at 84 boulevard Haussmann. His two sons, both graduates of the École Centrale, founded Kula Frères. The company closed in 1981.

21 *Catalogue général d'appareils sanitaires*, Kula ingénieur ECP, Paris, 1912.

22 Receipt of payment for the plumbing work, 1912–13, delivered 1 October 1914 by Charles Kula (AMNC).

23 The mansion had no laundry as such, but there were rooms for sorting and cleaning dirty linen on the attic floor. The most spacious was the laundry room, fitted with a number of glazed cupboards with gathered curtains, in which tablecloths and sheets were piled on white cotton-covered shelves.

24 René Sergent had worked with Achille Duchêne from 1903 at the Château de Voisins, for Count de Fels. See Henri and Achille Duchêne, *Le Style Duchêne* (Neuilly-sur-Seine, Éditions du Labyrinthe, 1998).

25 Flat rate work carried out for 16,560 francs by Collin from 14 September 1912, including terracing, gardening, tarmacking, drainage work and planting for the transformation of 1,630 square metres of garden (paths 400 square metres, lawns 520 square metres, flowerbeds and parterres 690 square metres) (AMNC).

26 Letter from Moïse de Camondo to M. Guillaume at the Duchêne agency, 19 December 1912 (AMNC).

27 Collin's estimates, 20 February, 2 May and 18 November 1913 (AMNC).

28 Letter from Moïse de Camondo to M. Poirier, 24 November 1919 (AMNC).

29 Supplied by Ebel in Strasbourg.

30 M. Collin, landscape gardener, 6 rue Fourcroy, Paris XVII; M. Poirier, florist, 16 rue de la Bonne Aventure, Versailles; M. Berthier, landscape gardener, 10 rue Dosne, Paris; MM. Moser et fils, 1 rue Saint-Symphorien, Versailles; M. Royer fils, horticulturalist, 44 avenue de Picardie, Versailles.

31 Letter from Moser Fils to Moïse de Camondo, 8 January 1925 (AMNC).

32 26–34 rue Washington, Paris VIII.

33 Bocquet also supplied the ten containers for the laurels in the courtyard.

34 The restoration of this trelliswork was carried out in 2003 by the Tricotel company; cf. Jean-Pierre van Reyndorp, Claire Frange-Duchêne, *L'Art du treillage* (Semur-en-Auxois, Éditions Spiralinthe, 2006), pp. 96–103.

35 It stipulates an annuity of 120,000 francs to cover the costs of the upkeep of the buildings and collections.

36 In 1928, justifying his refusal to lend the marble bust of *Summer* to the exhibition celebrating the centenary of Houdon, he wrote: 'it is the only ornament in my living room and, furthermore, I cannot subject it to the risks of transport and its exhibition in public'. In February 1923, Tédeschi had to remind Arthur Meyer, editor of *Le Gaulois*, that since he lived in the mansion with his family, the count deeply regretted being unable to open it to all.

37 The inventory was carried out by Georges Fontaine. The summary catalogue prefaced by Carle Dreyfus was compiled by Jean Messelet, who also added to the subsequent 1947, 1954 and 1960 editions. The 1976 edition was prefaced by François Mathey. The 1998 edition was revised and enlarged by Bertrand Rondot with the participation of Xavier Salmon and Béatrice Quette. The photographs of the rooms taken before the visitors' cordons were installed are an invaluable source of information. Scaffolding was even erected in the courtyard to enable the carpets to be photographed.

38 The 26 December 1936 number: the Large Study, the Large Drawing room, the Dining Room, the Salon des Huet, the Library and Moïse's bedroom.

39 The museum was open three days a week in the afternoon and all day Sunday. The cloakroom furniture was kept. It comprised 90 wall-mounted coathangers in brass with a hat shelf above, supplied by the Morea company (AMNC). Some items of wooden furniture, painted grey, including two marble-topped tables, chairs, a caned bench seat, a valet and an umbrella stand, were also made for Moïse's use.

40 As stipulated in the bequest, the mansion and collections belong to the French state and are managed by the Union centrale des Arts Décoratifs (now Les Arts Décoratifs). On 13 September 1952, the mansion was listed as a state-owned building. On 6 April 1981, it was included in the supplementary inventory of historic monuments and on 2 March 2005 it was classified as a historic monument, 'in its entirety, including the outbuildings, courtyards and garden at 61b and 63 rue Monceau, Paris VIII, located on plot no. 21, with a surface area of 34 ares 44 centiares, listed in the cadastre section 08–04 CM, the property of the state, allocated to the Ministry of Culture and Communication and conceded to Les Arts Décoratifs, 107 rue de Rivoli, Paris I.'

41 Under Didier Aron's presidency, the committee comprised prominent public figures, antique dealers and interior decorators.

42 It was the Florence Gould Foundation who enabled the restoration and presentation of archive documents, portraits and busts and the making of the short film now on permanent exhibit.

43 Gift of the Kraemer family (inv. CAM 1995.1.1.1 and 2).

44 Gifts of M. Katz (inv. CAM 2000.1.1-7) and Mme Vyza (inv. CAM 2000.2.1-5).

45 Gift of M. and Mme Serge Dassault (inv. CAM 2002.1-7).

46 A collection of 67 tie-pins by Boucheron was donated to the Musée des Arts Décoratifs by Moïse de Camondo in 1933; see Évelyne Possémé, *Épingles de cravate* (Paris, RMN, 1992).

47 William Desazars de Montgailhard and the Kraemer family.

48 See the work of Michèle Perrot, who edited volume 4 of *Histoire de la vie privée*, edited by Philippe Ariès and Georges Duby (Paris, Seuil, 1987), and Monique Eleb and Anne Debarre, *L'Invention de l'habitation moderne, Paris 1880–1914* (Brussels, AAM / Paris, Hazan, 1995).

49 Anthony Rowley, *The Book of Kitchens* (Flammarion USA 2000), Marie-Laure Verroust, *Cuisine et cuisiniers* (Paris, Éditions de La Martinière, 1999), Christian du Pavillon, *Éléments d'une architecture gourmande* (Paris, Monum / Adam Biro, 2002).

50 *Babette's Feast* (1987), by Gabriel Axel, based on the novel by Karen Blixen

51 In the châteaux de Vaux-le-Vicomte and Breteuil, several rooms in the basement may be visited. Many other state-owned buildings still have their late 19th-century installations, which could be restored, notably in the châteaux d'Eu (Seine-Maritime), Randan (Auvergne) and Champs-sur-Marne, formerly the property of the Cahen d'Anvers family. Mark Girouard devoted several chapters to domestic organization in *Life in the French Country House* (London, Weidenfeld & Nicolson Illustrated, 2000).

52 Christina Hardyment, *Behind the Scenes, Domestic Arrangements in Historic Houses* (London, The National Trust, 1997), Pamela A. Sambrook and Peter Brears, *The Country House Kitchen, 1650–1900*, (London, Sutton Publishing in association with the National Trust, 1996). In 1995 Uppark, tragically destroyed by fire, was reopened after five years of exemplary restoration work, and Petworth's servants' quarters were restored to their 1920–40 state: Christopher Rowell and John Martin Robinson, *Uppark Restored* (London, The National Trust, 1996), *Petworth, the Servants' Quarters* (London, The National Trust, 1997). Also noteworthy in this respect are Erddigg (Clwyd), Lanhydrock (Cornwall) and above all Castle Drogo (Devon), designed by Sir Edwin Lutyens in the 1920s.

53 *Du palais au palace, des grands hôtels de voyageurs au XIXe siècle* (Paris, Paris-Musées / Courbevoie, ACR, 1998).

54 Marie-Noël de Gary, 'Cuisine à la Camondo', *The World of Interiors*, May 2007, pp. 105–55.

55 *La Règle du jeu*, 1939; *The Remains of the Day*, 1993; *Gosford Park*, 2001, and in the 1970s the 68-episode BBC TV series *Upstairs, Downstairs* recounting the saga of an aristocratic family and its servants.

56 Prompted notably by the Jansen company, which wanted to train professionals in interior design. The school moved from rue de Monceau to 266 boulevard Raspail in 1988.

57 Except for the apartments in the left wing, lived in by curators of the Musée des Arts Décoratifs since 1936.

58 The glazed door at the foot of the staircase was next to the garage gate, both of which bore the number 61b, due to the enlargement of the plot during the mansion's construction (see p. 60). Beneath the arch, another staircase leads up to the caretaker's apartment on the first floor and servants' lodgings on the attic floor: five rooms with a communal bathroom.

59 The garage has a surface area of 110 square metres. The glazed awning was removed in 1961.

60 The restoration was supervised by Thierry Algrin, Architecte des Monuments Historiques.

61 Sergent housed the stables in the former mansion built by Violet. Their surface area is 83 square metres, and the grooming court 44 square metres. After consulting the Musgrave et Jardillier companies, an order for eight stalls for 8,300 francs was signed on 21 July 1911 with Mouton H. Oranger, 73, avenue des Champs-Élysées, but the interior decorator Feist's invoices mention nine stalls '2.72 m long...with fixed oak side partitions 1.25 m high surmounted by a 0.95 m-high grille...painting before assembly of 1,222 panelling boards, (each 1.25 x 0.14)...9 similar doors, 17 posts 2.65 m high, 9 troughs, 3 lamp stands, 1 chest in the middle, 1 oats chest, 2 chests near the drinking trough, 2 stable benches' (AMNC).

62 Until 1930, horses and automobiles could take the two wide side paths in the Parc Monceau (oral account by Françoise Petiet). The main roads in the district were still paved with wood, and rue de Monceau was repaved when Moïse moved into the Hôtel de Camondo in 1913 (see Correspondance, comtes Moïse et Isaac, p. 432, AMNC).

63 Plan (AMNC).

The Salon des Huet from the Gallery, *c.* 1936.

Chronology

Moïse de Camondo	Camondo family	Selected historical events
1860 Born 'in a stone house' at 6 Camondo Street in the Galata district of Istanbul. He probably learns French and English from a very early age.		**1860** Nice and Savoie become French. Garibaldi seizes Sicily. The City of Paris buys the Domaine de Monceau to create the present-day park. The Universal Israelite Alliance is founded.
	1861 Nissim de Camondo, Moïse's father, is made a knight of the Medjidie Order, 2nd class.	**1861** Victor Emmanuel is proclaimed king of Italy. Abdul Aziz made Sultan of the Ottoman Empire. Inauguration of the Parc Monceau and boulevard Malesherbes. The Pereire brothers acquire 81,000 square metres of land around the Parc Monceau . Première of Wagner's *Tannhäuser*, Paris Opéra.
	1862 'Schools War' in Istanbul (the Jewish community opposes measures concerning educational reform, the teaching of Turkish and French in schools, etc.). Abraham Salomon is excommunicated by the integrationist rabbi Akresh.	**1862** Bismarck is appointed prime minister of Prussia. Victor Hugo publishes *Les Misérables*. Birth of Claude Debussy.
	1863 Death of Rebecca Halfon, née Camondo, sister of Nissim and Abraham Behor. Founding of the central committee of the Universal Israelite Alliance in Istanbul, with Abraham Behor as president. Émile Pereire sells the plot at 63 rue de Monceau to Adolphe Violet, who builds the mansion that he is to sell to Nissim de Camondo in 1870.	**1863** Crédit Lyonnais is founded. The Imperial Ottoman Bank is founded. Manet's *Déjeuner sur l'herbe* causes a furore at the Salon des Refusés.
	1864 Creation of the Société Générale de l'Empire Ottoman, among whose co-founders is the family bank, Isaac Camondo & Co.	**1864** Founding of the Union Centrale des Beaux-Arts Appliqués à l'Industrie, to be amalgamated with the Société du Musée des Arts Décoratifs in 1882 to form the Union Centrale des Arts Décoratifs (Les Arts Décoratifs since 2006).
	1865 The Camondos relinquish their Austrian citizenship to become Italian subjects and swear their allegiance at the Italian consulate.	**1865** Birth of the architect René Sergent.
	1866 Death of Clara Camondo, née Levy, wife of Abraham Salomon. Death of Salomon Raphael Camondo, Moïse's grandfather (►). The records of Isaac Camondo & Co. are kept in French from now on.	**1866** Ottoman troops are defeated in Lebanon. Venice becomes part of the kingdom of Italy. Manet paints *The Fife Player*.
	1867 Abraham Salomon is ennobled by Victor Emmanuel II by decree on 28 April. He is granted the hereditary title of count, a coat-of-arms and a motto, *Fides et Caritas*. Abraham Behor is made a knight of the Medjidie Order, 2nd class.	**1867** Universal Exhibition opens in Paris.

Moïse de Camondo	Camondo family	Selected historical events
	1868 Abraham Behor and Nissim travel to Paris to prepare their move, staying in rue Marbeuf.	**1868** Death of James de Rothschild. Liquidation of Crédit Mobilier.
1869 Moïse de Camondo (►) arrives in Paris with his family. They move into an apartment in rue Presbourg.	**1869** The family moves to Paris (6 and 7 rue de Presbourg). Nissim stays in Istanbul to assist with Empress Eugénie's reception there on her way to inaugurate the Suez Canal. Isaac Camondo & Co.'s Paris office is registered at 31 rue La Fayette. Isaac passes his baccalauréat.	**1869** Inauguration of the Suez Canal. Death of Fuad Pasha (►), a friend of the Camondos, in Turkey.
1870 Stays in London with his family during the Siege of Paris. Lives with his teacher at Sir Edward Sassoon's house on Park Lane.	**1870** Abraham Behor buys the plot at 61 rue de Monceau from Émile Pereire; Nissim buys the mansion at 63 rue de Monceau from Adolphe Violet. Nissim is ennobled by Victor Emmanuel II by decree on 15 September. He is granted the hereditary title of count, a coat of arms and a motto, *Caritas et Fides*.	**1870** France declares war on Prussia on 19 July; suffers defeat at the Battle of Sedan on 2 September. Napoleon III is deposed and sent into exile in England. Proclamation of the Third Republic. Paris is besieged by the Prussians, September. Victor Emmanuel II takes Rome.
1871 Stays in Marseilles with his parents.	**1871** The architect Denis-Louis Destors draws up plans for Abraham Behor's mansion and alterations to Nissim's mansion.	**1871** Paris is bombarded by the Prussian army. Wilhelm I is proclaimed German Emperor at Versailles on 18 January. The Treaty of Frankfurt is signed by Chancellor Bismarck and President Jules Favre, ending the war. Popular uprising in Paris (March–May); the Commune ends in a bloodbath. Death of the statesman Ali Pasha (►), friend of the Camondos, in Turkey. Zola publishes *La Curée*.
1872 The family moves to 63 rue de Monceau.	**1872** Isaac Camondo & Co. becomes associated with the Banque de Paris et des Pays-Bas group. The family bank helps to found the Banque Austro-Turque and the Constantinople Tramway Company. Abraham Behor is granted planning permission to build his mansion. He buys several pictures at the Pereire auction. Isaac is made a commander of the Medjidie Order. Birth of Irène Cahen d'Anvers, Moïse's future wife.	**1872** Merger of the Banque de Paris and the Banque des Pays-Bas. Auction of the Pereire collections. Sisley paints *Flood at Port-Marly*.
	1873 Death of Abraham Salomon (►) in Paris, 30 March. He is buried in Istanbul on 14 April. Abraham Behor is elected president of the community's fund on the Consistory and made commander of the Order of the Crown of Italy. Nissim is promoted to officer.	**1873** Napoleon III dies in exile in Kent, England. France is liberated in September. Henri Cernuschi's mansion is built on avenue Vélasquez by W. Bouwens van der Boijen. Creation of the Salon des Refusés.

Moïse de Camondo	Camondo family	Selected historical events
1874 Enters the Lycée Fontanes (now the Lycée Condorcet). Stays with his parents at the spa at Luchon.	**1874** Isaac is officially appointed to work at Isaac Camondo & Co. He buys several Far Eastern artworks from the art dealer Sichel.	**1874** First exhibition of the Impressionists at Galerie Nadar.
	1875 Construction of Abraham Behor's mansion completed. He moves in with his family. Isaac buys five works by Millet at the Gavot auction. Alphonse Hirsch paints an interior at Nissim's mansion at 63 rue de Monceau.	**1875** Death of Émile Pereire. Inauguration of the Opéra Garnier.
	1876 Abraham Behor becomes a member of the board of the Banque de Paris et des Pays-Bas. Isaac visits Bayreuth to see Wagner's *Ring*.	**1876** In Turkey, death of Abdul Aziz and accession of Murad V, who reigns for three months before being replaced by his brother Abdul Hamid II (►). Ratification of the Ottoman Empire's first written constitution. Turkish repression of the Serbs in Bulgaria. Degas paints *L'Absinthe*.
	1877 Marriage of Hortense Halfon (Abraham Behor and Nissim's niece) to Alexandre Elissen. Reception at 61 rue de Monceau. Inauguration of the Portuguese synagogue in rue Buffault. Abraham Behor is a founder member; Nissim and Isaac de Camondo and Rebecca Halfon are donors.	**1877** Tsar Alexander II declares war on Sultan Abdul Hamid II. The telephone is first brought into use in France.
 Isaac de Camondo's apartment, avenue des Champs-Élysées.	**1878** Isaac buys several pieces of silverware at the Baron Pichon auction. Moïse is later bequeathed a pair of candlesticks (inv. CAM 97) and a pair of candelabra (inv. CAM 375 ◄) that were bought at this auction. Nissim is made an officer of the Order of Saints Maurice and Lazarus.	**1878** Death of Victor Emmanuel II and accession of Humbert I. Treaty of San Stephano signed by Sultan Abdul Hamid II. Universal Exhibition in Paris.
	1879 Nissim is elected president of the Société de Bienfaisance Italienne de Paris. Abraham Behor is made a commander of the Order of Isabella the Catholic; Nissim is made a commander of the Order of the Crown of Italy; both brothers are made commanders of the Order of the Redeemer (Greece).	**1879** Death of Napoleon, the Prince Imperial, in South Africa.
	1880 Death of Esther, Countess Raphael de Camondo, mother of Abraham Behor and Nissim, in Nice. Abraham Behor is elected president of the Paris committee of the Royal Portuguese Railway Co. Abraham Behor and Nissim are awarded diplomas for services rendered to the Universal Exhibition in 1878 and are promoted to Grand Officers of the Order of the Crown of Italy. Nissim is promoted to Commander of the Order of Isabella the Catholic and Isaac is made an officer of the Order of the Crown of Italy. Abraham Behor and Nissim rent the Château de Saint-Ouen at Favières (Seine-et-Marne) and its large hunting estate. Renoir paints portraits of Irène Cahen d'Anvers and her sister the following year.	**1880** Death of Isaac Pereire.

Moïse de Camondo	Camondo family	Selected historical events
	1881 Isaac Camondo & Co. founds the Compagnie du Ciment Portland et Boulonnais. Isaac is one of the most prominent buyers at the Baron Double auction. (**Three Graces clock, Louvre ►**). Abraham Behor is promoted to Grand Cross of the Order of Isabella the Catholic.	**1881** The Gambetta Ministry.
	1882 Isaac Camondo & Co. helps to found the Compagnie des eaux de Constantinople. Abraham Behor and Nissim are awarded the Légion d'Honneur, Abraham Behor is made Grand Cross of the Order of Our Lord Jesus Christ (Portugal) and receives the Grand Cordon of the Medjidie Order. Isaac is made Grand officer 2nd class of the Medjidie Order. Bonnat paints Abraham Behor's portrait (inv. CAM 1129 ►), Carolus-Duran paints Nissim's portrait (inv. CAM 785). The two brothers invite Gambetta to hunt at the Château de Saint-Ouen. Isaac visits Bayreuth with Léo Delibes for the première of *Parsifal*, then stays in Istanbul.	**1882** Death of Léon Gambetta. Milan Obrenovitch proclaims himself king of Serbia. The Union Centrale des Arts Décoratifs is declared a state-approved, non-profitmaking institution.
1883 Travels to Moscow for Emperor Alexander III's coronation celebrations. Made an officer of the Royal Order of Takovo (Serbia).	**1883** Abraham Behor, Nissim and Isaac lend objects for the Japanese retrospective exhibition organized in Paris by Louis Gonse. Abraham Behor and Nissim receive the Grand Cross of the Order of Takovo (Serbia), Isaac is made Grand Officer.	**1883** The Naquet Law authorizes divorce. Death of Wagner. The first De Dion-Bouton steam-powered car is made.
	1884 Léon Alfassa buys the Château de Montaleau at Sucy-en-Brie. Abraham Behor receives the Grand Cross of the Osmanie Order.	**1884** Founding of the Société des Indépendants and the first Salon.
	1885 The Alfassa affair: Léon Alfassa, Abraham Behor's son-in-law and a senior executive of Isaac Camondo & Co., speculates rashly on the financial markets and flees, leaving debts of over 10 million francs. Isaac rents the Domaine de Sainte-Assise in Seine-et-Marne for hunting until 1894. He is made Commander of the Order of Our Lord Jesus Christ (Portugal).	**1885** Death of Victor Hugo.
1886 Officially joins Isaac Camondo & Co. Buys the steam yacht *Rover* (resold in 1892).	**1886** Abraham Behor receives the Ottoman Iftikar and the Grand Cross of Charles III; Nissim receives the Grand Cordon of the Medjidie Order.	**1886** E. Drumont publishes the virulently anti-Semitic and hugely successful *La France juive*, reprinted around 200 times, in which the Camondos are frequently mentioned.
1887 Made commander of the Medjidie Order (Turkey) (►).		**1887** Construction of the Eiffel Tower begins.

1888
Becomes a member of the 'Par Monts et Vallons' hunt in Halatte Forest.

Moïse dressed
for hunting

1889
Nissim, Abraham and Isaac succeed one another as president of the Italian Committee for the Universal Exhibition in Paris.
Death of Nissim, 27 January.
Abraham Behor is promoted to Commander of the Légion d'honneur.
Léonce Tédeschi is appointed a senior executive of Isaac Camondo & Co.
A non-trading company is created to manage the Camondos' real-estate fortune in Turkey; an inventory of their property is drawn up.
Death of Abraham Behor, 13 December.

1888
The first long-distance car journey, by Berta, the wife of pioneering designer Karl Benz, from Mannheim to Pforzheim (40 miles).

1889
Universal Exhibition in Paris.
Milan I of Serbia abdicates in favour of his son Alexander. He spends some time in France, as the Count of Takovo.

1890
Death of Michel Halfon.
Clarisse Alfassa is put in the care of a guardian.

1890
Death of Vincent van Gogh.

1891
Marries Irène Cahen d'Anvers, 10 October.
The couple rent a furnished mansion at 21 rue de Constantine until June 1892 and the Villa Saint-Hubert at Cannes until January 1892.
Made grand officer of the Royal Order of Takovo (Serbia) and knight of the Order of Saints Maurice and Lazarus (Italy).

1891
Isaac is appointed consul general of Turkey and made a knight of the Order of Saints Maurice and Lazarus (Italy).

1891
Death of Jongkind.
Monet's first exhibition in New York.

1892
Birth of his son Nissim.

1892
The registered office of Isaac Camondo & Co. is transferred to 66 rue de la Chaussée-d'Antin.
Isaac buys Degas' *Dancer Holding a Bouquet*.

1892
Monet paints the first in a series of views of Rouen cathedral.

1893
Moïse and his family move to 11 avenue d'Iéna (►).

1893
The mansion at 61 rue de Monceau is sold to Gaston Menier; the furniture is sold at auction.
Countess Abraham Behor de Camondo moves to 43 avenue de l'Alma; Isaac moves to 2 and 4 rue Gluck and buys works by Degas, Monet and Sisley, mainly from Durand-Ruel.
In Istanbul, the family's residence at 6 Camondo Street is rented by the Universal Israelite Alliance, which uses it to house the Galata boys' school.

1893
Opening of Galerie Ambroise Vollard.

1894
Birth of his daughter Béatrice.

1894
Liquidation of Isaac Camondo & Co. in Istanbul.
Isaac buys a series of Japanese prints from M. Manzi, Manet's *Fife Player* (►), and four *Cathedrals* by Monet, whom he visits at Giverny.

1894
Indictment and trial of Captain Dreyfus, Paris: the 'Dreyfus Affair'.
Milan I of Serbia regains power.

1895
Buys the yacht *Le Géraldine* with his father-in-law, Louis Cahen d'Anvers, and his first car, a Peugeot with a Panhard-Levassor engine.

1895
Isaac is dismissed from his duties as consul general of Turkey. He buys Degas' *The Tub*.
Louis Cahen d'Anvers (►), Moïse's father-in-law, buys the Château de Champs-sur-Marne.

1895
First Cézanne retrospective at Galerie Ambroise Vollard.
Monet's *Rouen Cathedral* series is shown at Galerie Durand-Ruel.
Boni de Castellane marries Anna Gould.
Levassor wins the Paris–Bordeaux motor race.

Moïse de Camondo	Camondo family	Selected historical events
1896 Rents a villa at Villemétrie near Senlis for a year.	**1896** Isaac buys *The Crucifixion*, a bronze bas-relief attributed to Donatello (from the C. Robinson collection).	**1896** Ernest Sanson builds the 'Palais rose' for Boni de Castellane. René Sergent works in his office.
1897 Moïse and Irène separate. The yacht *Le Géraldine* is sold.	**1897** Isaac donates part of his collection to the Louvre with right of usufruct. He is a co-founder of the Société des Amis du Louvre.	**1897** Caillebotte's bequest to the Musée du Luxembourg in Paris. The Société des Amis du Louvre is founded.
1898 Shareholder of the Société du Théâtre National de l'Opéra-Comique (2 shares).	**1898** Isaac becomes a shareholder of the Société du Théâtre National de l'Opéra-Comique (8 shares).	**1898** Theodor Herzl founds the Zionist movement. Émile Zola publishes 'J'accuse'.
1899 Moves into a rented mansion at 19 rue Hamelin in the 16th arrondissement.	**1899** Isaac is elected to the board of the Union Centrale des Arts Décoratifs. He buys Cézanne's *House of the Hanged Man* at the Choquet auction.	**1899** The Dreyfus case is reviewed; he is reconvicted.
1900 General commissioner for Serbia for the Universal Exhibition in Paris (◄), for which he is awarded the Légion d'honneur. Made an Officier de l'Instruction publique (France), commander of the Order of the Lion and the Sun (Persia), grand officer of the Medjidie order (Turkey), and Grand Cordon of the Order of St Sava (Serbia). Travels to Cairo on business.	**1900** Isaac buys Sisley's *Flood at Port-Marly* at the Tavernier auction (43,000 francs). Boldini paints Béatrice's portrait.	**1900** Universal Exhibition in Paris. Construction of the first Métro line; Hector Guimard designs stations. Monet exhibits his *Waterlilies*. Jacques Seligmann opens his gallery at 23 place Vendôme.
1901 An Italian subject, Moïse becomes a French citizen in order to obtain a divorce (17 July). Competes in the Paris–Berlin motor race. Stays in Monte Carlo and Biarritz with his children. Takes the waters at Aix-les-Bains.	**1901** Isaac is elected to the board of the Banque de Paris et des Pays-Bas, which appoints him president of the Compagnie du Gaz pour la France et l'Étranger and of the Compagnie des Chemins de Fer Andalous. He is a shareholder of the Société P. Gailhard, which runs the Théâtre National de l'Opéra. He buys Jongkind's *La Côte Saint-André*, which he bequeaths to Moïse (inv. CAM 574 ▲). He is made an officer of the Légion d'honneur.	**1901** Death of Milan I of Serbia. Picasso's first Paris exhibition is held, at Galerie Ambroise Vollard. First Salon de l'Automobile at the Grand Palais.
1902 His divorce from Irène is granted on 8 January. Takes the waters at Aix-les-Bains.	**1902** Birth of Jean Bertrand, illegitimate son of Isaac and Lucie Bertrand. Isaac buys twelve watercolours by Jongkind. The architect E. Pontremoli begins building Villa Kérylos for Théodore Reinach, Béatrice de Camondo's future father-in-law (finished 1908).	**1902** Death of Émile Zola. Première of Debussy's *Pélleas et Mélisande* at the Opéra-Comique.
1903 Resigns as consul general of Serbia (29 April). Stays in Florence, Monte Carlo and Dinard with his children. Trip to Algeria.	**1903** Second donation by Isaac to the Louvre with right of usufruct. He is an honorary member of the Société du Salon d'Automne and sits on several juries. Birth of Paul Bertrand, illegitimate son of Isaac and Lucie Bertrand. Irène Cahen d'Anvers remarries, to Count Sampieri. Denys Puech sculpts a bust of Béatrice.	**1903** The first Salon d'Automne. Assassination of King Alexander and Queen Draga of Serbia, Belgrade.

Moïse de Camondo	Camondo family	Selected historical events
1904 Buys Villa Béatrice at Aumont. Stays in Antibes and Nice with his children. Takes the waters at Aix-les-Bains.	**1904** Isaac founds the new Société des Amis et Artistes de l'Opéra, of which he is president. Performance of his vocal and instrumental works at the Salle Érard. Sole shareholder of the Société Musicale founded by Gabriel Astruc. Nissim enters the Lycée Janson-de-Sailly (►).	**1904** The Entente Cordiale is signed by Great Britain and France.
1905 Stays in Monte Carlo (►), Rome and La Bourboule with his children. Competes in the Bennett Trophy motor race.	**1905** Death of Regina, Countess Abraham Behor de Camondo, 19 February. Auction of her jewellery, curios, etc. at the Hôtel Drouot on 17–20 April. Isaac rents the Villa Croix-Bosset in Sèvres.	**1905** Death of Alphonse de Rothschild. André Derain and Henri Matisse are dubbed 'the Fauves' when their paintings cause a scandal at the Salon d'Automne. Inauguration of the Musée des Arts Décoratifs in the Marsan pavilion of the Louvre.
1906 Joins the Association Consistoriale Israélite de Paris. Stays in Monte Carlo, Nice, Italy and St Moritz Dorf with his children. Takes the waters at Évian.	**1906** Isaac's third donation to the Louvre with right of usufruct. He composes an opera, *Le Clown*, which is premièred at the Nouveau Théâtre.	**1906** Captain Dreyfus's conviction is quashed; he is freed and pardoned. Félix Fénéon becomes director of Galerie Bernheim Jeune. Death of Cézanne.
1907 Begins to keep a written record of all his purchases of artworks. Stays in Pourville (►) and St Moritz Dorf with his children, and in Italy.	**1907** Isaac is a shareholder of Société Messager, Broussan et Cie, which runs the Théâtre National de l'Opéra. Nissim and Béatrice become members of the 'Par Monts et Vallons' hunt. Isaac leaves his apartment in rue Gluck for 82 avenue des Champs-Élysées.	**1907** The Triple Entente signed by Great Britain, France and Russia. Picasso paints *Les Demoiselles d'Avignon*.
1908 Stays in London and Egypt, and with Nissim in Istanbul.	**1908** Isaac draws up his will. He is promoted to Commander of the Légion d'honneur. *Le Clown* is performed at the Opéra-Comique.	**1908** Gabriel Astruc founds an international committee to fund the creation of the Théâtre des Champs-Élysées. In Turkey, the 'Young Turks' rise against Sultan Abdul Hamid II and propose a new constitution.
1909 Stays in St Moritz Dorf with his children.	**1909** Isaac is appointed president of the Société Nationale, that eventually forms the basis of the Crédit Foncier Ottoman. *Le Clown* is performed again at the Opéra-Comique and in Marseille.	**1909** Sultan Abdul Hamid II of Turkey is overthrown. Accession of Mehmet V. Louis Blériot becomes the first person to fly across the Channel. The Ballets Russes is established in Paris. Jacques Seligmann buys the Hôtel de Sagan in rue Saint-Dominique to create a gallery and his brother Arnold takes over the gallery in place Vendôme.
1910 Shortly after his mother's death, Moïse has his parents' mansion at 63 rue de Monceau demolished. Donates (with Isaac) about fifteen religious objects from the oratory at 63 rue de Monceau to the Temple Buffault and four pieces of oriental and Dutch silverware used in Jewish worship to the Musée de Cluny (now on loan to the Musée d'Art et d'Histoire du Judaïsme). Donates the borders of the Gobelins tapestries	**1910** Death of Élise, Countess Nissim de Camondo, 18 June. Auction of Nissim de Camondo's jewellery, objets d'art and paintings at the Hôtel Drouot on 15, 21, 22 and 23 November. Isaac buys three pictures by Renoir and Cézanne's *Card Players*. Henri Lebasque paints Jean Bertrand's portrait at the apartment on the Champs-Élysées. *Le Clown* is performed in Vichy.	**1910** Floods in Paris (▼).

Moïse de Camondo

The Martyrdom and Triumph of Saints Gervasius and Protasius (bought by his father) to the City of Paris.
Donates a watch by Boucheron (made by Bresighelli) to the Musée des Arts Décoratifs.
Stays in Seville.

1911
The architect René Sergent begins building the new mansion.
Member of the board of the Société des Amis du Louvre.
Member of the board of the Union Centrale des Arts Décoratifs.
Elected a member of the Association Consistoriale de Paris.
Stays in Scotland.

1912
Member of the board of the Société des Artistes et Amis de l'Opéra.
Rents 1,000 hectares for hunting from Robert de Rothschild, in the communes of Apremont, Aumont and Verneuil in Halatte Forest.
Stays in Provence.

1913
Moves from rue Hamelin to rue de Monceau, 15 July.
Represents the Consistory at the Temple Buffault.
Goes with Béatrice on the 'Revue générale des sciences' cruise to the Balearic Islands, Andalusia, Madeira, and the Canary Islands (▼).

1914
Stays with Béatrice at Arcachon in September.

1916
Stays in Deauville and Vichy.

Camondo family

Nissim passes his baccalauréat (►).

1911
Death of Isaac de Camondo, 7 April.
Decree of acceptance of Isaac de Camondo's bequest of his collections to the Musée du Louvre, 23 November.
Le Clown is performed in Antwerp.
Nissim begins his military service in a hussars regiment at Senlis.

1912
Posthumous portrait of Isaac by Henri Lebasque (inv. CAM 1132 ►).
Le Clown is performed in Cologne.

1913
Nissim completes his military service with the rank of sergeant and begins his training as a banker in the stocks and shares department of the Banque de Paris et des Pays-Bas.

1914
The Isaac de Camondo Collection opens to the public in the Louvre. Nissim, sergeant in the 3rd Hussars, 3rd Division 6th Army Corps, is mobilized on 3 August (►). First mention in dispatches (1 September, no. 4). Battle of Ypres.

1915
Nissim undergoes an operation for appendicitis and returns to the front in September.
Transferred to the 21st Dragoons. Promoted to second lieutenant. Defends the front in the Bois-en-Hache sector in Artois. Requests to be transferred to the flying corps.

1916
Nissim is posted to MF 33 Squadron as an observer in January. Photographs the Hill 304 sector at Verdun. Promoted to lieutenant in July. Second and third mentions in dispatches (16 May, 15 December, no. 428). Receives flying instruction.

Selected historical events

1911
The Mona Lisa is stolen from the Louvre, and does not return until two years later.

1912
Jacques Seligmann buys the entire Lady Sackville collection, inherited from Sir Richard Wallace.

1913
Inauguration of the Théâtre des Champs-Élysées.
Riotous première of Stravinsky's *The Rite of Spring*.
Inauguration of the Musée Jacquemart-André.
Marcel Proust publishes *Swann's Way*, the first part of his monumental *In Search of Lost Time*.

1914
Germany declares war on France, 3 August.
Beginning of the French retreat, 25 August.
The French government moves from Paris to Bordeaux, 2 September.
Battles of the Marne, Artois, Yser and Ypres, September–November.

1915
The French offensive in Champagne, September.
Joffre appointed commander-in-chief of the French army, December.

1916
Beginning of the battle of Verdun.
Fighting at Mort-Homme, around Douaumont, Hill 304, May–June.
Beginning of the Allied offensive on the Somme, July.
Joffre appointed Marshal of France.

Moïse de Camondo	Camondo family	Selected historical events
1917 Stays with Nissim in Vichy, July.	**1917** Nissim spends time in Champagne in April. Mentioned in dispatches for a fourth time (no. 275). Takes the waters at Vichy; takes leave (▼) at Deauville during the summer. Based near Lunéville in September. Dies in aerial combat on 5 September near Embermenil in Meurthe-et-Moselle. Buried in the military cemetery at Elfringen. Mentioned in dispatches (24 October, no. 169) for a fifth time. Death of Clarisse Alfassa, 18 October. Liquidation of Isaac Camondo & Co.	**1917** German withdrawal in Picardy, February–March. British offensive in Artois, French offensive in the Aisne (Chemin des Dames) and in the Monts de Champagne, April. Pétain appointed commander-in-chief of the French army, May. The campaign in Flanders, August–November. Battle of Cambrai, November–December.
1918 Moïse's collection is taken to Tours for safekeeping. Makes the Villa Béatrice available to the Medical Corps for use by the 'Mission de l'Ambrine' military ambulance service directed by Baroness Henri de Rothschild. Takes the waters at Évian.	**1918** 63 rue de Monceau in battle order (▼).	**1918** First bombardments of Paris by 'Big Bertha', March. Signing of the Armistice, 11 November. Accession of Mehmet VI of Turkey.
1919 Member of the finance commission on the board of the Union Centrale des Arts Décoratifs. Does not renew his mandate as member of the Association Consistoriale de Paris. Stays in Alsace-Lorraine. Takes the waters at Vittel.	**1919** Nissim's body is repatriated and buried in Montmartre cemetery (►). Béatrice marries Léon Reinach, 10 March.	**1919** The Treaty of Versailles is signed, 28 June.
1920 Elected vice-president of the Société des Amis du Louvre. Contributes to the purchase of Courbet's *The Painter's Studio* (10,000 francs). Donates 25,000 francs to the Union Centrale des Arts Décoratifs. Stays in Biarritz and in Germany.	**1920** Nissim is promoted posthumously to Knight of the Légion d'honneur. Birth of Fanny Reinach. Official inauguration of Isaac de Camondo's bequest to the Musée du Louvre	**1920** Georges Clemenceau resigns. Paul Deschanel is elected president of the French Republic, followed by Alexandre Millerand. The Treaty of Sèvres divides the Ottoman Empire into 'mandates'.
1921 Assistant secretary to the board of the Union Centrale des Arts Décoratifs. Donor member of the Société des Amis de l'Enseignement par les Musées. Organizer and member of the honorary committee of a symposium on art history in Paris. Honorary member of the Chambre Syndicale de la Curiosité et des Beaux-Arts. Resigns from the Comité France-Amérique. Stays in Wiesbaden.		**1921** Hitler becomes leader of the Nazi party in Germany.
1922 Member of the Conseil des Musées Nationaux. Member of the Commission Fondation Hannah-Charlotte de Rothschild. Member of the board of the Société des Amis du Musée Cernuschi. Cruise to Morocco. Travels by car to Wiesbaden.		**1922** In Turkey, accession of Abdul Medjid, the last Ottoman caliph.

Moïse de Camondo	Camondo family	Selected historical events
1923 Becomes a member of the Congrès International des Bibliothécaires et Bibliophiles. Serves on the honorary committee of the Vénerie française exhibition, Musée des Arts Décoratifs.	**1923** Birth of Bertrand Reinach. Georges Malissard sculpts a bronze equestrian statuette of Béatrice Reinach (inv. CAM 1967.1.1).	**1923** Proclamation of the Turkish Republic, with Mustapha Kemal (Kemal Ataturk) as president.
1924 Registers his will, in which he founds the Musée Nissim de Camondo. Becomes a member of the Société des Amis de la Bibliothèque Nationale. Founder member of the Société des Amis des Musées de Strasbourg. Honorary member of the Société des Amis du Vieux Saint-Germain. Active member of the Société Française d'Archéologie. Stays in Nice and Ostend. Travels by car to Italy.	**1924** Béatrice and Léon Reinach and their children move to 64 boulevard Maurice-Barrès, Neuilly-sur-Seine. Béatrice's former apartment is converted into the Blue Drawing Room.	**1924** The Islamic caliphate in Turkey is abolished under Kemal Ataturk. France begins to withdraw troops from Germany. Hitler writes *Mein Kampf*.
1925 Secretary on the board of the Union Centrale des Arts Décoratifs. Launches a 'modern frame' award, with a prize of 12,000 francs. Member of the board of the Société des Amis de la Bibliothèque Jacques Doucet. Founder member of the Société Française des Amis de la Médaille. Stays in Rome. Travels in Italy.	**1925** Fanny and her mother at a hunt meet	**1925** The Exposition Internationale des Arts Décoratifs et Industriels Modernes (origin of the term Art Deco) opens in Paris.
1926 Member of the honorary committee of the *From Le Nain to Manet* exhibition in Amsterdam. Stays in Nice and Bayonne. Travels by car to Rome.		**1926** Germany is admitted to the League of Nations.
1927 Member of the board of the Manufacture Nationale des Gobelins (artistic committee). Member-benefactor of the Société des Amis du Mobilier National. Vice-president of the Société des Amis du Musée Carnavalet. Stays in Bayonne. Travels by car to Venice.		**1927** Death of René Sergent.
1928 Titular member of the Club des Cents. Member-benefactor of the Amis du Musée de la Voiture et du Tourisme in Compiègne. Member of the honorary committee of the Houdon centenary exhibition at the Bibliothèque de Versailles. Stays in Nice, takes the waters at Bourbon-Lancy. Tours Spain by car.	**1928** Death of Théodore Reinach, Béatrice's father-in-law.	**1928** The Cognacq-Jay Donation to the City of Paris. Turkey switches from the Arabic to the Latin-based modern Turkish alphabet. Kellogg-Briand treaty (or Pacte de Paris) signed to outlaw 'war as an instrument of national policy'.
1929 Decorated by the Royal Order of the Redeemer (Greece). Stays in Aix-en-Provence and Barcelona, takes the waters at Contrexéville.		**1929** Death of Georges Clemenceau. The New York stock market crashes. Inauguration of the Musée Cognacq-Jay.
1930 Member of the Société d'Iconographie Parisienne. President of the finance commission on the board of the Union Centrale des Arts Décoratifs and vice-chairman of the board. Member of the Société des Amis de Sèvres. Stays in London, the South of France, Holland, Burgundy and Bordeaux.		**1930** French Prime Minister André Tardieu orders the withdrawal of the remaining French troops from the Rhineland. One-year conscription introduced in France.

Moïse de Camondo	Camondo family	Selected historical events

1931
Becomes a member of the Société de la Bibliothèque de Versailles.
Donates 100,000 francs to the Union Centrale des Arts Décoratifs for the Byzantine Art exhibition.
Stays in Cannes, London, Holland and Côte-d'Or.

1932
Member of the Commission des Arts Plastiques.
Member of the organization committee of the Exhibition of French Art at the Royal Academy, London.
Member of the honorary committee for the Manet exhibition at the Orangerie.
Stays in the South of France and Amsterdam (visits the Rembrandt exhibition).

1933
Donates 55 tie-pins to the Union Centrale des Arts Décoratifs in memory of his father, Count Nissim de Camondo.
Vice-president of the organizing committee of the Hubert Robert exhibition at the Musée de l'Orangerie.
Member of the patrons' committee for the Goncourt exhibition organized by the Gazette des Beaux-Arts.
Goes to London in March to see the Exhibition of French Art. Two journeys by car to Italy: to Naples and Venice.

1934
Member of the honorary committee for the Passion of Christ in French Art exhibition at the Sainte-Chapelle.
Stays in Biarritz. Tours in the south of England, visiting country houses and their gardens.

1935
Resigns from the board of the Union Centrale des Arts Décoratifs due to deafness.
Member of the honorary committee of the French Drawings in 18th-Century Collections exhibitions organized by the Gazette des Beaux-Arts.
Member of the honorary committee of the French Art in the 18th Century exhibition in Copenhagen.
Stays in Deauville. Visits the Universal Exhibition in Brussels.
Dies on 14 November.

1936
Decree of acceptance of the Camondo Bequest, 7 July (►).
Inauguration of the Musée Nissim de Camondo, 21 December.

1932
Death of Léon Piperno, executive of Isaac Camondo & Co. in Istanbul and manager of the Camondo's real estate interests in Turkey.

1933
Fanny Reinach's initiation at the Buffault Temple.

1935
Charles Cahen d'Anvers, Irène's brother, donates the Château de Champs to the French nation.
Death of Moïse de Camondo.

LE MUSEE
ANNEXE DU MUSEE DES ARTS DECORATIFS
A ETE LEGUE A LA FRANCE
PAR LE
COMTE MOÏSE DE CAMONDO
1860-1935
VICE-PRESIDENT
DE L'UNION CENTRALE DES ARTS DECORATIFS
EN SOUVENIR DE SON FILS
NISSIM DE CAMONDO
1892-1917
LIEUTENANT AU 2ème GROUPE D'AVIATION
TOMBE EN COMBAT AERIEN
LE 5 SEPTEMBRE 1917

1931
Paul Doumer is elected president of the French Republic.

1932
Paul Doumer is assassinated. Albert Lebrun is elected president of the French Republic.

1933
Hitler is appointed Chancellor of Germany. Fire at the Reichstag. Boycott of Jewish businesses. Germany leaves the League of Nations.

1934
Night of the Long Knives in Germany. Hitler becomes head of state.
Attempted right-wing coup d'état takes place in Paris.
Death of Béatrice Ephrussi, who bequeaths her villa to the Académie des Beaux-Arts de l'Institut de France.

1935
The Nuremberg laws are passed in Germany, establishing a legal basis for racial discrimination against Jews. Compulsory military service is re-established.
The Saar votes for unification with Germany.

1936
Victory of the Front Populaire in the legislative elections. The Blum Ministry.
Hitler denounces the Treaties of Versailles and Locarno and reoccupies the Rhineland.

Genealogy

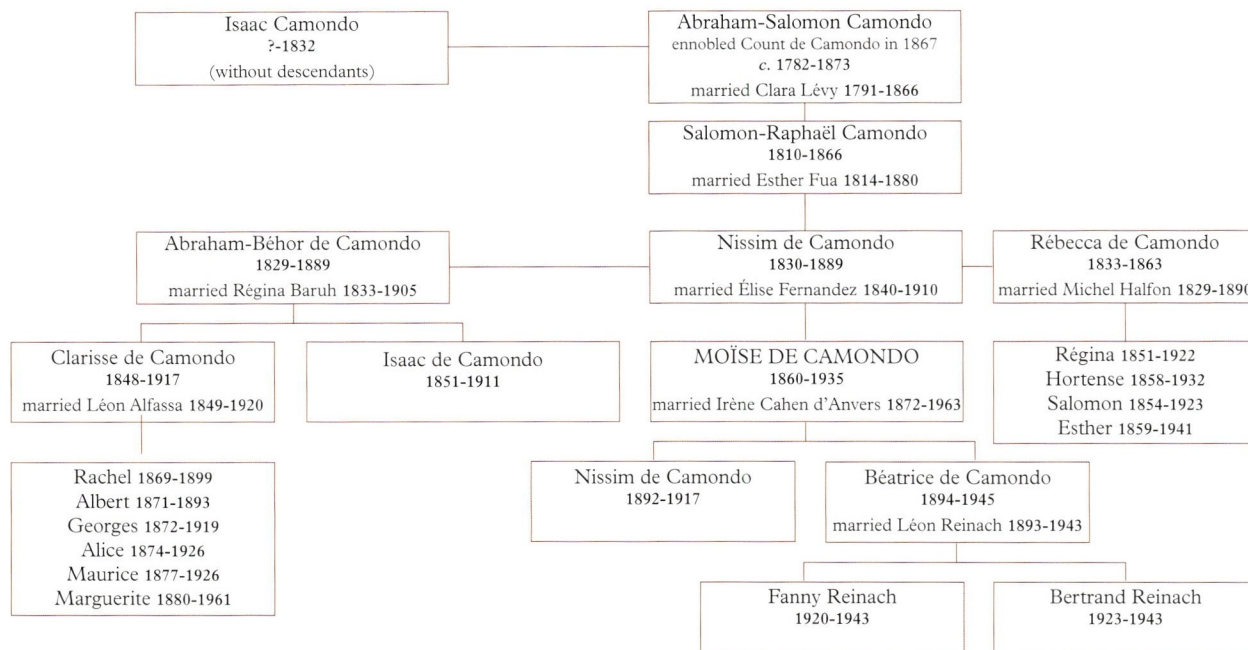

Isaac Camondo
?-1832
(without descendants)

Abraham-Salomon Camondo
ennobled Count de Camondo in 1867
c. 1782-1873
married Clara Lévy 1791-1866

Salomon-Raphaël Camondo
1810-1866
married Esther Fua 1814-1880

Abraham-Béhor de Camondo
1829-1889
married Régina Baruh 1833-1905

Nissim de Camondo
1830-1889
married Élise Fernandez 1840-1910

Rébecca de Camondo
1833-1863
married Michel Halfon 1829-1890

Clarisse de Camondo
1848-1917
married Léon Alfassa 1849-1920

Isaac de Camondo
1851-1911

MOÏSE DE CAMONDO
1860-1935
married Irène Cahen d'Anvers 1872-1963

Régina 1851-1922
Hortense 1858-1932
Salomon 1854-1923
Esther 1859-1941

Rachel 1869-1899
Albert 1871-1893
Georges 1872-1919
Alice 1874-1926
Maurice 1877-1926
Marguerite 1880-1961

Nissim de Camondo
1892-1917

Béatrice de Camondo
1894-1945
married Léon Reinach 1893-1943

Fanny Reinach
1920-1943

Bertrand Reinach
1923-1943

Index

318

Select Bibliography

The Camondo family and the Musée Nissim de Camondo

Pierre ASSOULINE, *Le Dernier des Camondo* (Paris, Gallimard, 1997).

Nadine GASC and Gérard MABILLE, *The Nissim de Camondo Museum* (Paris, Fondation Paribas/Union Centrale des Arts Décoratifs/Réunion des musées nationaux, 'Musées et monuments de France' coll., 1991).

Marie-Noël de GARY, 'Cuisine à la Camondo', *The World of Interiors*, may 2007, pp. 150–55.

Marie-Noël de GARY and Gilles PLUM, *Les Cuisines de l'hôtel Camondo* (Paris, Union Centrale des Arts Décoratifs, 1999).

Philippe LANDAU, 'Les juifs dans l'aviation française (1914-1918)', *Les Cahiers du judaïsme*, 21, june 2007, pp. 110–22.

Arnaud LE BRUSQ, « Chez le comte Moïse de Camondo », *Monuments*, L'Insulaire, 2006, pp. 11–26.

Sophie LE TARNEC and Bertrand RONDOT, 'Les Camondo et la vénerie', *Vénerie*, 164, december 2006, pp. 66–69.

Gérard MABILLE, *Orfèvrerie française des XVIe, XVIIe, XVIIIe siècles, catalogue raisonné des collections du musée des Arts décoratifs et du musée Nissim de Camondo* (Paris, Flammarion/Musée des Arts Décoratifs, 1984).

Bertrand RONDOT (ed.), *Musée Nissim de Camondo : catalogue des collections,* avec la participation de Xavier Salmon et de Béatrice Quette (Paris, Réunion des Musées Nationaux/Union Centrale des Arts Décoratifs, 1998).

Bertrand RONDOT, 'Moïse de Camondo and the Price of "Association" ', *Furniture History*, XLIII, 2007.

Anne SEFRIOUI with Bertrand RONDOT, Marie-Noël de GARY and Sophie LE TARNEC, *Le Musée Nissim de Camondo* (*Connaissance des arts,* hors-série, 2005).

Nora ŞENI et Sophie LE TARNEC, *Les Camondo ou l'éclipse d'une fortune* (Arles, Actes Sud, 1997).

Nora ŞENI, 'Diffusion des modèles français de philanthropie au XIXe siècle ; la famille Camondo', *PARDES*, 22, Le Cerf, 1996, pp. 230–51.

Nora ŞENI, 'The Imprint of the Camondos in 19th Century Istanbul', *International Journal of Middle East Studies*, 26, Cambridge University Press, 1994, pp. 663–75.

Filippo TUENA, *Le variazioni Reinach* (Milano, Rizzoli, 2005).

Emine Ğiğdem TUGAY and Mehmet Selim Tugay, *Kamondo Han,* (Istanbul, Orçun Türkay, 2007).

General reading

Philippe ARIÈS and Georges DUBY (ed.), *Histoire de la vie privée:* IV, 'De la Révolution à la Grande Guerre', Michelle Perrot (ed.); V, 'De la Première Guerre mondiale à nos jours', Antoine Prost and Gérard Vincent (ed.) (Paris, Le Seuil, 'L'Univers historique' coll., 1987).

Louis BERGERON, *Les Rothschild et les autres. La gloire des banquiers* (Paris, Perrin, 1990).

René BÉTOURNÉ, *René Sergent architecte. 1865-1927* (Paris, Horizons de France, 1931).

Monique ELEB with Anne DEBARRE, *L'Invention de l'habitation moderne, Paris 1880-1914* (Bruxelles, A.A.M./Paris, Hazan, 1995).

Grandes et Petites Heures du parc Monceau, exhibition catalogue (Paris, Musée Cernuschi, 1981).

Christina HARDYMENT, *Behind the Scenes, Domestic Arrangements in Historic Houses* (London, The National Trust, 1997).

François LOYER, *Histoire de l'architecture française. De la Révolution à nos jours* (Paris, Mengès/Éditions du Patrimoine, 1999).

Du palais au palace, les grands hôtels de voyageurs à Paris au XIXe siècle, exhibition catalogue (Paris, Musée Carnavalet, 1998).

Bruno PONS, *Grands Décors français : 1650-1800, reconstitués en Angleterre, aux États-Unis, en Amérique du Sud et en France* (Dijon, Éditions Faton, 1995).

Pauline PRÉVOST-MARCILHACY, *Les Rothschild, bâtisseurs et mécènes* (Paris, Flammarion, 1995).

Gérard ROUSSET-CHARNY, *Les Palais parisiens de la Belle Époque* (Paris, Délégation à l'Action artistique de la Ville de Paris, 1990).

Nora ŞENI, *Les Inventeurs de la philanthropie juive* (Paris, La Martinière, 2005).

The National Trust. Manual of Housekeeping. The Care of Collections in Historic Houses Open to the Public (Oxford, Butterworth-Heinemann, an imprint of Elsevier, 2006).

Illustrations Credits

Silhouettes of Nissim, Béatrice and Moïse de Camondo foxhunting, c. 1910.

Separations by Les Artisans du Regard, Paris.
Printing and binding by Mame, Tours,
February 2008.

Printed in France